Twice Sold, Twice Ransomed & Memoirs of a Southerner

Compiled By

JV PUBLICATIONS

©2010

This book consists of the following 2 titles:

Twice Sold, Twice Ransomed: An Autobiography of Mr. and Mrs. L. P. Ray:

By

Mrs. Emma J. Ray & L.P. Ray

Introduction by Rev. C. E. McReynolds

[1926]

&

Memoirs of a Southerner 1840 - 1923

By

Edward J. Thomas

SAVANNAH, GEORGIA

[1923]

MR. AND MRS. L. P. RAY

Twice Sold, Twice Ransomed: An Autobiography of Mr. and Mrs. L. P. Ray:

by

Mrs. Emma J. Ray & L.P. Ray

Introduction by

Rev. C. E. McReynolds

TO
THE MANY FAITHFUL FRIENDS
WHO HAVE LABORED WITH US
FOR THE MASTER
THIS VOLUME
IS DEDICATED BY
THE AUTHOR

INTRODUCTION

It is with pleasure that we respond to the request of our dear friends in Christ, Rev. L. P. and Mrs. Emma J. Ray, to write a brief introduction to their book.

We first met them in 1890 when pastor of the First Free Methodist Church of Seattle, Washington, which was located at 912 Pine Street. Brother and Sister Ray came to our services and we were impressed with their evident honesty and manifest desire to know the things of God. We have been intimately acquainted with them and their work for many years, and have noted with much interest their growth in grace and knowledge, their splendid success in the ministry of the Word, and in leading souls to Christ.

Brother and Sister Ray are held in high esteem by the Washington Conference and by all who know them. They are safe, sane and competent. They do not introduce fads and fancies into their revival efforts, but preach the whole gospel "with the Holy Ghost sent down from heaven." We are glad we ever met them. They have been a blessing to us, and we hope God may spare them many years to continue their good work.

We have read with much profit and pleasure the advance sheets of their autobiography. We predict for it a splendid sale, and believe it will prove a great blessing to all who may read it.

Rev. C. E. McReynolds,

Seattle, Washington.

PREFACE

For many years it has been laid upon our hearts to write our experiences and to tell about some of the incidents in our lives. Many of the pilgrims have persuaded us to do so. We bowed in prayer and inquired of the Lord if this would glorify Him, and the answer came, "Ye are my witnesses."

Just after we received this text, doubt came into my mind, which caused me to wonder if it really was the Lord who spoke to me. I felt I could not afford to make a mistake. Again I sought the mind of the Lord. After fasting and earnestly praying, I asked him to forgive me for coming to him the second time, and to give me one more passage of scripture; and to let it be a word concerning writing, and I would not doubt again. I turned to the twenty-sixth Psalm, and, not knowing what was in it, I began to read at the seventh verse. My eyes fell upon these words, "That I may publish with the voice of thanksgiving, and tell of all Thy wondrous works." My heart became hot within me and while I mused the fire burned. I said, "Oh, praise the Lord! The Bible says that I may publish it, and tell of all His wondrous works."

It was a prayer, and the prayer of my soul. The words, "publish it," kept turning over and over in my mind. I then ran and got my dictionary, as is always my custom when the Spirit impresses me with a word, as it is clearer to me when I get the foundation of the word. Mr. Webster thus defines the term:

1. To make known to mankind, or people in general, what before was private or unknown. Christ and His apostles published the glad tidings of salvation.

> "The unwearied sun from day to day,
> Does his Creator's power display;
> And publishes to every land
> The work of an almighty hand."

2. To send a book into the world; to offer for sale a book, map, or print.

I knelt down and thanked the Lord. I then arose to my feet, feeling sure it was the voice of God. At once I telephoned this experience to Sister S. A. Morgan, who, for twenty years, had requested us to write our experiences, saying that to do so she believed would glorify God.

Since that time many of our friends have made the same request, some kindly offering to assist us when we told them of our inability to perform the task. Thus by the help of the Lord and by the assistance of kind friends, we shall give personal testimony to what God has wrought in our lives, trusting that in so doing we shall glorify Him.

TWICE SOLD--TWICE RANSOMED

A land of sunshine, soft blue skies and bloom
Without, to charm the eyes, the heart to cheer;
Within, a filthy, crowded auction room,
The ribald jest, the oath, the heartless jeer.

And huddled close a brooding dark-skinned band
Of human chattels, waiting to be sold--
Children and parents, husbands, wives, they stand
To satisfy man's guilty greed for gold.

And from that cursed block, with downcast eyes,
Her baby girl pressed closely to her heart,
A gentle mother steps, and bravely tries
To thank her God--they are not sold apart.

A few years pass; the roar and shriek and din
Of war. And blood of brothers dyes the sod--
For blood must e'er atone for guilt and sin,
And cries have long assailed the ear of God.

The time was ripe, the bond-man should go free.
God had a man, gentle and strong and brave,
Who willingly a Joshua would be,
Who dared to strike the shackles from the slave.

His life the forfeit. But at last he gained
The goal, his heart had sought for many years.
Freedom and justice, peace and mercy reigned,
Union restored, though bathed with blood and tears.

The years slip by; and in a northern state,
Of fir and fern, where sparkling water plays,
The slave babe--woman grown, with chosen mate
In search of home and happiness, now strays.

They chose a city close beside the Sound
Builded, like Rome, upon her many hills.
Whose air and water, verdure, fertile ground,
Sing loud of health and freedom from life's ills.

Rejoicingly, these "dusky sons of toil"
Look on the scene, and boast their "jubilee."
Their's for the taking--water, trees and soil,
With all their stores--and dream that they are free.

And still, poor slaves were they, "Sold under sin,"
Her master, envy, vanity and greed;
His, rioting, tobacco, beer and gin,--
Worse bondage than from that they had been freed.

Like bondage all our race has sometime known,
Helpless to save ourselves from utter loss
Till one was found--God-man, who could atone,
Who nailed our fetters to His blood-stained cross.

They gladly "rose and followed," "at His call,"
Who paid their ransom, made them free again.
And for His service they "forsook their all,"
And He has made of them "Fishers of men."

Twice born, twice sold, and twice redeemed and free,
Yet still are "love slaves" "going out no more."
For at the breaking of the "Jubilee"
They craved the "ear-mark" at their Master's door.

..Affectionately inscribed to Mr. and Mrs. L. P. Ray, by their sister in Jesus, Mina B.
Spear.

Seattle, Washington, March 30th, 1925.

CHAPTER I
EARLY LIFE AND EXPERIENCES

I was born twice, bought twice, sold twice, and set free twice. Born of woman, born of God; sold in slavery, sold to the devil; freed by Lincoln, set free by God.

I was born in the State of Missouri, January 7, 1859, in a little town called Springfield. I was born of slave parents. My great grandfather was brought from Africa and sold as a slave in the State of Virginia. My father's name was John Smith, that being the name of his master. My mother's name was Jennie Boyd.

When I was one month old, I, my sister, who was one and one-half years old, and my mother, who held me in her arms, were sold at the auction block to the highest bidder. Two of my father's young masters bid us in, so our names became Smith.

My father was never sold, but lived in the same family where he was born until he became free. He was very much troubled at the prospect of seeing his wife, my mother, sold, and became restless, consequently his young master bought us in just to please my father, as he threatened to run away.

Every slave, after being made free, had the privilege of choosing a name for himself, but my father kept the name of Smith until his death. He was much loved by his owners. They moved to the State of Missouri when he was but a child. He was really the property of the young mistress, who refused to sell him, but kept him as chore boy in the big house, and the whole family loved him. This explains why they so readily bought us in at the auction.

At this time while he was yet young my father learned to read and write; although it was against the law for a slave to learn to read or write, he was thirsty for knowledge and stole what little education he had from his master's children. It happened on this wise; the boys were always spelling and repeating their lessons at home where they studied. He said he had a burning desire to learn to read. He would listen to them and would often steal their books, especially their speller, and have them tell him what these or those letters would spell. He studied in the field, or in the old log cabin, at night by the light from the old fireplace. In the field while resting the horses, he would take off his hat in which was hidden the spelling book and while he was pretending to be looking in his hat for vermin which were quite plentiful at that time, he was studying the words he was learning. He would then go on to the end of the row, spelling as he plowed. It would have been disastrous to him if he had been caught. A negro that could read was considered dangerous. He persevered until he could both read and write. In later years, when he became free, it was his habit to pick up a piece of paper, while resting in the garden, and read. My father never had an opportunity to go to school.

My mother was sold twice so far as I can remember. I remember mother's telling me about her only brother's being sold. He was in the orchard getting some apples to eat. The slave trader came and she was sent to call him, and she told him he was to be sold. He stopped eating and with a choking and pathetic voice he said, "Here, Sister Jennie, you may have all my apples." He was sold and sent south, and she never saw or heard of him again.

Soon afterward the Civil war began. I was only two years old and can not remember the beginning of it, but as it progressed the excitement became so great that even a child of three or four years old could not help but remember some things. I remember the Wilson Creek battle that was fought August 10, 1861, in Springfield, Missouri, my home town. I remember hearing the people talk with much excitement about the shells exploding and killing people, and being admonished to keep indoors, and if I saw one smoking not to go near it, nor to pick up one.

We were "run south" to Arkansas to keep from being taken away by the Federal soldiers as they passed through the country. My father and mother and the one sister that was sold, went with us. The other children, four in all, three boys and one girl, were on the farm from which my mother was sold. The older brother, about sixteen years of age, ran away with the Federal soldiers. My father said he asked for a pass before leaving, as no slave could leave the farm without having a pass. (They kept patrolmen in those days to watch the slaves and keep them at home.) My brother wanted to bid them goodbye, never expecting to see them again.

Our two young masters took us south along with a regiment of Confederate soldiers. I don't know what the name of the regiment was, nor how old I was at that time, but my father told me I would sing "Dixie Land" for the the soldiers at night around the camp fire.

My brothers that were left on the farm said they would miss "pappy" (as they all called their fathers then) and would go down to the field every day and look at his tracks made in the soft soil of the field, as he went away.

I cannot remember how long we were south; I don't think it was long, perhaps a few months. It was somewhere in Arkansas. There soon came a regiment of Union soldiers through Arkansas, commanded by General Fremont, and they took us back to Spring-field, under their protection, so I had the opportunity of singing to the Confederate soldiers going to Arkansas, and to the Union soldiers coming back.

I had a sister born on the way down to Arkansas when we stopped at the Bethphage camping ground. My mother named her Priscilla Bethphage. Priscilla was a very sad child, sick and delicate, being melancholy all her days.

When we arrived at Springfield, we went right back to our old owners; like so many chickens, we had nowhere else to go. But we did not stay there very long because General Fremont commanded every slave owner to give up all slaves who wanted to leave their masters. This was before the Emancipation Proclamation, and for this order General Fremont lost his position as Military Commander. We all left with great rejoicing. We had no place to live; we did not know how to provide for ourselves.

A neighboring slave owner, in sympathy with the north, let us (my father and mother, two sisters and myself) live in an old log cabin not far from our old home. My three brothers ran away from the Boyd family leaving my oldest sister on the plantation alone. She was the only slave left on the place. Around the fire at night, she had heard the other slaves talking about running away, and our mother had told her that she could run away and come to her. It was not very long before she started at night after getting the chores done, traveling at night, creeping through the underbrush. She had to come about two and one-half miles from the plantation into town. As she had heard them talking about the "underground railroad" and run-away negroes going north, it gave her a little idea of what to do. When the slaves ran away, the only thing they knew to do was to follow the north star. My sister came to us in the log cabin.

I remember hearing the slaves talk about getting to Canada over the "underground railroad," with the help of sympathetic northerners.

I never go across to the British side now, but I feel like lifting my heart in gratitude to God. It takes me back to the days of slavery, when our poor fathers and mothers prayed so earnestly to see that land and never had the opportunity and yet I, their offspring, reaped the fruit of their faith and prayers. God surely works in a mysterious way, His wonders to perform. Amen! Hallelujah!

My sister's liberty was short-lived, because the old master and the two daughters came after her. We were all happy, playing on the floor in the log cabin. The old mistress came to the door and said, "I have come after my nigger." My sister screamed and started for the back door, but someone was there to catch her. We children cried and our mother begged and prayed but our sister was taken back and they put a ball and chain on her and kept her chained down until she was subdued and would run away no more. But in a few days she was back again; this time mother ran with her to some Union sympathizer nearby, and they kept her until the Proclamation was issued.

When the glad tidings came that we were freed, and the war was over, such rejoicing and weeping and shouting among the slaves was never heard before, unless it was the time that the Ark of the Covenant was brought back to the children of Israel. Great numbers of the slaves left their masters immediately. They had no shelter, but they dug holes in the ground, made dug-outs, brush houses, with a piece of board here and there, whenever they could find one, until finally they had a little village called "Dink-town," looking more like an Indian village than anything else. There they sang and prayed and rejoiced. Later on, the soldiers began to come through, returning from the war. They brought many negroes with them who were searching for members of their families. I remember my mother, with me holding on to her skirts, standing watching the soldiers as they passed in their blue suits, and the colored people all shouting "Hurrah for Marse Abe," and cheering the Union boys as they passed. That was a glad day. That certainly was a year of jubilee for the poor black slave. They had heard about the Liberation from Bondage of the Children of Israel from the Egyptians and their prayers were always to the Almighty God, and the God of Abraham, Isaac and Jacob that they too someday might be delivered, and now it had actually come. Oh! what joy!

My father was the only colored man that could write. Slaves were not allowed to learn to read and write, under penalty of flogging, but my father was a house servant and had stolen his education from the young masters as they said over their lessons. He was kept up for hours at night, and sometimes almost all night, writing letters trying to find out where loved ones were. Some had been run south, some were sold away, and they could not tell their names, only the first names. Mothers were hunting children, and husbands hunting wives; they kept my father very busy.

It was also very hard upon the slave owners, as there were none of the white women that knew anything about work, and they were left without a single servant. It was hard for both blacks and whites to become used to the change, for the slaves had no idea how to earn a living. Some of the slaves that had good masters never left, but stayed on the plantations the rest of their lives.

It was not long until my brothers came home and we were all gathered together. Soon after that came the assassination of Abraham Lincoln. That brought great sorrow over all the land, and especially to the blacks. I remember the village of huts where the negroes lived; everyone would have a little piece of black cloth hung on it. They could not afford crepe, but it was merely a piece of old black pants, or coat, or anything in order to show their bereavement and their sorrow, that one so great had been taken from them; they loved him as their friend and deliverer. I heard them speak so much about "Marse Abraham" in their prayers, and sermons, and talk, and about "resting in Abraham's bosom" that I thought for a long time that Abraham Lincoln, and Abraham in the Bible, were the same man, until I began to go to Sunday-school and learned the difference.

CHAPTER II

EDUCATION OF THE COLORED PEOPLE

It was not very long before the white missionaries came from the North and schools were started, the children going to school by day and the older ones at night after work. Everyone was eager to get an education. It was amusing sometimes to see them reading the signboards and grocery advertisements, and as soon as the small children began to learn to read, they would inquire, "Child, what does dat say?" or, would say, "Read dis for me." It was astonishing how rapidly they learned, even the older ones.

They began to build churches at the same time. Money came in from the whites of the North, also from those in the South who were in sympathy. The slaves belonged mostly to the same denomination as did their masters. My mother was a Cumberland Presbyterian, and she helped to build the little church within a few blocks from our home, and to get a little Sunday-school started. How earnestly they prayed for means to build that church. They wanted the church more than homes to live in. I remember, when it was finished, that mother gathered all the children together and went to church, after making great preparation with our new dresses and bonnets. I remember the preacher talked very loud and with great unction, and many of the older ones shouted and cried. I got excited and could not understand it, and I cried too and wondered what it was all about. I was not long in finding out that Jesus died for me and that if I was a good girl I would go to heaven when I died and that I could see Him.

Soon after that we leased the ground near where the majority of the other colored people lived and built a little shanty of our own.

Some would never go to bed until late, but would wake up about midnight to pray and would keep it up sometimes for two or three hours; sometimes the neighbors would awaken and join in the singing and prayer and ofttimes souls in neighboring houses, would get under conviction and be converted. Those were great days. They would go from house to house to tell all the neighbors that they were converted, and would tell what a dear Savior they had found.

It was not very long after that my mother's health broke. She had been worked hard as a slave and she died in the fall of '68 leaving nine children. She called us around the bed and had us sing for her. The colored people had a song that they always sang, either at time of death, or when they were sold away from each other, that goes something like this:

> "Oh mother, adieu, I am sorry for you,
> My heart's filled with sorrow. What more can I do?
> If I see you no more 'til the last trump shall blow,
> I'll see you in heaven, where parting's no more."

Mother wanted to live to raise her children, as she had prayed so long for freedom, now it had come and she had to leave them. She asked the Lord that she might be reconciled to His will: finally she got the victory and was blessed. She called us all to her bedside and told us she wanted us to meet her in heaven.

> "O, death, where is thy sting?
> O grave, where is thy victory?"

I really did not know what it would mean to me to lose mother at this time, but I was not long in finding out, as my father had several little ones left, one being a baby not over a year old.

Before she died, my mother had requested him not to separate the children, but to let them "work out" and always keep a home for them. This request was kept until the last child had grown up, or death had taken it away. A doctor took me to work for him, and different persons took those that were old enough to work. I was nine years old and just old enough to take care of a baby and to wash dishes. I was much afraid of this doctor, as he was a very cross man. When he took me, I had no clothes. I remember their making me two little calico dresses and gingham aprons, and I was very proud of them. I cried every day and wanted to go home because he treated me so harshly. He let me go home on Sunday morning to stay until four o'clock in the afternoon.

I remember his telling people to come and look at his little negro that had been given him, but I had learned from father the blessings of freedom and liberty, and I felt all the sadder. Finally, after spending the day at home on Sunday, my father told me I would have to go back; that he had not given me away, but just wanted me to work and get some clothes and something to eat. He said that he would never give me away; that I should always have a home to come to and that I should be good and obey them.

I, too, got the spirit of "run away," as I was so afraid of the doctor. I took my clothes, hid them under the steps, did my chores, and, towards night I went downstairs to my supper, and, taking my bundle of clothes from under the steps, ran as hard as I could until I got home. My father told me I should not have left, but as I cried and was afraid of the doctor, who swore at me, father said perhaps he could find another place for me. The next day the doctor came after me. When I saw him coming I ran under the bed and began to cry, and as I would not come out, he asked for my clothes. Oh how I hated to give up that little cotton dress and gingham apron, but when I thought of being delivered from the doctor, it was a great consolation to me after all. I always felt that he might have given me one of the little dresses or aprons at least as I had no mother and had worked awhile for some of my clothes.

In the fall of the year, after working in the summer time, the children that were old enough were sent to school. Two of us girls were old enough; our three brothers and oldest sister had no chance to go; they had to work. Our white school-teachers, sent from the North, were devout Christians and missionaries. They taught us not only to read, but also to study the Bible and to learn the ways of God. There were sent to us as teachers a man by the name of Hayes with his three daughters and two sons. I did not go very steadily. I worked out in the summer and went to school in the winter.

I soon got to the place where I wanted pretty clothes, and I was ashamed of my dresses, but father could not give us any better.

Part of the time I did not have enough to eat. I have gone to school many a day without having anything to eat until night, with the exception of a piece of cold corn bread. When I saw other girls, who had mothers, have good things to eat in their dinner pails, I would hide mine. I thought then as much of a white-flour biscuit as I would of the finest fruit-cake now. Everybody ate corn bread, and, if we had that and bacon, we fared well. This was also the fare of many of the poor whites. I ofttimes took my little sister and went off by myself and ate my corn bread with sorghum molasses, if I was fortunate to have that, and I would never let them know but that I had dined sumptuously. One time when I saw the white girls coming home from school I called to them and asked what they had left in their dinner pails. One girl gave me a biscuit with peach preserves on it. It was made of white flour and I think it was the best biscuit I ever tasted. I am sure it was, for I have never forgotten the taste of it, and as I write it almost seems that I can taste it now; old-fashioned peach preserves, made as only a Southerner can make them.

As poor as we were, our father did not allow us to beg, especially for something to eat. He told us it was a disgrace to beg. He thought it better to go hungry than to beg, and if he saw a person, especially a white person who had been free all his life, begging, he would say, "I can't see how persons that have had their liberty all their lives need to come to such want." He told us to wait. He would get it for us. I praise the Lord it was no worse, for if I had to go hungry all day, he would be sure to come in with a little meal, and ofttimes with bacon, at night.

I went to school until I entered the fourth grade. Of course our privileges were not such as they are now, but I learned to read, and write, and spell, and that was considered among our people a pretty good education. My father wanted me to keep up my studies, but I soon got to the age when I wanted to work and buy some clothes, as I would ofttimes have to go to school with the sole of my shoe all loose and tied on with a string, through deep snows and zero weather. When I look back now and see how other girls who were clothed so much better than I, sickened and died from catching cold from exposure, I realize it was only the mercy of God that I lived through it, and that He had a purpose in it all. I can see plainly that it was all in answer to my mother's prayer.

There was a very kind white Methodist woman by the name of Mrs. Timmons. She took me to live with her. She felt sorry for me, and told my father she would let me work for her through the summer seasons. For awhile she let me go to school, but later on she could not keep me and let me go to school regularly through the winter seasons. I worked for her in the summer and went to school in the winter. She was very kind to me, clothed and fed me well, and she was a very devout Christian woman. She belonged to the Methodist Episcopal Church, North. They had their family prayers morning and night regularly, and were very consistent in their lives and claimed the blessing of sanctification. She never allowed any cooking or dish-washing on Sunday. I was a nursemaid for her little daughter until she was a large girl, and then I did the housework.

MRS. M. E. TIMMONS AND DAUGHTER

After awhile I tired of this place and wanted to go to dances and parties, but, as she was a very good Christian woman, she did not give me permission. Oftentimes, I went as a nurse girl with the white people to the white Methodist camp meetings, and other revival meetings, and took my seat in the back of the house, or up in the gallery and waited till the meetings were out. There I took care of the baby.

They had great revivals in those days. They were of the old-fashioned kind, where people would get blessed, sinners would be converted by the score, and whole communities would get stirred.

I remember about some revivals in our town. Those were days of great awakening in our little town of Springfield. There was a public square in the town, and men brought their products and sold them on the public square as they do now in public markets, and they were struck under conviction on their loads of wood, and their wagons of corn. Meetings were held in the Court House or in any place--sometimes on the streets, also in the jails, and they would get right down off the old wagons and pray to God and get saved. And in our own churches I have seen some of them, as the preacher exhorted, get up and start for the altar, fall under the power of God, and lie for hours and sometimes for days.

While the preacher was preaching, others would be struck under conviction, and oh such praying and preaching and singing. Those that were mourning prayed through to victory and came out with bright shining faces--Praise the Lord. Old grudges were put away before they were justified, wrongs were made right and there was a deep and godly sorrow for sin. Some saw visions and hell seemed to be before them, while the saints would rejoice and sinners were being converted in the old-fashioned way.

There was nothing said about sanctification among us, as we had not the light on it; but there were quite a few of the old pilgrims who enjoyed the experience. We have often heard them say, "If you ain't just right, you're just wrong," and they would say, "You will have to come clean."

We had some great camp meetings in those days. We often went to the woods between meetings, and we called that "seekers' prayer." The men took the men seekers and went in one direction, and the women took the women seekers and went in another direction, quite a distance from the camp to a spot of ground and put in the time praying. Some got saved, others got under conviction, as a great many sinners went along with the seekers. The old-fashioned horn was blown and they were given time to come back for their lunch and be ready for the night meeting. At the evening meetings the ministers dealt faithfully with souls, and pungent conviction led to thorough conversions. All sinful pleasures were put aside, and the converts became loyal followers of Christ. Oh, Lord, do send us a wave of the old-time, devil-driving, sin-killing, soul-saving power of salvation.

"Oh for that flame of living fire,
Which shone so bright in saints of old;
Which bade their souls to heaven aspire,
Calm in distress, in danger bold.

"Where is that spirit, Lord, which dwelt
In Abraham's breast and sealed him Thine?
Which made Paul's heart with sorrow melt,
And glow with energy divine?

"Is not Thy grace as mighty now,
As when Elijah felt its power;
When glory beamed from Moses' brow,
Or Job endured the trying hour?

"Remember, Lord, the ancient days;
Renew Thy work; Thy grace restore;

And while to Thee our hearts we raise,
On us Thy Holy Spirit pour."
Amen, Lord, let it be so.

These conditions grew brighter and better as we children grew older. The boys were old enough to leave school and work. My older sisters went into service, and my father would collect their wages. Our rations became better.

CHAPTER III

HOME LIFE

Our oldest sister was a mother to us, and when she was fourteen years old could do a woman's work. She was a good cook and housewoman and was a blessing and help to us all. In those days, Southerners who were able did not eat warmed-over food. All such was given to the slaves or help. As the people were fond of hot biscuits, the cook always made up a good quantity of dough, and served them hot. As they began to get cold, they were taken off the table, and more hot biscuits were served, and the cold ones were scraped into a bucket with other leavings, and, in a couple of days or less time, the cook had a bucket full to carry away. Our sister brought these home.

All the ex-slaves did not fare as hard as we, having mothers to help them shoulder the responsibilities; but my father's was a lone man's struggle, with nine motherless children, and it was also a struggle to pay for our home. But the pressure grew lighter as the children grew older.

We soon got our little home paid for. As I have previously mentioned, it was a two-room shanty with an attic and with one acre of ground.

Father was a good gardener, so now the dark clouds of poverty were beginning to break a little, and silver linings were more vivid, and our intellectual skies began to shine more clear.

I would often hear my father say, although he was not saved, "I thank my God for the chance of being a man, and I'll come out all right yet, if I have half a chance."

I remember my first earnest and sincere prayer. My two older sisters had been working out, and they had come home for awhile. I was the housekeeper, and I had not kept it as they thought I should. They began to give me orders and sent me out to gather brush from some acreage of underbrush nearby and I failed to obey. They chastised me for it, and I suppose I did deserve a flogging. I began to get angry and cry, and it was hard for me to stop, so I went alone into the woods and began to pity myself, saying, "I have no mother; no one loves me, and I wish I were where mother is." All at once I found myself praying, and I kept it up for quite awhile, and finally I crept back into some underbrush and hid myself. I prayed, "Oh Lord, have mercy upon me, please have mercy upon my soul."

Of course I had heard others say these words as they were praying. Nevertheless I was sincere but I did not know how to trust the Lord, and to exercise the appropriate faith. I had heard older ones say, "pray through," and I had often heard others tell about how the Lord shook their dungeon and the chains fell off, and how they had seen the devil go. Others would tell how they had asked the Lord to let a certain star shoot or to give them some sign that the work was done. I had heard and seen them as they were taken into the church. The elders were called to the front and they were asked to give in their experience, and, if their testimony did not ring clear they were told to go back and pray through until they were sure, without the least shadow of a doubt, that the work was done.

As I did not understand what faith was, I waited a long time upon my knees, and after my flow of tears ceased, I wondered why the work was not done, and I began to doubt. Now as night was approaching, I began to feel frightened and crept out into the open, picked up my sticks and dry brush and went home. I ofttimes sang when I was sad and I began to sing. I can not just remember the song I sang, but I believe it was this one, as I sang it so much when sad or lonely.

> "I'm a-rollin', I'm a-rollin',
> I'm a-rollin', through an unfriendly world,
> I'm a-rollin', I'm a-rollin',
> And I'll praise God when I get there.
> Oh, brothers won't you help me,
> Won't you help me to drive old Satan out of the way?
> I'm a-rollin', I'm a-rollin',
> And I'll praise God when I get home."

In the meantime father had arrived, and my baby sister had told him my trouble, and he admonished us all.

I kept this experience to myself, and I pondered it over in my heart. Later I joined the church, and was baptized, but I did not have a clear conception of the new birth, because I did not know clearly how to believe.

Later on, the Christmas holidays arrived. Everyone was making presents for the Christmas tree in the church and I knew we would have no presents because we were poor, and I hated to see my little sisters left out, so I began to plan some way to have our names called. Right here I practiced my first church deception. We got together and said, "We'll put something on for you if you'll put something on for us, and we will just wrap up wooden chips in paper and put them on as though they were presents. We won't open them in the church, but we will have our names called." So we each did this, our names were called; and we received our presents, and yet there was a consciousness of guilt on us, but we never told it. We watched the other children get their presents and, as we started away, one said to the other, "It's better than any." We meant it was better than none.

Nearly all the churches have dropped the old-fashioned Christmas tree from their entertainments. Would to God that every church entertainment might be removed, and that the Holy Spirit's infilling might take its place, for many a young girl or boy has gone to ruin and shame after taking part in some church play, or other amusement. The church entertainment became too tame for them so they took on the theater, or ball, or other sinful pleasures.

At the age of eleven, Mrs. T. took me to St. Louis. She kept a millinery shop and would go to St. Louis to buy her stock each season. You will notice the picture with the child in my arms. She loved me almost as well as she did her mother, and I loved her like a mother.

Her mother desired to have the child's picture taken. She didn't want to sit for it. The photographer couldn't get her to sit still; she cried for "Emmy" as she called me. They told me to take her and to get her pacified. I did so. She put her hand against my face and pressed her cheek against mine, and the mother said, "There, take her just as she is."

You will notice the way my hair was dressed. It was the style to wear at that time what was called "chignon" or waterfall. It was a great big amount of hair with wires run through to hold it on and make it light and puffy.

I was very proud and had no mother to plan my clothing and I wanted to dress and keep up to the fashion. I am surprised now, that Mrs. T. allowed me to wear such, but as long as the servants were clean, they were allowed to take their choice. Older persons told me that I was too young to wear such things. From that time on, for upwards of twenty-seven years, I wore some style of false hair, changing as the fashions changed. As I grew older I became more vain. No more school for me after leaving Mrs. T. I loved to dress and go to theaters.

Wages were better, my father did not need my help, and the home was paid for. My two younger sisters were old enough to work themselves, and in the meantime the sister older than I and the one younger died, also one brother. I found out that I belonged to a tubercular family. But, notwithstanding, I forgot all about my religious training and all I could think about was having a good time.

I left home and went to Western Missouri. I worked out, and came home every once in a while to see my father, and then went again. I tried to make myself believe there was no God, but I soon gave that idea up. I was afraid to die and did not let myself think about it.

"NURSE EMMY" AND THE CHILD
WHO LOVED HER

CHAPTER IV

MEETS MR. RAY

I met my future husband, L. P. Ray, in Carthage, Missouri, in '81. He was young like myself and had not been from home very long. Mr. Ray's home was in Emporia, Kansas. We were married in Fredonia, Kansas, in '87. He learned the trade of stone-cutter and mason. We were very happy for a short time. Later, my husband began to drink, not so very heavily at first. I knew that he drank when we were married, but I didn't think much of it at that time. I thought so long as he could take a drink or let it alone when he liked, it was all right. I thought it looked manly for him to smoke a cigar. I didn't give it much thought, until it began to come so often--then our trouble began. When I woke up I found that he had become a drunkard. The class of men that he worked with was made up of drinking men, and he always said that he felt he had to be a man among men. When they got their pay they would all take a drink around. It soon came to pass that he began to lie about his wages. He got despondent afterwards, and declared that he would never take another drink, but it would not be very long--a space of possibly a week--until he would be at it again and I got to the place where I had no confidence in him. And he would say, "I'll prove to you that I will be a man yet," and then he would get morbid and say, "I'll leave this town. If I can get away I'll go where I am not so well acquainted, and I will do better." He went ahead, as we never had money enough left to go together, but he would always send for me as soon as he could, and then we would start again to live a new life. It would not be very long before it would be the same old drink, the same old devil, the same old sin. I had a temper equal to a tigress. And a drinking man and a woman with a high temper make a home a hell. Many a night have I wept all night and wet my pillow with tears. He would always be sorry afterwards and say, "I will never do it again." But of course the habit was on him, and his associations were bad, and he had not the power within himself to resist the temptation.

I got tired of moving. It seemed as though we could never settle down, or get anything together. Ofttimes he would put a little money in the bank, and take it right out again; once he told me I could put it in the bank myself. He brought his wages home Saturday night when he was not drinking. I put it in the bank on Monday, and for once I thought we had some money ahead. I noticed that he came home drunk at times. I asked him where he got his drink, and he said, "I didn't spend any money for it, the boys treated." Finally I found out that we had not a cent in the bank. As fast as I put it in he was writing it out on a check; then it would be the same old quarrel, until my soul got sick and faint within me. At first he was not a quarrelsome man; I would do the quarreling, but later on when he was drinking, he got so he would quarrel with me, and not only with me, but with others. He went into saloons and once got into a fight over a dog and was arrested and put into jail. He never laid in jail more than over night, as he always worked and had many friends, also, who drank. I found out that my married life was a disappointment to me as well as to him. I often felt that I would leave him, if I had a child, or some one to love.

I was of a jealous disposition, and then after attending dances we came home and quarreled. I got so sick of it, that one time after he was arrested for drunkenness, I said to him,

"Let's get religion." He told me not to start something, and of course I did not say any more to him. When he came home he always brought the Salvation Army paper, "War Cry" for me to read on Sunday. In one of the "War Crys" was a cartoon of a Salvation Army band going up the street blowing its horns and beating its drums, and back up in the alley was an empty barrel, and a poor old drunk had heard the music of the band and was creeping out of the barrel. He had been awakened by their songs and music--oh, I remember what an impression it left upon me, and I wondered whether my husband would quit his drinking, if he was saved. We seldom went to church, as I could not get him to go with me. I got books--novels--and read all day to him to get him to stay at home.

Although a sinner, I did my cooking on Saturday. The influence of Mrs. T. stayed with me, and I never worked on Sunday. I always kept my little house clean and did everything to make it attractive, hoping that I could win him. He was not unkind, except when he had been drinking. He was not unkind then, unless I disturbed him, and when I saw him coming in drunk,--(perhaps I had waited all day or maybe late at night)--the minute I laid my eyes on him, as the saying is, "the devil would be to pay" and I could not hold my tongue, as he always wanted to make believe he was not drunk. With a drunken man and a high-tempered woman you can imagine what the result would be. Every time I went to a ball I came home with a conviction on my heart that I was doing wrong. Even while I was on the floor dancing, a sadness would come over me. I often wished I was dead and would threaten to kill myself, but did not have the courage to do so. I was afraid of hell. Oh, praise the Lord for deliverance.

He had promised before coming to Seattle, that when he got here he would quit drinking and would buy us a little home. We would pay no more rent and would live in a shanty until we got money enough. He bought a little shanty, and we lived there until we were converted. There were but a few of our own people in Seattle when we came, and at times I got very lonely. I had a dear friend who died after giving me a birthday party. I went to see her one day and found her sick, very sick. I remained with her all day and promised to come back the following day. The next day I went back, after doing my work in the morning, and found there was crepe on the door and oh, it was such a shock. We had just had a dance a night or two previous. We had talked the day before, and she was called away so suddenly. It seemed to take my strength, and I seemed unable to get over it, and something began to tell me that if I did not get right, I was liable to die and not be prepared. (This friend of mine belonged to the Catholic church.)

In the meantime a colored church was organized in Seattle--The African Methodist--and there was a conference being held. I persuaded my husband to go with me, and we went on Sunday morning, and I sat and cried throughout the meeting. I hardly knew why. I felt somewhat ashamed when I got home. On Monday I was very blue and felt that life was a failure, and I wondered whether I should go and see another friend, with whom I often talked about my troubles. She would send out and get a bucket of beer, and we would sit and tell about our sorrows and our husbands. I did not know I was under conviction. I felt I should die. I started from the house, reached the corner of the street and something seemed to say, "Why not go to the church?" I stood for a few minutes and I decided, "Well, I'll just go." I had on a new dress Sunday, and I also had another new dress. I said, "I'll wear this one today." I thought I would show my good clothes. When I reached the church, a young man was preaching. I shall never forget the text. He was preaching for the first time--his first sermon--and it seemed as though the bishop and the rest of the preachers were all sleepy. The text was, "Behold, I stand at the door and knock, and if any man open, I will come in and sup with him and he with me."

He remarked, "He is knocking at the door of some heart today," and I felt that he was talking to me. As the Spirit began to move, the bishop woke up. The preacher went on to tell about a friend of his (a school teacher), who was under conviction at one time and he did not yield to the Spirit's wooing. Finally he went into the country to teach school, and he was taken ill suddenly and when the preacher went to see him he said, "I can't pray now. Oh, I wish I had prayed when I was at church that time; I wish I could feel now as I did then." The tears began to roll down my cheeks. I was afraid to use my handkerchief for fear people would notice it. The brother of this friend of mine that had died, had lately been converted. He came over and spoke to me and asked me to come to Jesus, when the call was made to the altar, and I told him I could not go there. I would go some day, not now; the thoughts kept running through my mind, "You can't be a Christian and live with that man, and you know the Odd Fellows are going to have a dance. If you get saved, your husband will go to the dance, and he will be flirting, and you will have to go and watch." We never went to any place alone. With all our troubles, one would never go without the other. This helped to hold us together. So I said, "Not today," and yet the preacher kept saying, "Behold I stand at the door and knock." He kept rapping on the pulpit, and I felt as though a hammer was striking my heart and breaking it in pieces, and I wept all the more. Just about that time, a sinner, an old friend of ours, got up and made a bee-line for the altar, and the Christians began to say "Amen," and the preacher seemed to plead more earnestly. Then this young man who was talking to me spoke about his sister, and the thought of her sudden death flashed through my mind. I said, "Oh, I can't be a Christian now and live with the devil. I will some day." A voice seemed to say, "This is your last opportunity to be saved." I could not sit any longer. I felt as though some unseen hand had taken hold of me, and before I knew it, I ran to the altar, fell on my knees and said, "Yes, Lord, have mercy on me and I will serve you all my life."

Sister Roy, a very devout sister, and others came and spoke to me and said, "Just give up; this is the very best step you have ever taken in your life." I said, "I will. Lord, have mercy upon me and save me." Right then and there my burden rolled away, and daylight broke into my soul. Oh, praise the Lord. I sprang to my feet and said, "I am saved," and began to sing. At the same time there were two others saved beside myself. Oh, that was a happy day. I felt it would be good to die then and there. The Christians all rejoiced and said, "We have got the queen," as I was quite a leader in the dances and in society. We gave quite a few dances in our home. They seemed to feel that the dancing crowd was broken up. As I started to my home the devil began to talk to me. He said, "Now what will you do? You know you can't live with him and be a Christian." As I went into the door he was at home. I felt so new and so light; it was a new world, for I was born again, this time from above. I said to him, "I have been to church today and am saved." He looked very much surprised and could not say anything. I looked at him a little while and began to cry. He would not talk with me about it, and I could see right then that I should have a battle if I kept saved. Then I said, "I have promised that I would serve the Lord, if He would take the burden off my heart, and that I would be true to God, if I had to leave you." But, oh, how my heart yearned to have him come with me. He did brace up for awhile, quit drinking and went to church with me Sunday mornings. He was glad I was a Christian, and wanted me to say my prayers before retiring, and when I failed to to so, he would tell me about it. I prayed to myself, not audibly, I did not have courage to offer prayer with him. He wanted me to keep saved, but would not come with me. I was so happy for awhile, it seemed I was in a new world. I was not afraid to die, and had great peace of soul until I got my eyes off from the Lord upon him. I was ignorant of the Way. I did not know what the word consecration meant. How I do praise the Lord for being so patient with me.

Later my husband tried to encourage me, and I persuaded him to go with me to church. After awhile, he began to drink again. I did not feel like getting angry as before but would cry, get heavy hearted, and discouraged. Some of the older Christians visited me, and I would take courage as they asked me out to church on Sunday, saying, "We missed you." Again I took courage and said, "I'll stick to it and not give up." I want to stop right here and say, "How many opportunities for doing good we let slip, because we are not awake to our privileges. Many a heart is aching, if we could read them all, and a kind word or a prayer would go a long way in helping a groping soul out of its misery." So it was in my case.

There were real mothers of the church, especially Sister L. Roy. For though we had ten thousand instructors in Christ, yet we had not many mothers. I went to church on Sunday mornings, but I never got out at night. I was afraid to leave Mr. Ray for fear he would go off to the saloon. For awhile he stayed at home on Sunday mornings while I was away. Later on when I came home from church he would be gone, and I would sit and wait all day long, get dinner, but I could never eat if he didn't come. It would take away my appetite. Then I would begin to get angry and try not to. I would look for him and wish he would arrive. I would get real mad, and just about the time I was the maddest, he would come in, or I would look and see him come staggering down the road, and then I would think, "He must not speak a word to me, or he will hear from me." When he came in, he would want to talk, and I would say, "Keep your mouth shut, and we will have no trouble. If you don't we will have trouble," and then he would get mad, and I would say things I should not have said. As he would swear at me, it hurt me so bad I would use the same words back at him, and then he would say, "Now you're a Christian; you're a fine one; you had better go and pray." Then I would turn my tongue loose, as I felt that I had already given away to my temper, and give him a piece of my mind--later I would wish I had it back again. I would cry all night and repent the next day, and I would think "It's of no use; I will not go to church again." Therefore I did not grow in grace and was not strong. If I went to church, I could not pray and I could not testify. I was backslidden in heart. I became tired of it all; it seemed so hard to live a Christian life. I did not thoroughly understand what consecration was and did not know that the Lord could take that distrust out of my heart, and let me trust Him entirely. I wondered where it would all end. I was afraid to go back, and yet I was back, but had not confessed it.

Later on there came a little evangelist from Texas, who was filled with the Holy Spirit, to hold a revival for us. He held a revival in our church, and my, how he uncovered sin, especially in the professed Christians. I went to church Sunday morning. He said, "You professed Christian women who have husbands that are not saved, you don't pray enough. What one of you will lead the prayer meeting tomorrow? We want to have a prayer meeting every evening at seven o'clock. We want to put these unsaved husbands on the prayer list." My, I felt bad. A friend of mine that also had an unsaved husband came out with me, and we happened to meet the evangelist and she told him, "I cannot pray in public, because I have heart failure," and I said, "Don't expect me to, I don't believe in women praying in public." He didn't say a word.

The next night I persuaded my husband to go with me. I thought the evangelist would excuse me, as the other preachers always did. That night he got right up and said, "We have some women here that have asked me not to call on them to pray. We want no cowards in our band who will their colors fly." He looked right over at me, and I felt that everybody knew he was talking to me. I got mad and when I came out I told my husband what I had said to him, and he began to make fun of me. "That's right, if you cannot pray, get down and out," and he laughed at me. I felt so ashamed, yet I felt I dared not try it.

All the next day I kept saying, "Well, I am neither a Christian, nor am I a sinner. I am not having the pleasure that I had before I was saved." As I thought over this, I said, "I'll go and try to pray and do the best I can, but if I do so, my husband will leave me, because he will be at the saloon every night while I am at church. I will have to give him up, but I have started now and I am going through, so I will go tonight and try." I thought, "I will have to give him up, I am going to leave him, or he will leave me. I am not happy anyway, so I will go and do my duty." Then the thought came to me. Treat him with courtesy, ask him to go with you, and if there is any leaving done, let him do it. I thought again, "What shall I do? I am not able to do hard work," and then I thought, "I will go out nursing children," and I had it all planned out, as to what I should do. But I asked him that evening if he would not go with me, and he said, "No." I said, "All right, my dear, I have followed you as far as I can, and if you will go to hell, you will have to go by yourself. I am going to serve the Lord from this time on."

I never shall forget how I went up the hill. It was seven o'clock in the summer time, and as I went up the hill I looked up to the sky, and said, "Oh, God! I love him so, but I will follow Thee. I have never had a mother or anyone to love me, and now my life is a disappointment." All at once it seemed that a voice said to me, "You can love me," and I said, "Oh, Lord! Do take that love, that foolish love that I have in my heart for that man, and let me love Thee, and I will serve Thee as long as I live." And oh, how light my heart got. Right there I was reclaimed. I told them that I would lead the meeting, and when I went in, I walked up to one of the older sisters and said, "I will take the meeting," and she said, "Praise the Lord." She was glad.

I don't know what I said, and I don't know what I read, but it was very few words and oh! it was such a relief, and such a blessing came to my heart, because I had obeyed. That night when the preacher preached, he took the subject, "You must come down." It was very touching. I followed him all through the sermon, and he told how everybody had to bow the knee and confess to God, and I wondered to myself if it would ever be possible that Lloyd Ray would confess, or come down, and I said, "No, not he; he loves drink too well." As I went home that night from the meeting very much blessed I said, "Well I know he will not be there; he will be in the saloon; but I will go home and say my prayers and go to bed, because we are going to part. I have the Lord now and He loves me."

To my surprise, when I got on the side of the hill, I saw a light in the window and I said, "What, can it be possible that he is there, and has not gone to the saloon?" As I opened the door and went in, I walked over to where he was sitting and said, "Oh, you should have gone to church tonight and heard the sermon. The preacher says, "You must come down. I am so glad you will have to come down some day, maybe when it will be too late." He didn't answer me a word. I knelt down beside the bed, took up my cross and prayed.

The evangelist had asked the people to pray for him, and we had put all those on a prayer list who wanted to have prayers for their people. He called the prayer list a chain, and every person was a link in this chain, so that when we prayed for them and they were present, they would know for whom we were praying, and we would just ask the Lord to break the chain. He had everybody pray unitedly in the morning at four o'clock, to break the chain.

The next day, I sang all day. I sang old songs I had forgotten, songs I had heard in my childhood days. Husband was not working, and he never came home through the day. He stayed in the saloon until night. This day he went away, and it was not long until he was back, but I did not say anything to him, I just sang and prayed. He went into the woods and sawed logs all day. When evening came, we did not hold much conversation, but I said to him, "Will you go to church with me tonight?" He said, "After awhile I will come over." Oh! how I ran up that hill. It seemed as though my feet hit only the high places. I had such joy in my heart, and I kept saying, "After awhile, after awhile." I was surprised that he was so willing to come. We had a good prayer service, and when the time came for the evening service, he came in and walked right to the front seat and sat down beside me. I was delighted. The preacher spoke of the Love of God that night, and then he spoke of woman's love, how a mother loved her children, and a woman, her husband. He said, "I have heard them say, 'I could take my heart out for him'." As he said these words, my husband twisted and turned from one side to the other. It seemed as though the very bench he sat on was afire. Finally the preacher made the altar call, and he said, "You Christians go back there and speak to those sinners." I thought, "Oh, whom can I speak to? I never spoke to these sinners. I have gone to parties and dances with my husband, and though I have stopped dancing, they know I have not been a good Christian; I am ashamed to speak to them." But he said, "Move out," and I remembered what I had promised the Lord. I looked around to see whom I could speak to with the least embarrassment. There was a little woman that I was well acquainted with, very kind, who always had a smile on her face, although she was not saved. I walked up to her and asked her to come with me to the altar. She laughed right in my face. That made me feel ashamed, but I took courage and said, "I know I have not lived as a consistent Christian should, and have never said anything to you before, but from this time on, I intend to do so, and walked away." Later on we had the privilege of seeing both this lady and her husband saved in their own home, while my husband and I were making our house-to-house visits. She said she laughed that night because she did not know what to say. She lived and died in the faith several years later. Her husband is a member of the Baptist church at this writing. We give God all the glory. Amen.

I was afraid to speak to anyone else, so I started back to my seat feeling I had tried to do my duty, and as I returned, I noticed there was an old lady speaking to my husband, and he was all broken up and was standing there weeping. It struck me so hard I got weak in the knees, and the first thought that came to me was, "let me get away, I don't want to go near him," and I went in another direction. I remembered how I had sworn at him; how angry I had gotten at him and I couldn't think he had any confidence in me, so I didn't want to spoil a good thing. He didn't go to the altar. The meeting closed, and some one spoke to me and said, "Your husband is coming," and I said, "I hope so."

We walked home and we didn't speak a word to each other. When we got ready for bed, I said, "Will you pray with me?" He didn't answer me a word and went off to bed, and I prayed. The next day he got up early and went down to the saloon. I had started washing, and about nine o'clock he came back. I was surprised to see him come home, and I saw the change on his face and he looked very sorrowful. He walked in and asked me, "Do you want the clothes line put up?" Oh! such softness and tenderness there was in his voice! I said, "Yes, dear," and as he went out to put up the line, I ran behind the front door and knelt down on my knees and said, "Oh, God, kill him, kill him, kill him!" as I knew he needed nothing less than a thorough purging and killing. As he came back in I kept singing, said nothing much to him, only prayed in my heart. The day was spent very quietly between us. When evening came I said to him, "Will you go with me to church tonight?" "I will be over after awhile," was the reply. Oh! it seemed as if I were in a new world, although I had been converted. I could see that the Lord was dealing with him, and after the prayer services he came, walked up to the front where I sat and sat down by me, and I felt I had a real man. After the preaching was over the altar call was given. He got right up and walked forward and knelt down at the altar. I did not go near him, I was afraid he would think of my life as a Christian, but I knelt and prayed where I was. Finally, he rose to his feet and said that he believed that the Lord had saved him, and oh, such a bright smile was on his face. The Christians gathered around him, shook hands with him, and rejoiced, but I didn't go near until the last. I wanted to let him tell it and be sure of it before I went near him. Finally, I went up, and as I got near him we embraced each other and stood and wept on each others shoulders. The preacher said to the congregation, "How many of you converts will go home and will pray with me at four o'clock this morning?" He told my husband to set up his family altar and be praying at four o'clock in the morning. We went home that night and had our prayers. As we knelt by the bed side, I prayed first as I was older; then he prayed and trembled just like a leaf, and said, "Oh, Lord, bless my wife," and I cried and raised my head up and looked at him and thought, "Is it possible this is he praying?" It seemed almost too good to be true.

I assure you there was no sleep that night. We talked and sang and prayed and cried and laughed all night long. Then we began to confess our sins to each other, and he said, "Emma, you know that time I got drunk at a certain time and spent that money. I wouldn't have done it, but you accused me wrongfully. Will you forgive me for it?" And I replied, "Yes, I will," and then I said, "You remember that time I hit you with a cup? I knew it was wrong, but you provoked me. I am so sorry, will you forgive me?" And so we would confess, and then we would sing, and then we would cry, and then we would laugh.

The preacher, before we left the church that night, said, "When you pray, don't pray the way the old colored man did when he said, "Oh, Lord, rub our heads against the wisdom post." The minister said, "God was our wisdom and would teach us," but as we talked it over, we said, "Thank God we can see now what the old-time fathers meant. The Lord surely has rubbed our heads against the wisdom post."

Oh, such rays of light flooded our vision that we could see our mistakes and our sin and the enemies of our souls. No wonder the Lord said in His Word, "If the light that is in thee be darkness, how great is that darkness."

We were up at four o'clock in the morning and prayed again. Mr. Ray said, "As soon as you get my breakfast, I want to go down and see Bill." This was one of his associates that he drank with, and he said, "I will be back at noon, and then we will go again to our friends and tell them what the Lord has done for us." He went down to the old corner where he drank. It was called "Billy-the-Mug's" saloon. There he met his friend Jack with some others and he told Jack all about it. He will tell you of his conversion in his experience later. But he was home at noon. We had prayer and started out again.

In the afternoon we went to those with whom we had danced, drank beer, and played cards, and told them what the Lord had done for us, and everywhere we went we sang and prayed, then went right out and left them weeping.

CHAPTER V
MR. RAY'S TESTIMONY

I was born in 1860, February 8th, in the State of Texas at Kentucky Town. I was born of a slave mother; I am told that my father was white. I know nothing of a father's counsel, and if I am anything at all, it is because I am what I am by the grace of God and my mother's prayers. My mother was a devout Christian, the mother of seventeen children, and a Baptist by faith. All the rest of my family are Baptists. We remained in Texas after we obtained our freedom until I was ten years old, then we went to Emporia, Kansas. I did not have much schooling, as times were hard and most of us had to work, so we got along in some way. Like most boys, when I was large enough to earn wages I quit going to school; so I have had to face the world with a meager education. I thank the Lord that He found me and saved me just as I was, in my ignorance and sin.

I left home at the age of nineteen and I have never forgotten how my mother cried over me at that time. While I was at home she would pray for us, especially on Sunday mornings. She would gather us in and, oh, how she would pray for us! She would clasp her hands and then raise them up and cry, and then she would bring them down on the chair and repeat her prayer, and it would make me feel so bad. If mother would only stop crying.

MR. RAY AT SIXTEEN
YEARS OF AGE

MR. RAY AT SIXTEEN YEARS OF AGE

She said she wanted me to be her preacher, but I replied in my heart, "Anything but a preacher," and said all kinds of mean things about preachers. I did not like them, as she always entertained the preachers in our home, and I remember the time when she had a number of them at dinner, and she put the good things on the table for them to eat. We were not accustomed to eating biscuits in those days, and I watched her take the biscuits out of the old-fashioned skillet, cooked with a lid in front of the fire place, with coals over the top and coals in the bottom. My, how my mouth watered for those biscuits! I was so afraid that the preachers would eat them all, and she kept saying to them, "Have another one;" and they would say, "Yes, Sister Mary, I will;" and they would brag about her good cooking. I watched her until she had taken out the last biscuit and put it upon the table, and as she passed the plate around, she told them to help themselves, and when they had taken the last one, I said to my brother who was sitting with me, "There, Ben, the last biscuit is gone." She didn't say anything to me then. I knew when the last one went that it meant corn bread for my dinner. But after the preachers all left I got a flogging, so I did not like the preachers and said I would never be one.

Mother's prayers followed me wherever I went. Like most boys, I wanted to become a man. So I began to drink and do the other things that went with it. Drink got the best of me from time to time and at last it got me down. I quit writing home. Oftentimes I would get under deep conviction and get drunk to drown it. When I was in the saloons, and the Salvation Army women came to sell their "War Cry," because I was under conviction and wanted to do something good, I would buy one. Oftentimes we would get into disputes over religion. I always respected it in a sense and did not want to hear any person ridicule my mother's religion and sometimes got into a fight over it. There are others who feel the same way.

I wandered from place to place until, finally, I came to Seattle, July 6th, 1889. The city was burned down in ashes and I came to help build it up, as I was a stone mason and cutter by trade. It was first built up of tents, and saloons were at every door. The temptation was terrific and drinking everywhere. Beer by the water buckets was on the job from morning until night. Thus it got me farther down. But my mother's prayers followed me wherever I went. I could not get away from them.

About this time a revival meeting was held in the African Methodist church. This was the time I was born again. I praise the dear Lord that the same fire burns in my heart now, as I think of God's mighty power to save. That night the conviction was pungent. I had been under it for two days. I was in the habit of going to the saloon every morning when I was working, to get my "morning's morning" as I called it. I thought I would go down and take a drink this morning, but my sins lay heavy upon me. I went into a saloon and took a drink and came home, something I was not in the habit of doing. I stayed at home all day, and the next day I went back. I thought I could fight the conviction off. I went to the bar and called for a whiskey, but something came up in my throat, and my heart was so heavy I could not drink. I shoved it to one side and said, "Give me a beer." They gave me the beer, and the same lump came in my throat, and I could not drink it. I shoved that to one side and said, "Give me a cigar," and paid my bill and walked out, never to go in again. As I started up the hill towards home I said, "What's the matter with me?" I said I would pray, but I never had prayed and I found myself standing still in the street, wondering if I could be saved. I came to the house, and when I saw my wife I felt sorry for the way I had talked to her about her religion, and at times after casting it up to her I would feel bad, but would not tell her so. I did not want her to backslide. At times I would tell her to go pray or say her prayers,--if she went to bed without them, and said so in the way of a joke. I am glad she did not give up entirely, and I thank the Lord that she held on to Him for me. I went to the church that night and went to the altar. I don't remember many of the words that I used.

"I said, "I cannot pray," and someone said, "Say, 'God be merciful to me, a sinner'." I repeated that prayer until I knew I was saved. Talking about moving pictures, I saw them before they were ever put on. That night my whole past life passed before me and, as each sin flashed upon the screen, the Lord would say, "Will you give up that sin," and I would say, "Yes, Lord." "And this one," and I would answer, "Yes." They continued to pass this way until I had said, "Yes" to the last one and I felt clear before God, and my sins were all washed through the blood of my Savior, praise the Lord. Oh, praise the Lord, the fire is burning now and has been for thirty years.

We had a glorious time when we went to our home. Then I set up my family altar and it has never been taken down. The first thought that came to me was of my mother as she had not heard from me for nineteen years. I sat down and wrote her a letter and told her that I was saved. I told her that I was delivered from the drink appetite, and I have never wanted it from that night up to the present moment. I praise the Lord for taking away the tobacco appetite also. I had one equal to the worst you could think of, and as to swearing, I had no equal, but it went with all of the devil's goods. When my mother received my letter she was the happiest woman in Emporia. She took the letter and went to the other children and had some one read it, as she went from home to home. She could not read herself. Then she would shout and praise the Lord for what He had done for her boy. At this time most of her children were alive and lived close to mother. She said she wore the letter out, carrying it around with her and having it read. She would take it with her when she went to wash, and have the white people whom she was working for, read it. I wrote her eight pages on foolscap paper. I thank the Lord for the privilege of sending for her later on. She came to my home and stayed with me for one year. I went back and visited her twice afterward before she died at the age of ninety-five. She was converted when but a child, in the year that the stars fell, in 1833.

On the third day of July, 1906, I was baptised in Lake Washington. I wrote to her and told her the day I would be baptised by immersion. They say she got very happy at church that Sunday. While visiting here she received the blessing of full salvation. Oh, mothers never stop praying for your boys! Hold on to God, He will answer prayer. Prayer changes things and, in spite of my dislike for preachers, I am glad of the privilege of now being a preacher of righteousness for His name's sake.

CHAPTER VI
MRS. RAY'S SANCTIFICATION

Soon after Brother Ray's conversion, some white people came to our church. We thank the Lord for them. They had the experience of full salvation. A man by the name of Clark and his wife, also an aged man whose name I have forgotten. All gave their experiences, telling how the Lord had cleansed them from inbred sin. They gave us some chalk-talks from the blackboard, describing the natural heart, the justified heart, and also the sanctified heart, illustrating by drawing three hearts and showing the fruit of each one. It was very interesting to some, but I did not understand it.

Our pastor seemed to be hungry for a clean heart and so were several of the members, and he advised us all to seek the experience. He said it could be obtained, and that we could live without sin. We were both then walking in the light, keeping up our family prayers, and were praying in secret three times a day, sometimes oftener, reading our Bibles, and were hungry for the blessed experience, as our pastor took the lead. We could see such a difference in his preaching.

The old gentleman referred to, visited from house to house and prayed with us. He said the Lord sent him to us. I was very much blessed. He gave us some tracts to read, but later went away. We have never heard from him since. We have often wished we knew where he was, so as to write and tell him that we had sought and obtained the blessing. Some of our church members did not believe we could live without sin, and ridiculed the preacher and persecuted those who had the experience. Nevertheless we often found ourselves yearning for the Holy Ghost. We would weep when others would tell about it. I had some very previous times in my secret devotions, and ofttimes was blessed and happy. I had quit my backsliding, didn't get angry outwardly, and if anyone spoke evil of me I didn't like it, but could keep still. Oh! how I longed for that perfect peace which I saw in others' lives. I heard a white lady preacher, a United Presbyterian, tell that the baptism of the Holy Spirit was the promise of the Father, and He could fill us with Himself and cleanse us from all unrighteousness. After preaching, she would say, "Now all who want this experience arise." We did so. Then she would say, "Stay right there," but she didn't give us an opportunity to seek. She did not tell me the way through to victory; and I became so hungry, and craved the baptism of the Holy Spirit day and night. I did everything that others told me to do, and tried to get it just as they did. My pastor said he went into his closet, and told the Lord he would stay there until he received the blessing. I tried that, got tired and came out, as my mind began to wander upon other things. I found myself, while washing, at a standstill over my tub, praying for the baptism of the Holy Ghost. I went to see Sister L. Roy, my mother in Christ, and inquired of her how she got the blessing. She said they told her, when she prayed, to believe that she received, and she did believe and the Holy Spirit fell upon her. She was so blest that she ran through the room, praising the Lord, for His Holy Spirit had come into her heart to abide. Her joy seemed to be so great that it made me hunger all the more. I went home and tried that out, saying, "Lord, I believe; give me Thy Holy Spirit's baptism." Then I said, "Now I have received Him." I remained quiet for a few minutes, and before I knew it, I said again, "Oh, Lord give me the Holy Spirit, wash my heart and make me clean." I kept this up all night, and the next day was the Sabbath. I went out to our little church. We had no preacher. The conference had moved our former pastor, because some objected to his preaching holiness.

A few of us knelt to pray, and while I was praying, saying the same thing over, "Please sanctify me," the Spirit whispered softly, "Why do you pray longer? Can't you believe?" I stopped for a few seconds. It seemed that I could pray no farther. I reminded myself of a chicken dying with the gaps. I had gapped and gapped until I died, and right there I died and said, "Have Thy way." It flashed upon me that I was seeking the experience my way and was trying to feel like others did. The Spirit then said, "Believe the Lord and receive the Holy Spirit." I said, "Lord, I take Thee at Thy word; I believe Thou dost sanctify me just now." One of the sisters was praying and I could hardly wait until she was through, to tell it. As she finished, I arose to my feet and said, "I am sanctified, I take the Lord at His word right now." The pilgrims rejoiced, and I felt as peaceful as though my struggles were over, and yet I did not have the demonstration that they had manifested. I then said, "I don't feel as you do, but I take the Lord by faith." I returned home in a very quiet attitude, and went about my home singing, Blessed Assurance, Jesus is mine," not expecting any more witness of His Spirit, only a quiet, peaceful soul rest. On Wednesday afternoon I lay down upon my couch reading a little book on "The Assurance." The question was asked in the book, "Reader, have you met these conditions?" I said, "I have," and as I answered, "I have," all of a sudden it seemed that a streak of lightning had struck over the corner of the house, and it struck me on the top of the head, and went through my body from head to foot like liquid fire, and my whole body tingled. I tried to rise and was so weak I fell back upon the lounge and I said, "What, Lord?" and there came another dash of glory through my being and a voice inside of me said, "Holy." I tried to rise, but had not the strength and I cried, "O, glory! The Holy Ghost has come into my heart." As my strength began to return, I felt a passion, such a love for souls as I had never felt before. I saw a lost world. My heart became hot. A fire of holy, abiding love for God and souls was kindled at that hour and I felt to say with Isaiah, "Here am I, Lord, send me." It was the fire that still burns in my soul this very moment, and I feel it will last until Jesus comes. I have often been tried and tempted by wicked men and devils. There has never been a moment that I have had a shadow of a doubt concerning my baptism of the Holy Ghost and fire. Oh, hallelujah! He abides. He abides. I am glad the Spirit helped me to receive Him by faith. I can see now it would have been injurious to me to have the feelings when I wanted them, for now when I have no feelings I walk by faith. Otherwise I would always be in doubt as to my baptism by the Holy Spirit. Since then I have made many blunders and mistakes. The judgments of my head are at times imperfect, but, thank the Lord He keeps the motives of my heart pure through the power of the Holy Spirit.

There came to us another pastor, and he did not believe in the experience of entire sanctification. Many of the members did not understand us and there was considerable persecution. They told us we professed to live without sin, which was impossible. We tried to explain to them how we could sin if we desired to, but as we walked in the light and trusted in the cleansing blood of Jesus, He could keep us the rest of our lives without actual transgression. This we purposed to do. The persecution grew hotter until we were forbidden by our pastor to testify to it. About this time there was a big convention held in the First Presbyterian Church by Rev. A. B. Simpson, and Stephen Merritt, of New York, under the auspices of the Christian and Missionary Alliance. Some of us attended. There the Lord wonderfully poured out His Spirit in sanctifying and healing power; our souls were encouraged and helped. Brother Ray came home. He said he had been seeking while away and was hungry for a clean heart. He fasted and prayed and read his Bible. It did not take him so long to enter into the experience as it did me.

He went one evening to a Mission on Third Street. There he heard a Bible Reading on the baptism of the Holy Ghost. He had also read the Scripture in Acts, 2nd chapter, and in Acts 19:4, 5, and other chapters about receiving the Holy Spirit. It seemed so easy for him to believe. After praying at the altar a short while, he did not demonstrate, but I could see that he had received the blessing. He said "I am satisfied now." It came like a still, small voice. It seemed to settle him down so deep in God. He did not seem to have a shadow of a doubt about it, and his life was so steady and calm. He loved his Bible. It was a new book to him as well as to myself. We saw new beauties every time we opened it. We said to each other, "O, how precious is this new light!" We never knew there were so many words about the Holy Spirit and its workings. We could not keep it. We told our pastor and all our friends. We thought they would all be glad, but some did not understand; others ridiculed. Now we were consecrated and fitted for service, the burden for lost souls came on our hearts with greater zeal and joy than ever.

A great light flooded our souls, and immediately the Holy Spirit began to lead us out into deeper depths. We found Him to be a Comforter and Reprover. The Scriptures plainly say, "When He comes He will reprove the world of sin, and of righteousness, and of judgment" (John 16:8).

He didn't give us all the light at one time, but later, little by little, as we were able to receive it. Neither did we speak in tongues, but He gave us a new tongue to testify and tell the glad tidings. We could also see the fields that were white, and our work lay before us as we caught the vision.

Old wrongs had been made right, old debts paid, the tenth of our income was being given to the Lord. We were standing in our places ready for the battle, and waiting for orders at the Spirit's command.

THE COLORED W. C. T. U. OF SEATTLE, WASHINGTON. MRS. L. P. RAY (FOURTH FROM LEFT IN CENTER ROW) WAS FOR MANY YEARS THE PRESIDENT

THE COLORED W. C. T. U. OF SEATTLE, WASHINGTON. MRS. L. P. RAY (FOURTH FROM LEFT IN CENTER ROW) WAS FOR MANY YEARS THE PRESIDENT

CHAPTER VII
COLORED W. C. T. U. ORGANIZED

Some ladies of the Woman's Christian Temperance Union came to our church to organize a union among us. We were finally organized and I was made president. Everything was new to us. There were fourteen or fifteen other sisters in the union. What a revelation it was to us! There were forty-two departments in the W. C. T. U. work at that time. We were anxious to work, but didn't know how to start. Mrs. Mary Wade was the County president, and Mrs. Emma Wood was the secretary. We received great encouragement from Mrs. Libbie Beach-Brown also.

I shall never forget the first County convention that was held soon afterward, and our little union had the honor of entertaining them. Each department gave its report. How my heart did go out for the lost and the drunkard. I sat and listened eagerly and wondered what I could do, or how to begin, and as I listened, the tears rolled down my cheeks. I said, "Oh, how blind I have been; I want to do something, too!" I prayed the Holy Spirit to show me my special work. I sat and cried through the meeting at every report, saying, "How blind I have been; what can I do?" When the afternoon session came, they said, "We have just fifteen minutes for testimony." I said, "Oh, thank the Lord, I can tell of Jesus' power to save," and when the opportunity was given, I was on my feet and that was a great consolation to me. I remember, while I sat weeping, I had looked into my song book and I turned to a song--

> "Come, ye disconsolate, wher'er ye languish,
> Come to the mercy-seat, fervently kneel,
> Here bring your wounded hearts, here tell your anguish;
> Earth hath no sorrow that heaven can not heal."

I took courage from that moment and said, "The Lord will give me, too, something to do."

At our next local meeting, we decided to hold our meetings monthly. We went out and hunted those that were sick, and wherever we could get an opening. It was wonderful how the Spirit led and we began "to do with our might what our hands found to do." It seemed as though there were many opportunities for helping the sick. We had our prayer meetings with our friends, and the Lord began right there to pour out His Spirit in a marvelous way. Some were converted in their homes. We had the opportunity of going with Sister Roy to visit the jails at that time. I testified to the prisoners--told them of a better way, and how the Lord had delivered my husband from drink.

One evening, soon after, we were sitting in our home reading, and all at once, a stone came through the window. My husband went out and looked around, but could see no one. Finally, he hid himself and watched, and soon another stone came. This time he saw the youngsters and ran after them. To his surprise, they were girls, two girls, not over twelve or fourteen years of age. He caught one and the other one ran away. I came out myself and he held her until I came up the steps. She screamed so loudly that it brought out the neighbors. I told her that we would either take her to her mother, or call the police. We didn't let her go, because we felt it was our duty to inform her parents, and so she consented to go to her mother. We went with her down near Yesler Way, and as we entered the house, we found the mother in a very drunken condition, drinking beer and smoking. We told her we had come to bring her daughter home. She swore at her. It made our hearts ache to see such a scene. There were a drunken man and several other persons in the house. The mother promised to take care of her girl. A little later, we went one Sunday to our jail work, and as we lined up before the bars and began to sing, we saw a man who stood back in his cell. As he looked out and saw Mr. Ray, he stepped out and began to cry. He cried all through the meeting. Mr. Ray told of his conversion,--what a drunkard he had been, and how sin had got him into jail through drunkenness. The man wept sorely. As soon as our meeting closed, he came up to the window and said, "Well, Ray, is this you? I am surprised. I know what a drunkard you were. Would to God I had what you have." Mr. Ray asked him what crime he had committed, and he told him, "I killed a man last week. I stabbed him in my yard after he left my house." And he said, "Oh! If I had only known of this salvation, I might not have been here, but it is too late." During the testimony, I had given my experience too. He said, "I remember the time Mr. Ray had a fight in the saloon, and how I took his part. I am so glad you are saved, and your wife also." He asked us to go and see his wife. He said, "She drinks hard, and I was jealous of the man I found in my house, as he hung around so much. I do love my wife and I want her to quit drinking. If you tell her your testimony and tell her I sent you, perhaps she will quit." We promised we would do as he requested. We went to a house down below the sidewalk on Yesler Way, a little dirty, dingy room, and there to our surprise we found the girl who threw the rock and the mother, beastly drunk on the bed, and the girl was smoking cigarettes. Oh! Such a sad home of sin and depravity! I could not help but weep, and thought perhaps that would have been our fate, if we had not been delivered from sin. We told her that her husband had sent us. She was almost too drunk to talk intelligently. She said, "Charley was a good man, but it was the drink that got him. I know he would not have killed the man if he had been sober."

We told her he wanted her to give her heart to the Lord, and he also wanted us to tell her what the Lord had done for us. As we told her, she sobered up a little and wept. We asked for the privilege of prayer and she said, "It's too late now. Charley is liable to be hung, and I feel that I am the cause of it." We read the Bible, prayed with her, and left her weeping. She had sorrow, but it was not of a godly sort. It was because her sins had found her out. Her husband was given a light sentence, twenty-two years in the penitentiary, and the last we knew of wife and daughter they were still leading a life of sin and shame. My prayer to the Lord for them was, "Lord, I pray Thee to stop them in their mad career, before it is eternally too late."

From this time on the Lord gave us work. We found much to do. We felt so sad to see what sin had wrought. We kept up our monthly meetings, visited homes and sat with the sick. We were delighted to go into homes and clean them up, scrub and wash and do anything we could. Then, too, the sisters were very faithful and worked with us. Finally, as our meeting progressed, our pastor began to find fault and thought we had plenty of work to do in the church, and that it was the church's work that should be done. He didn't see any need of working around with this class of people and he kept objecting until some of the sisters became discouraged. He wanted them to give entertainments and do all they could to get the church out of debt. When we went to church on Sunday we came home sorrowful. After awhile some of the sisters began to drop out; thought their first duty was to their church, and this was only a W. C. T. U. Oh! how sorry I felt when they began to get discouraged, because the Lord had saved so many at home and we had our mothers' meetings. Quite a number had been converted and had joined the church, but our pastor did not believe in the work of the W. C. T. U. At our next monthly meeting, several of the women gave in their resignations and said, "We will have to work in the church." I said, "This is the church work." It seemed as though my heart would break, and I wept. Just before kneeling in prayer, the song came to me, "Nearer, my God, to

Thee, e'en though it be a cross that raiseth me." It seemed as though, when I sang my second line, I was being brought nearer to Him, although it was a great cross to give up my sisters; but I told them I would come to the church and would help with their prayer meetings, but would not take part in their socials, as the Lord had shown me a better way to labor for Him. I attended for a few times but the interest seemed to subside and finally the meetings closed. I told my companions that there were two of the sisters who thought the meetings ought to go on, but they were not able to attend, so I gave it up. But husband and I decided to go right on and work together. He was an honorary member. I would attend the white unions. The women all seemed nice and sympathetic, and did all they could to help me. They said they were sorry, because we had sent in better reports than any other unions in the County.

Husband and I kept up our jail work. We worked with a Mr. Blake, a member of the First Methodist Church, and the Lord abundantly blessed and saved souls. After awhile, Mr. Blake had other engagements, and the work was turned over to us. After giving in satisfactory reports to the W. C. T. U., I was elected County Superintendent of Jail and Prison Work. The Lord gave us a few white workers to go with us. We kept this work up for about four years with wonderful results. The Lord helped us to get the favor of the jailers and sheriffs. We held Sunday afternoon meetings. The prisoners would always take hold and sing with us. There were many boys and young men among them. Not all that you find in jail are "down-and-outs," as one might suppose. Some had committed the first crime, and some were hardened criminals. We met all classes there. In the south end of one of the tanks there was a bath tub which we used as an altar. After service we would ask the men who wanted to lead a new life to step forward. We invited them to kneel at the bath tub, and there many souls were converted.

There was a young man by the name of Howard Holmes, who was in for murder. There was a desperado in at the same time by the name of Blank. One night Blank made a wooden pistol, held up the jailer, took his keys, unlocked the door and let almost every prisoner out. Holmes was a colored boy and he came out with the others. It was a rare case in those days to see a colored prisoner. Most of the work was exclusively among the white people.

It was very rainy weather and the colored boy caught a bad cold. When he was finally captured, he was sick and they placed him in the hospital. They kindly let me visit him at any time, as they knew he wouldn't live long. He was very sorry for his crime. He was condemned to be hung. He asked us to pray, but it seemed hard for him to believe that the Lord would save him. He would say, "Oh, if only I could feel as I used to when I went to church, but I can't pray, and it is no use for you to pray with me, for I am lost." We plead with him, but finally he died. He thanked the jailer for his kindness, and thanked myself and Sister Roy for visiting him, and went out into eternity without hope. This experience seemed to urge us on to "Rescue the perishing, care for the dying," and to warn others of the awful results of sin.

We always carried with us religious tracts, and flowers. We always sang some of our own songs. They seemed to grip the hearts of the hearers more than some other songs we sang, and blessed our own souls also. We were not ashamed of them; they were given to our forefathers under the pressure of slavery. We had sung them all when we were young, and now when we were getting older we did not forget them, especially after we were saved.

Sometimes we held the meetings in the morning. Later we got access to the jail at almost any time to do prison work. There were many other workers also that held meetings there on Sunday, each one having his own department with the privilege of visiting any part. Some of the prisoners who started to serve the Lord, having no home to go to after coming out, would go down into sin again. The policemen would hound them and tell them to move on out of town, and they would often commit crimes, since they had no place to which they could go.

Occasionally there would be one that the Lord would lay upon our hearts to take to our home. We felt that if he had a chance, he would make good. We would never take them unless they seemed to have a good experience in salvation. We would tell them when they got out to come and see us. We would always help them to get a change of raiment and invite them to the Mission, or to church, and we want to say right here that we never had one in the house who betrayed our trust. We would tell them that we had confidence in them; ofttimes leave them in the house alone; trust them to go to the market for us, and, although some of them had been desperate criminals, we thank the Lord today that they proved good, at least while they remained with us. We would not keep them very long (a week or two, sometimes less) until they got work enough to get out of town. Some returned to us again.

CHAPTER VIII
WORK WITH MOTHER RYTHER IN SLUMS

As opportunities for a broader field of usefulness kept opening up, we helped in the missions. By this time we were going to the hospitals and my husband was doing personal work on the streets, or in any place to which the Lord led him. Those were great days to us, as we were young and full of zeal for the Lord.

We also had the privilege of forming an acquaintance with Mrs. O. S. Ryther. She is now known as "Mother Ryther." She is one of the oldest missionaries in Seattle, having one of the largest homes for children at the present time. At that time she had a Mission and also a Rescue Home. On Wednesday afternoons we would go into the slums together and hold meetings, and also into the houses of shame below the "dead line." We found the inmates mostly very courteous. One house in particular was called the octoroon house. Most of the girls were bright mulattoes. The landlady was always willing to stop their dancing and music and to call every girl into the meetings. The Lord gave us good results from this work, and some were saved out of this house.

Occasionally Mrs. Ryther invited us to come and sing and talk to the children in her Home, also to the girls that she had upstairs. We have known her to have at one time seventeen babies in one ward, and a more loving woman I never met. She had to solicit funds for the Home throughout the city. She was always full of smiles and kind words for everybody. We never heard a girl speak evil of her. At one time she had five dope fiends in her house-- morphine fiends. They were taken up on the streets by the police on account of their low and nude condition, as they were not capable of taking care of themselves.

Mother Ryther went to the jails and begged them to let her take the girls and break them of the dope habit. It would usually take about six months. She could not take the drug away from them all at once, so she would lessen the amount as they could stand it, and keep them until they were healed, or in a respectable condition to be turned loose. She had some awful experiences that a person would not believe unless he actually saw them. The girls had to be locked in with bars on the windows until they could be trusted outside. It was something awful when the appetite came upon them. If they could not have the drug, they would go into convulsions, and if they could not get it then, they would go crazy and die.

It seemed that the only salvation for them in that condition was in our Jesus and His blood, and this proved to be a remarkable cure. There were five of them in particular that ran together, and among them was a colored girl. She had been very well reared, but sin had gotten her down. She was in a worse condition physically than the rest, at this time. Her name was Lucy. She had a large carbuncle on her neck, and her limbs were nothing but boils and sores. Bent over, and with head twisted to one side, she looked more like an Egyptian mummy, and a deformed one at that, than a real human being.

Mrs. Ryther seemed to have the love that was kind and "beareth all things and endureth all things." One day the girls got away from her and went down in the slums again. They lived under the wharves, upstairs in old deserted buildings, and sometimes they were found in deserted outhouses in the mud flats--anywhere they could hide away in the daytime from the police. About twelve o'clock at night they would come out into the streets to beg and get dope. They told me they had gone for weeks with hardly anything to eat and they would imagine at all times during the rainy weather that the policemen were on their tracks. They would creep along the wharves, or along some back street, and run and dodge around all night long with the fear that they would be arrested. Once they came at night, knowing where Mrs. Ryther's cream for her babies was, and stole all the food that they could find in the basement, and took away the milk. Mrs. Ryther had that love which "suffereth long and is kind." When they were arrested, she went and begged for them again and said she would try them again, as she knew the mothers of two of them. They had come from good Christian homes and had got their start as fiends through the doctors and sickness, and this led them down in sin.

One day this girl, Lucy, became very sick. She could not get away and was put away from the other fiends, and, as they let her come into the prayer meetings, she would listen attentively to the words of the preacher and finally got under conviction. She did not want to die and hoped to get well, but she could not give up the drug.

One day Mrs. Ryther called me up to her home and told me she would like to have me talk to Lucy, as I might be able to help her, for she was one of my own race. Mrs. Ryther was very busy and couldn't put in so much time with one, although she was very kind to her. I sang and prayed with Lucy and went away, and in a few days I was called back again. They thought she was dying. The carbuncle seemed to be eating through, and the doctor said it would only be a short time before it would eat through to a vital spot and cause death. They had taken quite a portion of the drug from her, but they could not take it all. She had to have it three times a day, morning, noon, and night. She tried to pray but could not, she was full of tears, looked up in my face and said, "Oh, Mrs. Ray, do you believe the Lord will forgive me?" It really seemed to me as though the death rattles had already come into her throat, for I had seen several die, and I felt sure she was nearly gone. I said to her, "Yes, Lucy, but you will have to give up that dope. You don't want to go before the Lord full of dope." She said, "Oh, I am thinking of when six o'clock comes." I said, "Lucy, the Lord says, He is your Shepherd, you shall not want." I felt desperately in earnest. I knew what I was saying and was repeating Scripture, and then it came to me that He could take the desire away, and I said, "If you will give it up, I believe He will stand by you. If I were you I would go out clean." Immediately she said, "I will never touch it again." I knelt beside her bed in prayer, as Mrs. Ryther was busy and had told me to be led of the Lord in what I did. After praying myself, I told her to pray and to tell Jesus just how she felt. She did so and such a blessing seemed to come over her, and she began to praise the Lord and to say, "Oh, I am saved! I am saved!" When Mrs. Ryther came into the room, she told her about it and we all rejoiced together. Then I told her I would stay by her, as it looked as though she was sinking again and I did not think she would live until morning. I sat by her all night and she slept the whole night, and I sat there and prayed and told the Lord that I believed He had saved her soul. I thought she would go at any minute, but she lay quiet, like a child. The next morning about five o'clock I went home and went to bed. About nine o'clock I was called on the telephone to come quickly and bring Lucy's "gun," as she called it. I had asked her to give it to me. It was lying on the chair by her bed and was ready to be used when the drug was brought in. I had taken it home with me, and, as Mrs. Ryther had gone into the city on business, the nurse called me, and told me to come quickly and bring the "gun," as Lucy seemed to be getting wild, and the doctor said to give it back to her as she could not live without it. I rose and took it to her immediately. When I went in she was wild and she said, "Oh, Mrs. Ray, give me just a little pinch, I can't stand it. The habit is on me." I didn't know for a moment what to do, and the thought came to me, "If God could help her all night without it, He could help her forever." So I knelt by her bed and said, "We will pray, Lucy, look up!" and immediately the pains left her and she got better, and she has never called for the drug from that hour until now. We had no thought of her getting up and well, as we had not asked for this.

She was in a semi-conscious condition, and we planned for her funeral, thinking that she was so far gone that she did not know what we were talking about. Her limbs were cold to her knees and she was blue, (she was a bright mulatto) and we thought she was going to pass out at any time.

I went home that night. Mrs. Ryther watched with Lucy. The next morning, she called up and said, "Come quickly, I want you to hear Lucy. She is shouting and praising the Lord, and oh, she looks so well. She can't stop praising the Lord; come right away." As I entered the room, she was preaching, and said she was going to live to tell the other fiends, and our hearts rejoiced. Surely the Lord had done more than we could ask or think. Mrs. Ryther sent for a brother, Con Johnson, and had him come and anoint Lucy with oil in the name of the Lord. I and his wife both prayed and she healed rapidly. The carbuncle went off her neck soon, and one of the arms which was crooked straightened out, and the hump in her back disappeared. Many came to Mrs. Ryther's to see the converted fiend.

Then we said we would go down below the dead line and find the other girls, as they were away from Mrs. Ryther's place at that time. We hunted until we found them. There was a young lady, Miss Warren by name, who worked in the Seaman's Bethel Mission in the slums, who was very kind to these girls. We inquired of her and she told us where we could find them, hidden away under a sidewalk. They looked more like rats than they did like human beings. They said, "Yes, we will go and see her." I took them to a restaurant and got their breakfast, three of them. Then we went up the back streets, as they were ashamed to go the public way. They took me under some old houses to a place under the wharf and showed me their home. You would not believe anything except rats could exist there. Not even dogs would be satisfied to live in such a place: it was damp and mouldy and dark. Such a place for what had once been bright, intelligent human beings!

There is no telling how depraved the human soul can get, when the enemy gets hold of it, and we find he is no respecter of persons. He can take the most cultured and refined and bring them down lower than the beast. I am so glad that where sin abounds, grace can so much more abound,--praise the Lord!

When we came to Mrs. Ryther's and the girls saw Lucy rejoicing, they seemed to be glad and told her to stick to it. Two of them had once been converted and they told their experience and said that some day they too would try it.

There was another fiend who knew this girl, Lucy. She had been arrested as a vagabond. She had been in jail about a month and they were giving her less of the drug all the time. She asked the jailer if I could come in and stay with her. She had seen what the Lord had done for Lucy who was up and out preaching the gospel. The jailer told her I could. By this time I was becoming well known to the jailers.

When I was asked, I decided to go. I fasted and prayed, and told her to fast. She said she had fasted and prayed, and I went in to stay until the work was done. She had taken a bath that morning. There were other fiends in the cell next to her. They said, "We will do all we can to help you. We will not come around you." Then when I went in we had prayer right away, and she prayed earnestly and asked the Lord to save her soul first. She seemed to break up and weep, and I believe if there ever was a soul saved, she was. She seemed to have the evidence every way. We went into our cells. They gave me a hammock right along side of hers. I had taken from my home a pillow and a blanket. They locked the door beside us, and there we were to wait upon the Lord until we got a sign that the appetite was gone. She went right off to sleep and slept quietly all day only waking to get her lunch. The jailer and the matron would come and look in at the window. The name of the jailer was Burkman. They would look in and say, "It's wonderful," and walk away. We stayed all night and until late in the evening of the next day. The girl wanted to see Lucy, so we telephoned Mrs. Ryther about it and she and Lucy came immediately. After talking awhile, Lucy asked the girl to come home with them. The jailer told me that I could have the girl, but I felt that I ought to stay with her there for awhile. They thought it was wonderful because she had had to have the dope every six hours, and here she had got by for two days, and the jailer said, "If this proves successful, I shall publish it in the papers." She insisted on asking Mrs. Ryther to let her go home with them if I did not object. She would be with Lucy and she thought Lucy would be a help to her. I did not object then, but as I have thought it over since, I should have asked to stay longer with her in the jail. Mrs. Ryther took her home and said, "Lucy will watch over her as I am busy."

I went away feeling a little uneasy for her as Lucy was young and Mrs. Ryther was loaded down with her other duties, and I knew it would take some person who knew how to prevail with the Lord in a case of this kind. The next morning I called up and Mrs. Ryther answered the telephone and said, "The girl has gone, our prisoner has escaped." Lucy said she didn't know how long she had been gone, but when she woke up in the night she was gone.

It wasn't very long before the policemen had her and put her in jail again. This time they did not let her go for six months. We all felt very sorry. The jailer was an unbeliever but had begun to think there was something in it, but after she got away, it seemed as though his faith failed him. She didn't undertake it again, but stayed her time out. I asked her why she went away after the Lord had healed her and she said, "I was helped, and I know the Lord helped me, but I was awakened all at once and I felt the habit coming upon me and I slipped out of bed and got my things and ran away as hard as I could go until I got down to the drug store where they sold the drug to the fiends. I just had to have it. I felt ashamed of it afterward, but I could not help it." She came out of the jail partly cured, and she told me that she felt that no one would take an interest in her after treating Mrs. Ryther and myself as she had. Something seemed to say to her, "If you are ever anything and get out of jail no one will care for you, you will have to care for yourself." She braced up and never used it again, and went to a strange city. Years after, I went to that city and did not know her. She is a beautiful woman and very fine. She invited me up to her home. She said she was married and wanted us to come and meet her husband. She did not claim to be saved at this time,--said she was backslidden. She had sent east and had her mother with her, and her mother never knew she had been so low down in sin. We had prayer with her and came away trusting that the Lord would yet get hold of her and bring her back to Himself.

On one of our visits to the "Octoroon House," as we entered the hall, a very pretty girl, an octoroon, stepped out of her room. As soon as she saw us, she exclaimed, "This is my last year. After this year I will stop my life of shame."

Mrs. Ryther stepped inside of the parlor and we were alone for a few minutes. I said to her, "My dear child, you may not live another year. Better stop now." "No," she said, "another year. I can't quit now, I am in debt; beside there is no one that would care for me. I have got to get some money and good clothes and then I'll stop." She said, "I read my Bible and say my prayers." I said to her, "Do you see that carpet?" and pointed down at the floor at the same time. She looked down. "Well," I said, "the constant tread and wear upon it will soon finish it. So will it be with your poor little body if you do not quit. Better stop now." We passed into the parlor, leaving her to think it out. We would often lift our hearts in prayer for the poor little girl in her prison house, for indeed she was imprisoned, soul and body. She told us she was in debt to the landlady and she could not get away until her debts were paid, and that if she did not have good clothes, no one would notice her. There is many a poor girl today selling her soul for fine clothes.

Just about a year from that time, Mother Ryther called and said, "There is a girl here who is dying of tuberculosis. Perhaps you can help her. She is in a bad state. We want her saved before she passes away."

When we went upstairs they told us, "Perhaps she will let you talk to her. She drives everyone out of the room. She says she sees devils, and she keeps saying, 'Drive those devils out of here.' "

When we went in, sure enough, she was possessed. The devil had her spirit, soul and body. She said, "Go out. There is a snake in your lap." (I was sitting beside her bed.) She actually drove me out.

To my surprise, 'twas the same girl whom I met the year before worn out and crushed by the tempter. I went home with such a burden. Some of her associates in sin went to see her and they told her about her actions. They gave her a good lecture, telling her to give up. They told her that it was evident she would never get well. They warned her not to die in sin, and said, "You let Mother Ryther and Mrs. Ray pray for you."

The next day she quieted down and there was a calm look on her face. It was in answer to our prayers. She told Mother Ryther to call me in. We prayed with her and asked forgiveness for her sins. She prayed although she was very weak. We did not see the manifestation of joy that some have, yet she was so sweet and restful. We did our best and the results are with the Lord. Eternity alone will tell the rest. We laid her body away and her soul went out to try the realities of another world. The last day she lived, she received a letter from her dear old grandmother, who thought she was away out in the west working. She never knew the life she lived. The girl was not strong enough to read the letter, but held it in her hands until she died. She had been decoyed from home by the promise of work. As to the madame of this house, she too had seen better days. But the spirit of the world and the love of money had caused her to sell her soul. Her paramour came down with tuberculosis. He didn't want to believe he was dangerously ill. She sent him to the Providence Hospital. The doctor told her he had but a short time to live, and although she was in sin and shame, she didn't want him to die unsaved. I feel sure this was the result of the meeting we held in her house. She insisted upon our visiting him. She said, "He will not receive you kindly, but don't mind him. Speak to him about his soul. I don't want him to be lost."

We went to see him. He told us that he felt all right. That he had only a little cough and would be out soon. He didn't care to hear us pray or talk. We came away feeling so sorry for him. A night or so afterward while we were at the Mission, the woman came to our house and finding we were out, she waited on the porch until we arrived. She was half drunk and was so distressed about him. She insisted we go once more and pray and sing for him. She said, "He can't live but a few hours and I want him to get saved." We did not think it necessary to go again, but for her sake we went. We met the same results and as it was a Catholic hospital the sisters did not want us there.

He was failing rapidly and did not notice us. However we did our duty. The woman told us, when she saw he was dying, that she could not stand it and in her distress she begged the sister to baptize him. She cried and prayed until the sister took a pitcher of water and poured some upon his face.

Afterward the sister begged that nothing be said about it as it was against the rules.

The man passed away just as he had lived. We laid him away to await the judgment. The madame promised to forsake her sin and to close up her house. I visited her and she was under conviction but not deep enough to give up. Everything was the same as it had been. She was grieved more about his soul than her own. She thought she had plenty of time. The next time I visited her she seemed so different. She had been to see a spiritualist fortune teller to find out if he was lost. The fortune teller told her that he was very happy. That settled it and with this delusion and lie of the devil she rallied and went on with her dirty work destroying souls. When we went east we lost track of her and when we returned her house had broken up.

"There is a way that seemeth right unto a man but the end thereof are the ways of death."--Bible.

About a month ago we visited Mother Ryther's home. We had not seen her more than three or four times in twenty years as our later work was on different lines, hers being the maintenance of a children's home exclusively, and ours, evangelistic work. We were glad of the privilege of meeting Mother Ryther again. She seemed to possess the same sweet spirit as in former days.

There was a little afflicted boy hanging on to her skirts and trying to talk to her. She said that he had the rickets but was much better than when she had taken him at three weeks of age. She took him because no one else would have him. He was blind and a cripple and was a great care for her. She would take him to her room at night in a basket and bring him down in the morning when she came to her work. She cared for all the rest of the children with this little tottering cripple at her feet. She seemed to have more compassion on the weaker ones, although she loved them all.

As we left the Home, we praised the Lord for the privilege of meeting such an one and with a prayer in our hearts that she might live many days to honor and glorify Him.

> "O Lord of harvests, send forth laborers,
> Send them forth. To Thee we pray." Amen.

CHAPTER IX
WHERE WE FIRST MET THE
FREE METHODISTS

During our first experience in jail work, a band of Christian workers came from the Free Methodist Church at Ross, near Fremont, in this city. These meetings were conducted by a Sister Griggs, who has since died. She was assisted by several young people, from the Seminary, a Free Methodist school in the vicinity, in charge of Rev. A. Beers and his wife. This school was called at that time The Seattle Seminary, but is now known as Seattle Pacific College.

A young colored boy by the name of Kraft was converted in the county jail through the efforts of these workers. His was a remarkable case. He was doing time for some petty offense. After hearing Sister Griggs' message and the testimonies of the young students, he got under pungent conviction, and afterward prayed through to victory. His testimony was clear and sound. He was bold to witness and to live the right life there in the presence of his fellow prisoners. The band took a great interest in him. When he had served his sentence, he had nowhere to go. We gave him a temporary home with us until he could get work. During the time he was with us, the students invited him over to the Ross Church. He went the following Sunday. He came home with his face beaming with the glory of God. "Oh, Brother and Sister Ray, I wish you could have seen what I have seen today. There were about seventy-five saved young people there. They testified so freely and some got blessed; others shouted and praised the Lord. I did not know that white people had such good religion. You must go out with me next Sunday. Those young men advised me like a brother. I never saw such a lot." We told him we would go. We went, and the half had not been told.

Later on there was a Free Methodist conference held by Bishop Jones. At Tenth Street we could hear the amens before we reached the church. The singing was glorious. There was such a spirit of freedom and liberty among them. They were not afraid to say, "Praise the Lord." It was evident that in these meetings the Psalmist's prayer was answered, when he said, "Oh, that men would praise the Lord, for His goodness to the children of men." Young Kraft stayed with us for a short time and, as work was scarce (that being about the time that Coxey's army marched across the country to Washington, D. C.) he went to California.

We continued to visit the Free Methodist church occasionally. They always treated us with courtesy. In the meantime we got a new pastor at our own little church. We felt glad that we had a change, but to our surprise we found that he had been prejudiced against us by our former pastor. When we attended church, the persecutions were just about the same or worse. Some of our older pilgrims who got the experience at the same time we did, treated us kindly, but as new ones came into the church which was growing in membership, they, seeing the pastor did not fellowship us, did not understand us. Although the persecutions came pretty heavy, the Lord in the meantime was pouring the oil of joy into our souls. We were kept very busy at work in the slums. Some said we were crazy. One of our old friends remarked that he would kick us out, if we came to his house to pray. We felt very free when we went to minister to the poor. They always received us gladly. We were made to feel some of the sufferings of Christ. "He came unto His own, and His own received Him not." It was a great pleasure for us to go on the streets, for there we had willing hearers, and it rejoiced our hearts to sing and testify to the poor down-and-outs on the streets. We felt it one of the greatest privileges of our lives to sing and preach out in the open, just because our blessed Redeemer lived in the open. He was born in a manger; He was crucified in the open; He is coming again in the open, and if we had a thousand tongues to sing our great Redeemer's praise, we would gladly go out into the hedges and by-ways to bring them in from the fields of sin. We want to follow the Lamb whithersoever He goeth. Even though we were misunderstood, by many, both white and colored, we knew that Jesus understood us. Oh, 'tis so sweet to follow Jesus, and to know that you are in divine order. The Lord wanted to use us in the slums. This line of service took us away much from the church work. We had four different pastors and none of them seemed to understand us, and did not want us to testify to the experience of entire sanctification, although it was a Methodist doctrine. We decided to go where we could have fellowship.

CHAPTER X
HOSPITAL WORK

As we walked in the light, new opportunities for doing good presented themselves. Now the doors for personal work at the hospitals opened up, especially at the County Hospital. Here we met a brother worker from the Seaman's Bethel and a Mrs. Rockwell from the Woman's Christian Temperance Union who were conducting meetings Sunday afternoons. We soon found ourselves making regular weekly visits, and ofttimes on Sunday afternoons we took with us flowers and tracts, and these proved to be a blessing to them and to us, as it gave us an opportunity to speak a word to them. They also seemed pleased to have us sing. Afterward we would offer a short prayer. They soon began to expect us on visiting days, and later the matron let us come at any time to visit the sad ones, and we believe many souls were saved during our labors at that place. To God be all the glory.

The reader will notice on page 36 a picture of me when I was eleven years of age, the time that I put on the false hair. I wore this for over twenty-five years and it became a part of me. As I had no mother and as I was very proud, after wearing it for a certain length of time, I was ashamed to take it off. I changed with the fashions, and I kept this up until after I was saved and sanctified. The Lord did not give me light on it at the time I was sanctified, and I believe if He had, I would have had a desperate struggle before taking it off, because it had become a part of my nature.

One time while in Mt. Carmen Mission, a sister gave her testimony and she said that she wondered that if when Jesus came, she would be ready to meet Him, and she thought, "What if I should be curling one side of my hair and should run out to meet Him with the other side uncurled, I wonder if He would take me up," and it brought her under conviction, and she decided to wear her hair as the Lord gave it to her. She did not know I wore false hair but, if she had taken a hammer and struck my heart, she could not have hurt me worse. I said, "That's all right for her; she is a white woman and has got plenty of hair; the Lord doesn't mean that for me, and then my husband doesn't want me to take it off. He would be ashamed of me." I had worn it so long that it had killed the roots of my hair, and I was partially bald, and I would not listen to any suggestions about putting it away. I felt all right for a while, but afterward the conviction came back with a little stronger force. It took me a long time to get my hair all fixed and curled. I had to dye it to keep it black. I spent many dollars upon invisible pins and nets, besides a whole lot of worry as to whether I had it on straight or not. I did not want anyone to know I wore it, and many times I was late getting to church Sunday morning because I would stand before the glass to see if I had it good and secure, and I often tried my husband by taking so much time. I began to get tired of it and I would do it up Saturday nights all ready for the Sabbath, but somehow I could not fix it right. I would pray over it, get some relief, and after awhile, when I would be in prayer, it would come up before me again. How true the Spirit is in His dealings with us.

There was a Baptist preacher present at one of the special meetings of the Mission, and he called all the Christians forward and said, "Let us ask God to search our hearts, if there is anything in our way that would hinder our souls from being converted." I did not go at first. I said, "I am all right; there is nothing between me and the Lord. I don't know of a thing that I am holding onto" and then I came to a standstill. The next moment I said, "Lord, I don't know of a thing unless it is that hair." I held still for a few minutes longer until I knew that it was the Lord speaking. The devil said, "Woman's hair is her crowning glory," but the Spirit said, "That is some other person's hair; it is false; it is not yours." Then I said, "Lord, I will take it off, if I have to go bald-headed the rest of my life." By this time, the prayer service was over, and I arose in my seat and told them that the Lord had shown me something He wanted me to do. I said, "Now I want to say right here that I do not believe the Lord calls every person to do as I am doing, but this was needless and it was in my way and the Spirit has dealt very gently with me." As I went home that night, I told my husband what I had done. He said that he prayed the Lord to give him grace to go out with me, because it brought such a change in my looks. I went to the stove and threw it into the fire and said, "Praise the Lord, Amen." I took my comb and brush and brushed what little hair I had. I made me a little bonnet and put streamers of ribbon and tied them under my chin. The ribbons cover the bald places on the back of my head, where the hairpins had worn the hair off. That night my sleep was so peaceful.

The next day was hospital day. I took my tracts, fruits, and flowers and went upon my errand of mercy, full of assurance that the Lord was with me. As I went into the hospital, it seemed as though the Spirit had gone ahead of me. Everyone whom I spoke to had tears in his eyes. All were glad for me to sing or pray, and I could feel that the blessing of the Lord accompanied every word. We went into a ward which was called "Billy-the-Mug's" after a saloon in the city, where there were many sick and broken-down men from the effects of strong drink. Right near the door was a young man about twenty-five, and he was a Catholic. They were all very glad and greeted me heartily. I handed this young man a tract and some flowers. He began to tell me his sorrows, and I told him that Jesus had a balm for every sorrow. He seemed glad to have me talk. I told him to give his heart to the Lord and He would save him. I asked him to pray and he said, "Yes, sister, do pray." After I had prayed, I asked him to pray and he began, oh, so earnestly to plead for forgiveness of sin. While he was praying, the men on the cots were under conviction, and one especially who was reading a paper. His paper shook in his hands and he looked as though he could hardly keep from crying out. Finally, this young man prayed clear through and began to shout the victory; and, I tell you, I shouted too right there in that hospital. We forgot where we were and the glory of the Lord seemed to fill the place. I told him I believed the Lord could raise him up and that I would pray to that effect. As I left that place and got seated in the streetcar, it seemed as though my soul was like a bird up in the air flying along ahead of the car. It was unspeakable joy to know that a soul had been converted, and I could see that it paid to be obedient to the Spirit. Oh, these little things that seem to be so small that stand out like mountains in our way! When I consecrated my life to Jesus, I gave up all I knew, and all I did not know. But I found more in the unknown than in the known. The Holy Spirit teaches me and gives light, as I am able to receive it. I praise the Lord for my teacher, my guide. This experience brought more light to me. I was growing in grace and in the knowledge of my Savior. This was my first convert.

To my surprise, one Sunday who should come into the Mission but this young man, healed and his face shining with glory. It pays; it really pays to be obedient to the Spirit's whispers. "Whatsoever He saith unto you, do it."

About ten years ago, I went into a camp meeting in Snohomish, and whom should I meet but this man, still professing to be saved. It had been fifteen years since I had seen him. I never would have known him. He asked me if I remembered where I had seen him, and if I remembered the Catholic boy who was converted and healed in the King County Hospital. He was a businessman in Snohomish at that time and he introduced me to his wife.

On Sunday night, after I was out there I had a dream. I dreamed that all at once, we heard a noise in the sky, and Jesus had come, and a voice said, "Go ye out to meet Him." I thought I went out doors and as I looked up the heavens were filled with angels and Jesus was in front and the light and the glory was so great that I fell on my face and shouted, "Oh, glory to God! Glory to God!"

I am glad I pulled off that hair, and I have never doubted from that day to this that it was the voice of the Lord.

CHAPTER XI
THE ALASKA GOLD CRAZE

In 1896 and 1897 came the Alaska gold craze. People came in from all parts of the world and outfitted in Seattle. Previous to this business was at a standstill.

The Coxey army, made up of men without work, started from Seattle to march to Washington, D. C., to demand work. There was general dissatisfaction among workmen everywhere. Work was scarce in Seattle. Mr. Ray was fortunate to get a job as porter in one of the large dry goods stores here, McDougal and Southwick's. As soon as the Alaska boom struck the country, business picked up right away and in a short while, the city was full of strangers, preparing themselves to go to the Klondike. Thousands of them outfitted from this business store. With them, they took only clothing suitable for that cold climate. Hence, they left their old clothing and trunks and such things behind them. The shipping clerk then turned many a parcel over to Mr. Ray to help clothe the poor. I'm sorry to say that many of the men leaving for the North left their Bibles behind, and I suppose many left their salvation also. They went forth "to pierce themselves through with many sorrows." To speak after the manner of men there is no great loss without some small gain. We had an old attic in our house which was full of these old clothes that we gave to the poor. There was a great opportunity for doing good in the store, as Mr. Ray would hand out tracts to the men and talk salvation to them as they passed through.

In about a year or less time the city was flooded with men who had had their feet and arms frozen from exposure. During this time, there was a young Swedish man, by the name of Antone Lynn, who asked us if we would let them have a prayer meeting at our home as there was quite a number of the Mission workers and others who felt it would be a good idea to have a cottage prayer meeting. We gladly consented and we set Friday night as the time. To our surprise, the people came from all over the city. At times, there would be as many as sixty present and I must say, to the glory of God, that I never was in a series of prayer meetings where the power of God was so manifested. There was such harmony. Souls were saved and some were healed. There were pastors from different churches. They were all of one accord. The Lord graciously poured out His Spirit in our midst.

During these meetings, we decided to go east and in a short time, we were packing up. One day while I was busy packing, a young colored girl came to the door hunting some place to stop for the night. She, too, had got the craze for gold, and came to do housework in the city. I wanted to take east with me some souvenirs and I spent hours gathering some starfish, and I was very busy with them when she came to the door. I told her that my house was full, but I sent her to a neighbor not far away. I asked her if she was saved and she said, "No, but she would like to be." I told her that I would see her that evening, as I was very busy then. As soon as she left, the Spirit spoke to me and said that was a good chance to do that girl some good, as she had told me she had no mother, and the thought came to me, "You were too busy with your souvenirs." I felt quite bad over it the rest of the day, but I had told her I would see her that night.

I worked with the fish all day putting them on boards and in the sun to dry until I became quite nervous as they were ugly things. After I got all through for the night, my husband came and I told him about the girl. After supper we went to inquire for her and the neighbor to whom I sent her had gotten her a job and she had gone to it. Then I began to feel bad and saw what I had done. She was a stranger and I could have been as a mother to her, but it was too late then. I asked the Lord to forgive me, promising that I would be more thoughtful next time. When I got home the girl was on my mind, and the starfish were on my mind, and it seemed as though I could see nothing else but starfish and I could think nothing but starfish. When I got to bed I could see nothing but starfish, green ones, red ones, blue and black and horny ones, in fact most all colors, as I had a tub full of them. I could not go to sleep. I wakened my husband and told him that I couldn't see anything but starfish. I covered my eyes and I could see the starfish under the covers and I said, "O Lord, please take this away from me. I see what I have done. I did not obey the Spirit and was too much taken up with the things of the world and let a soul slip by me. If I had taken time and prayed with her, I believe she would have been saved, as tears were in her eyes when I talked with her. Lord, if You will forgive me, I will never turn anyone away when there is an opportunity to speak to him." As quick as a flash the starfish disappeared, and I could see plainly this scripture in Col. 1: 12: "Give thanks unto the Father, which hath made us meet to be partakers of the inheritance of the saints in light."

> "Have Thy way, Lord, have Thy way,
> This with all my heart I say,
> I will obey Thee, come what may;
> Dear Lord have Thy way."

I caught the vision and said, "O Lord, I am thankful for the chastening and hereafter will, by Thy help, be obedient to Thy voice."

Mr. Thomas Lippy, a Christian man, had just returned from Alaska and bought the place we lived in with the intention of tearing it down to build the Seattle General Hospital. How glad we were for we felt this ground to be sacred as here was where I received the baptism of the Holy Spirit and the Lord had blessed us in ministering to others. Mr. Lippy, when we told him we hoped that this place would bring the blessing to the patients in the hospital that it had to us, told us that if Mr. Ray would tear down the house he might have the lumber. So Mr. Ray tore down the house and turned the lumber over to the African Methodist Church. They used some of it for building their new parsonage. So those grounds and the house are sacred and are being used for the glory of God to this day.

We never visit the sick in this hospital, but that it takes my mind back to my consecration and the baptism of the Holy Ghost that I received upon those grounds, that sanctified my soul and has kept me up to this time. I have made many mistakes and blunders but I praise Him for keeping my motives pure and my heart clean.

REV. CHARLES H. WITTEMAN

REV. CHARLES H. WITTEMAN

CHAPTER XII
OUR VISIT TO THE EAST

On the first day of May, 1900, I started from Seattle to go east. I had been praying for a long time that God would open the way that I might go back and tell the good news, to my relatives and friends, as to what the Lord had done for me. When I left there I was in sin and darkness. I had been in great expectation, waiting for the time to come to start back to my old home. I left the house on Fifth Avenue, where the Lord had so wonderfully blest my soul, and bade good-bye to my friends in Seattle. Brother Ray remained behind, as he had a job of work to finish. He planned on coming a couple of months later. As I left Seattle, and the train passed through Georgetown, I looked out on the old County Hospital where I had seen so many poor souls saved and started for heaven. I couldn't help but shed a few tears. After I got out of the city, my mind turned toward the old state of Missouri, where I was born. My joy was so great I could hardly sit still in the train. I would ride for about an hour, and then I would go back into the dressing room and get down upon my knees, right while the train was moving, and thank God for every mile-stone along the way.

When I came west and would cross a canyon or high bridge, or any dangerous place, I would become frightened, for the time being, but as soon as I was safe, I forgot all about it. I had heard from childhood that if a person could say, "Lord, have mercy," quick enough when in danger, he could be saved. I was told that if a horse threw a man, that there was a chance for him between the stirrup and the ground. I am so glad that I didn't have to take any such chances. I was saved and could pass the rough and smooth places with great peace of mind and soul. There was one song especially that I was singing in my heart,

> "Leaning on Jesus, leaning on Jesus,
> Safe and secure from all alarm,
> Leaning on Jesus, leaning on Jesus,
> Leaning on the Everlasting Arm."

I had no fear of a train wreck or anything else. I was thinking of the time when I should look into the face of my dear old father once more and tell him of the joy I had in serving the Lord. My father was past seventy-five years of age and had never been converted. I prayed the Lord not to let him die before I could see him and persuade him to turn to the Lord. I also had a brother who was a hard drinker. I had prayed for them these years and now I was going to see them again. I read my Bible and then sang a song. It seemed as though the blessing of God was upon the fields, and mountains, and the cattle. I could see God in the rivers, in the little streams and in the flowers, and it all made me think of heaven. After an hour or more I would think it time to pray and bless God, and I would go into the dressing-room and fall upon my knees. It seemed as though the very wheels of the train were saying, "Praise the Lord, praise the Lord!" When the engine would scream it seemed to say, Glory to God! Glory to God!" I felt this glory in my soul, and my heart was saying the very same thing that the locomotive said, and the scenery seemed to be saying it, too. I shouted for joy all the way from Seattle to Kansas City, Missouri, over two thousand miles.

When I arrived in Kansas City, my sister and husband met me at the train. I had not seen her for thirteen years. As I stepped off the car and we greeted each other, I said, "Praise the Lord!" Her husband said, "What did she say?" and my sister said, "She is saying, 'Praise the

Lord'." When we got to their home in the city, my sister said that I looked good in my face and young, but that she missed that false hair. She said that there certainly must be something that would make me take off that false hair, and that she was going up to the city to buy me some more, as she did not like the looks of me. I told her that I did not come back to Kansas City to backslide. We talked almost all night. I told them of what the Lord had wrought in the lives of my husband and me.

On the following Sabbath she took me with her to church. It was a very large, fashionable church, and the people were dressed in the latest styles. The choir sang well, but I missed that old-fashioned spirituality and hand-shake that they used to have when I was a girl. Things had changed with the times, and while they had progressed wonderfully, financially and intellectually, I was sorry to see that in many of them the old-fashioned spirituality had died out, and a new era of things had set in. I was with my sister a couple of weeks and visited some of the smaller churches. We found them not so formal as the larger ones. We met a few of the old-fashioned kind of people. She took me to look over some parts of the slums, and we found the slum work much different from what it was in Seattle. There was no work being done among our own people in the slums. There was Salvation Army work among the whites and lots of missions, but no rescue work of any kind in the slums where the colored people were. We could see sin and vice on every hand. I began to cry as I looked around and saw so many of my own race in sin, drunkenness, and misery. Among the better classes of our race they had schools, and we found just as cultured people as we had ever met among the whites in the north. We had an opportunity to speak to the pastor of one of the leading churches and he told us that there was not a work of the kind in the city. My sister said that I had better stop over and work, as there was plenty to be done among our own people. I wrote to my husband and told him of the conditions as I had found them. The saloons down among the lower classes were one to every block. Men, women, and children carried beer by the pail. I saw children from four years up with buckets of beer, and, oh, how my heart bled for them. I began to hope that some way the Lord would redeem some of these poor souls from their debauchery and shame. "Sin is a reproach to any people, but righteousness exalteth a nation." I had seen sin of a different type and slums of a different type, but were caused by the same principle, that of sin. My sister begged me to come there, with my husband, and work. These people of my race had come to this city from the farms

JOHN SMITH, FATHER OF MRS. RAY, AT THE AGE OF NINETY-SEVEN.
HE LIVED TO BE NEARLY ONE HUNDRED YEARS OLD.

and plantations of the south. Being illiterate and helpless, they had drifted down into this part of Kansas City. Some of the people of the better classes told me that if these people down in this low section wanted to make anything of themselves, they should come up from there. They did not think it right to go down and mix with them. We saw some of the same conditions among some of the poor whites, and Italians. I would cry everywhere I went, as I looked out on these awful sights and I saw that there was no one to rescue them, only as they came up to the churches. This they scarcely ever did. I wrote to my husband about it and wished he were with me to hold street meetings.

I left there after visiting with my sister. I went back to my old home at Springfield, Missouri. Three of my sisters and one brother had passed away. My father had become tired of living alone and had married again. There were left just four of us, one brother in Arkansas, this one in Springfield, and a sister in Kansas City, Missouri, beside myself. My husband met me there after a few weeks. Things were different. This was a smaller town than Kansas City and had a better class of people generally. There were no slums among our own people and I really enjoyed my visit there. My father had moved from the old home-place, and I was desirous of seeing the place, where I had had so many hardships, with some pleasures, because it was home. As soon as I got rested I went over to the old home, crying as I went, both for joy and for sorrow. I was sorry that I had not known when I was young what the Lord had taught me since I had become older. Everything had changed. I looked for that spot of ground where I prayed the first time. There were large factory buildings on this ground, but I located the place as near as I could, and as I walked upon the soil I said, "Oh, Lord, how I thank you that I understand this now. How ignorant I was when I was on this ground, and how earnestly I prayed on this spot but could not understand. I know I am saved now, and I have returned to this spot to give you the glory for all you have done for me."

I met many of the mothers and fathers who had known me when I was a child. I told them what the Lord had done for me, and they told me that I was like my mother. She had prayed so hard for us before she died, and I was glad to walk in her footsteps. I met my old Sunday-school teacher and he was glad to see me. I told him his labors had not been in vain, and he rejoiced with me.

On Saturday night my brother came to see us. He had been working in the country. He had a family there in town. It had been years since I had seen him. As he started to leave my step-mother brought in a Bible that had been in our family for years. After reading a passage in it, I told my brother that I had come all the way from the west on purpose to see him saved. I told my father the same thing. This seemed almost to break my brother's heart. After praying, I asked him to promise me that he would give his heart to the Lord. He said he would. I told him that I thought he would regard me as pretty bold, but he said, "That's all right." After he left I talked with my step-mother and father awhile. I told my father that I had come home to hear him pray, as I had never heard him. He did not answer me, but I could tell that he felt the weight of my conversation. The next day was the Sabbath and I was so glad to meet the old acquaintances, and, one by one, the old mothers and fathers who had known me in my childhood. As it happened, it was on Old Folk's Day, and they had sent out carriages to bring all the old people, who were not able to walk, to church. Some came who were nearly a hundred years old. There was one who was one hundred; one, ninety; and some from sixty-five to seventy-five, most all of whom I had known when a child. This was a Presbyterian church. I could do nothing but sit and weep, as I watched these old people brought in the church. After prayer and reading of the Bible, the meeting was open for testimonies before preaching. I could hardly hold myself until time to speak, and then I rose and told them of what the Lord had done for me. How I thanked them for their prayers for me when I was young and couldn't realize what it meant, although I belonged to the church. I didn't know then what vital salvation was. I thanked them for their godly lives, and they began to shout and it seemed like old times when I was a child. Well, it really seemed like getting into heaven. I went home a very happy woman. I wrote to my husband of my joyful experience. It was a pleasure to me to go to some of their homes, although there were great changes. Instead of some of the old log cabins there were cottages and beautiful yards, and I could see a wonderful improvement intellectually and financially, for which I was very thankful. I also visited an old spring near the old home from which I had at times carried many a piggin of water upon my head for about a quarter of a mile. We had no well on our place. We used water from the wells of first one and then the other of our neighbors. I could carry the piggin on my head and at the same time one in my hand. I broke quite a few piggins before I learned the art. I don't believe that I could carry one now. It was a common thing then to see a woman with a pail on her head and one in each hand. We carried all our wash water, and water for the pigs and chickens to drink. I wonder now how we did it. There was one woman in the neighborhood who had a well. She was so selfish. We could scarcely ever get water from her place. I remember one of the women called my attention to the well and said that the old woman had died and that she did not believe that in the end selfishness paid.

About this time my husband came east and we remained there for a few weeks. While we were there we hunted up a Mrs. Timmons, the one spoken of in the first pages of the book. She was not there, but we found out her address and wrote to her. She was glad to know we had been converted, and she wrote to me, saying, "Emma, surely the ways of the Lord are past finding out. I took you when you were small, I was sorry for you because you had no mother. Now I'm glad I did. There was a well-to-do woman who once said to me, 'Why do you keep that homely little creature. I don't see how you can keep her.' That woman died a drunkard and see what the Lord has done for you."

My brother had three boys and one girl in his family. We asked his wife if she did not feel the need of being saved. She was very agreeable to talk to, as we had been girls together. One night I asked her when her husband would be home. She could not tell me. However, one evening we went over and waited until he came. He did not act so pleased as when we first came, as he had begun to get under conviction. I asked him to let us pray before we left. His wife seemed so tender and we asked her to join with us in prayer and she did so. The next night she was converted. Then she helped us to pray for her companion. It seemed as though his heart had become somewhat harder, but in a night or two he yielded unto the Lord and was graciously saved. We were glad to see them united in one bond of Christian love.

We visited all our churches and my brother's wife went with us. Everybody seemed glad to see them saved. We spoke to some of the members and begged them to pray for my brother and to visit him, as a young convert needs to be mothered and cared for just like a child. Some of them promised me they would do so. We stayed at my old home about a month after my husband came. Then we left there to visit his mother. My brother left us at the train and I can see him now standing weeping. He promised to be true, but I feared for him. I knew that temptations would be very strong. I was afraid that unless he watched and prayed, he would fall back into the old habits again. He endured it for a while, but I'm afraid the preacher and the Christian people did not take the interest in him that I would have been glad to take in one that the Lord had plucked as a brand from the burning. I will stop right here to say that if the church of Christ would do its duty to rescue the perishing, and would care for them until they are on their feet, there would not be the backsliding that there is. May the Lord send an awakening along this line.

CHAPTER XIII
OUR JAIL WORK IN KANSAS CITY, MISSOURI
Hick's Hollow

Before leaving Seattle, the Woman's Christian Temperance Union, of which I was a member, being County Superintendent of Jail and Prison Work, thought it advisable to give me a letter of recommendation to the Woman's Christian Temperance Unions at the different places we visited. I did not visit the Union until after my husband and I started home and stopped over at Kansas City the last time. I found out through the papers where it met and went to a meeting. This Union was a white one, as there were no colored W. C. T. U.'s in Kansas City. They greeted me quite heartily. After bringing them greetings from the W. C. T. U. of Seattle, I told them that we had decided to stop over in Kansas City and work among our own people in the slums, jails, and workhouses. They were very glad to help us in any way they could. We saw the need of it, and we hoped to get up an interest among the colored people along this line. They voted to give me a recommendation to the sheriff, so that I could immediately begin my work. We consulted with Sister Clayton and a few of the special workers. The next week we visited the sheriff and gave him the recommendation. He gladly consented to have us come in and work among our own people. There was only one colored woman in Kansas City who had done any special work along this line. She had been working with the whites. Her name was Mrs. Moore. She had quit this work and was a matron at the Old People's Home, so we were the first band of colored people to organize themselves for work in the jails and workhouses of Kansas City, Missouri. The Lord graciously rewarded our labors.

It seemed my heart would break the first time I went in and saw so many of my own women, men, and girls from fourteen up, also boys. Their quarters were not pleasant, as they were dark closets. Some were thrown in there for the smallest trifles, but some had committed crimes as dark as those we had seen in other places. We soon found out that the devil is no respecter of persons. He will destroy every soul that he can. The prisoners were very glad to have some of their own people come and pray for them, as they were not used to it. Some white missionary had taken the gospel to them occasionally on Sunday. When there, we lined up before the bars and told them that we were going to come every Sunday. We gave them books and asked them to join with us in the singing. Oh! what beautiful voices. How my heart went out to them, and I coveted those bright talents for the Lord. The jailers and the prisoners were glad when we came, because they could hear these voices throughout the whole jail. The singing brought cheer to all. They listened attentively to our preaching, and many a one came out of that place to go in no more. They heard some things that they had not heard on the outside. Of course there were others who were natural criminals, as are found among other races. We gave them tracts and an opportunity to seek the Lord. Some of those in for the first time would weep bitterly, and eternity will tell the results and the good that was done. We kept this up weekly, and when we could not go ourselves, we sent some of our workers. This was twenty-five years ago, and the work is going on yet, and one of the workers who started in with us, Elder A. B. Ross, is still holding the meetings there. He has had many conversions and quite a number of the criminals condemned to be hanged have been converted. They have had their sins forgiven and have been washed in the blood of the Lamb. We are still in touch with these workers in the jail. We are glad God gave us the privilege, through the W. C. T. U., to open up this much needed line of work among our own people. We give God all the glory.

As we were strangers in Kansas City, it was quite a while before Brother Ray could find work. Finally, he secured a job in Armour's Packing House, but there came a cold spell and, as his work was outside stone work, he had to lay off. This cold spell lasted for six weeks or more, and our means were becoming limited. We prayed and fasted and waited upon the Lord.

It seemed a long time before the weather broke enough, so that Brother Ray could go to work. We here learned the meaning of the word, "Hardscrabble." My sister would give us a basket of food occasionally, and Brother Ray had a sister in Kansas City, Kansas, who sent us some fruit just at the time we needed it. I suppose my hard experiences as a

child taught me how to economize. I would buy a piece of cornbeef and boil it with rutabagas or other vegetables and was careful to save all the juice to cook the next meal with. I would skim the grease off for frying. A brother and sister who worked with us gave us eggs occasionally, and at different times they gave us a dollar and a half.

Still the weather was cold. Brother Ray would get up in the morning and walk about two and one-half miles, as he could not afford street car fare all the time. By noon he would be back, saying, "No work today." The devil tried to discourage him and sometimes his face would look long. Then we would pray and say, "Lord, we believe that you sent us here. We believe you will see us through." As we prayed, the Lord would give us the victory.

One day a woman came to the house and asked me if I wanted a day's work. It was very cold, down below zero. I had street car fare and rode out to the suburbs of the city. There was part of the washing to put out, and a half-a-day's ironing. The woman had told me she would want me for the whole day, but when I got there she said she would let me go at one o'clock. I looked at the big basket of clothes to be ironed. After putting out the washing, I got down by the table and prayed the Lord to give me strength to work, and I thanked the Lord after every piece I got ironed. When I finished the work, I was hungry and the woman gave me a cup of hot water and a very slim lunch, and when I left she handed me fifty cents. I thought I would get seventy-five cents. It had taken ten cents of the fifty for carfare and, my, how I suffered that day with the cold, but I said, "Praise the Lord, you sent us to this place." When I got home, one of the workers gave me a dollar and some more eggs, and I thanked the Lord for the day's work. Soon after this, the weather broke and my husband went to work again, and from that day on, we had no more hard times. We had learned our lesson of faith and would not exchange our experience for anything, because the bread and the rutabagas we ate tasted sweeter than when we did not trust the Lord so fully.

One day I began to laugh when I looked into the cupboard and saw that it was almost empty. The Lord blessed me pretty near to death. Husband was not out of work from that time until we left for home. We soon learned that if we expected to win souls in this part, we would have to practise what we preached to the very letter, and for once in our lives, we lived out the "Sermon on the Mount" to the letter, during all these tight times. These people were expert borrowers. They would borrow the broom, the tub, some coal, some bread, some soap, an apron to go to work in, a sunbonnet--anything you had to loan. They would ask to borrow the lamp out of the Mission to go to bed by. We did not refuse them, as we had come there to win them. The coal man in these places came through every fifteen or twenty minutes. The people bought coal by the half-bushel or peck. There was not a half hour through the cold weather but that you could hear the song of the coal man, "Coal, coal, buy some coal." One man hardly passed before another came. These coal sharks robbed these poor souls and that is why we had to keep a fire in the Mission, to keep the children warm.

Some of these children would come, a half dozen at a time, to our place. At first we never ate a meal which we did not divide with them. We were not able to give them a full meal, but we gave them each a share of what we had. They knew when it was time to eat, and they were always on hand. Their mothers would leave them without fuel, early in the morning, to go to work, and then they would come into the Mission, poor naked little tots, with their shoes untied and their hair unkempt and ofttimes they would be holding their ragged clothes together with their hands. They would pray and say, "Lord, if my mamma had a loaf of bread, she would give a little boy or girl, who was hungry, some." After such a prayer, we could not have the heart to refuse them anything to eat. The children would come in by the fire, and, as there were no sidewalks around the house, they would bring the sticky mud in on their feet and then put them on the rounds of the chairs. It was some work to keep things sanitary. Sometimes husband would help me clean and he would say, "If the Lord isn't in this, there is a lot of unnecessary work going on here." Then he would pray and take courage. I remember our first New Year's night. The room was packed with children. We had to keep the windows up and we kept chloride of lime in the room because some of them were so unclean. That time we held a meeting almost all night. Quite a number of the children and one or two of the older people were saved. It was a great night. From that time things took a change. We had the children to help us pray. It would astonish any older person to hear them. From that time rags began to come out of the windows. The parents began to clean up their homes. They began to put shoes and clothes on their children and our Sunday-school became larger. Whenever some of the older ones came in, the children would get down on their knees and plead for the souls of Miss Sue, or Miss Molly, or Mr. Johnny. They called everyone by a given name. This was a habit of the whole hollow.

When we left the place, my clothes were all shabby, but how it paid. The suffering was nothing compared with the glory and blessing we received while working with these precious souls. Some of the little ones were great soul-winners. They would find a little boy carrying beer and they would tell him it was wrong, and then the little boy would be ashamed to be seen carrying it. One little boy would ask others to come to the Mission. Sometimes two or three would be persuaded to come, and they would bring them to the door and say, "Mrs. Ray, here is a little boy whose mother drinks, and he wants to be saved. He says he don't want to swear any more. He wants to be a good boy, too." I would stop my work and they would get the song book and how they could sing, and then they would pray with this little boy, and he, too, would give his heart to Jesus. Many were the times they came in to sing and pray. They were very well-behaved and I could do anything with them. I had the good will of the parents, and the children all loved us.

Through the summer season we pitied these poor children. There was not a sprig of grass growing around there. Sometimes they would have wild sunflowers, as they were plentiful there, but not any grass for them to play on. We would take them on outings to some park occasionally through the summer. Their mothers would clean them up and some of the Christian workers would come down and help us prepare a lunch. It was amusing to watch them when the car stopped and they got into the park. They would run, and as soon as their feet touched the grass, they would roll over and over, the same as a horse that had been shut up in a barn for some time. Then they would get up and run to the swings and it was a joy to watch them. If we had any hard cases, we would always ask the children to pray. It was remarkable how they could repeat Scripture. We would teach them the Scripture verses and they learned them very readily. On Children's Day we would take them up among the better classes to their exercises, and we had the best behaved children of all. They knew the Scriptures better than those children who had had better experiences.

We were getting ready to move into our new home, and Brother Ray was delighted, but I felt troubled about it, as we had a temporary place on the hill with some workers. From this place we could hear the noises of the people at their night revelry, on the hillside. It was very insanitary down there, and I told my husband I did not believe the Lord wanted us to live in the same place with those people. However, he thought it best. I cried mightily to the Lord about it, and I wasn't really satisfied until I had a dream.

I thought I was passing through the city on a trolley car. The car was running along on a hillside and there was a muddy stream in the valley, which was very shallow. I thought the car I was in broke loose and rolled down the hill stopping right by this narrow stream. I stepped out and looked down. There were a great many human souls struggling in the muck and slime. I ran and plunged into the slimy, black water. I thought I swam like a duck and that every time I dived I caught one of those people by the hand or arm, holding my breath all the time I was under the water, and then swam to the bank and then gave him a toss and threw him high and dry on the hill. Then I blew the water from my mouth, so as not to get any of it on the inside, took a good breath and made another dive. I kept this up until I had rescued quite a number of human souls. I awoke and thought, "Well, this is only a nightmare and I am glad." Then it came to my mind about this place and I thought I wouldn't say anything about the dream, but I couldn't put it away from my mind. I asked the Lord if He was speaking to me through this dream to make things plain. Then I turned to my Bible and opened it to Isaiah, fiftieth chapter, and second verse, "Wherefore when I came, was there no man? when I called, was there none to answer? Is my hand shortened at all, that it can not redeem? or have I no power to deliver? Behold, at my rebuke I dry up the sea, I make the rivers a wilderness."

I read the whole chapter, but settled it with the Lord from the second verse, and then said, "This is of God. Yes, Lord, I am willing." I called husband and told him my dream and about the Scripture. We prayed eagerly with a "Yes, Lord," in our hearts. We decided to move and we had the place papered and cleaned and moved right into one of the roughest and most notorious corners at "Hick's Hollow," 590 Lydia Street, in the same building as our Mission. Some good saints came to help us and we prayed the Lord to clean up that place.

The people that came to the meetings, in their testimonies, would frequently say, "Sister Ray's Mission," as they always found me there and Brother Ray out working. I did not feel that it was fair, because Brother Ray made it possible for me to get out to the day meetings to work with the children, by going out and making the means of our living. I always said, "Don't say Sister Ray's Mission and work. It is Brother and Sister Ray's work. Husband works through heat and cold and never seems to tire. He is always willing to put in every cent for the salvation of souls or to help them." I would ofttimes say, "I'm preaching the gospel and he is working to pay expenses," which was a real truth. I heard a sister tell of once taking a voyage across the sea on a large liner. She said the most prominent man on the ship was the captain. Every one was saying, Captain, the Captain this, or the Captain that, or the Captain says so and so, or "I will talk with the Captain. He is running the ship." This woman said she would like to see the stoker and asked some one to take her down in the hold of the ship to see him. When she got in the engine room there was the man with his face all dirty from the coal and perspiration. He was poking the coal in the furnace and keeping the fire going to keep the steam up to run the engine. The woman said, "That's the man I feel like praising. If he failed at his job, the Captain would-not get very far." I got a lesson from this story and

MR. AND MRS. RAY'S MISSION IN KANSAS CITY, MISSOURI

from that time on I didn't want anyone to say "Sister Ray's" for by the help of the Lord and by the backing and cooperation of my husband I was able to do the work and felt that we were workers together. To God be all the glory.

Husband was a good sleeper, but I could not sleep at night. From that time they began to vacate the other rooms one at a time, and it was not long until we had all the rooms overhead to ourselves, but the basement was still occupied by people who were very noisy. We could hear the noise of the whole neighborhood and, with two or three exceptions, the people were drinking, dancing, singing, some playing guitars, some mandolins, and some even had pianos. I could put up with the noise from the outside, but I couldn't see how I could stand it to have it inside too.

A Notorious Character, "Penny West"

One hot summer evening quite a number of the people from around the neighborhood was gathered right in front of our place, as it was on a corner. There was a gas light there, and the ground was smooth. They sat on the sidewalk and on the steps under our window and door and drank beer and shot craps. I could tell that I was not going to sleep and asked the Lord to help me through the night. I got tired of hearing the awful grunts and peculiar noises they made while playing the dice. These people had a peculiar way of playing. They would throw the dice and would grunt like a hog and say, "Come seven, go eleven," and then grunt, and such a grunt. It sounded like the demons in the pit. After they had played for quite a while, they began to get pretty noisy as they kept bringing beer, which they called "rushing the growler." Of course they lost money playing.

I stood it until about two o'clock in the morning. As it was very hot I had been sitting in the window over them and heard everything they said. Some of the women were with them and when one of their men would lose they would get angry and try to get them to go home. This would cause a row. Finally I decided I would speak to them as Mr. Ray dared not, for they would not stand a man's talking to them about their noise. I stuck my head out of the window and said, "Gentlemen, do you know this is the Sabbath." They had started on Saturday night and it was now after two on Sunday morning. "I have been sitting here and haven't been able to go to bed because of your noise. I believe you know better than this and have been taught better than to gamble like this." Penny West, one of the gamblers, spoke up and said, "We are on the sidewalk, you know." However, that sidewalk was right under our window. Some of the women said right away, "That is right. Let us go home," but the men grunted louder, and said, "Come seven, go eleven." I felt like crying. I felt sorry for them and I didn't know what to do, so I decided that I might just as well pray. I began to sing before I started to pray and sang just as loud as I could, "Preaching the Gospel will soon be over."

> Preaching the Gospel will soon be over,
> Preaching the Gospel will soon be over,
> All over this land.

> *Chorus--*
> All over this land, all over this land,
> All over this land of sorrow,
> All over this land.

> Sinning times will soon be over,
> Praying times will soon be over,
> All over this land.

> Pleading times will soon be over,
> Pleading times will soon be over,
> All over this land.

By this time Brother Ray was awake and he got up and began to sing with me as loud as he could. The louder we sang, the louder the men grunted, but we wouldn't stop. We sang one song right after another, songs we had learned in our childhood, songs of our own. They understood what we meant, but it didn't phase them. We sang quite a while and then we began to pray. I don't believe that Daniel in the lions' den could have felt more earnest in prayer than we did at that time.

Finally we heard a noise, and something struck the door and some one walked up the steps and we felt sure the men were coming after us and in their drunken condition we didn't know what they would do. We didn't take time to think, but cried to our God and kept it up until four in the morning. In the meantime we heard a wagon, but we didn't know what was going on outside. We didn't stop to talk, but prayed on with all our might and as loud as we could. After a while we both prayed through. Day light came and we ceased praying. Everything was quiet outside. We didn't go out side or look out, but said, "Thank God," and went to bed.

After we had our breakfast at twelve we began to prepare for the children to come to Sunday-school. We couldn't have it until one o'clock, as the people caroused all night and didn't get up early enough in the morning for the children to come at the usual hour. Mr. Ray went outside. Some of the people were peeping out of their doors and there were several standing in a little group talking in low tones, and others were looking out of their windows. One of the men approached Mr. Ray and asked if he had sent for the police the night before. Mr. Ray told the man that he had not come there with the intention of calling the police, or anything of that kind, but that he trusted God to move their hearts and stop them from their sinning. We knew that it wouldn't pay to have them arrested or to interfere with them in any way, if we expected to do them any good, so we trusted the Lord fully. The man believed what Mr. Ray said, as he had confidence in him, so Mr. Ray asked him why he had asked that question. He said, "A bunch of policemen slipped up on them while they were playing and one struck Penny West over the head with his club and beat him up, and threw all the men into the Hurry-Up Wagon and took them to jail. Didn't you hear the policeman come up the steps? When that one hit Penny over the head his club flew out of his hand and up the steps and hit your door." Mr. Ray told him that we heard some one come up the steps, but that we were talking with our God and didn't know what was taking place. They accused them in court of disturbing those Mission folk's peace and getting them to screaming and praying. We never from that time on had any crap shooting or drinking beer under our window, or upon our steps. That was the beginning of the breaking up of one of the worst rendezvous there was in the place. The people didn't get mad at us, and Penny West told Brother Ray that he was sorry, but that they were all drinking and didn't know what they were doing. They had always played dice on that corner as the police couldn't get down there without their seeing them, as they had to come down a long flight of steps, and the men always kept one man watching while the others played. This time they were all too drunk to watch.

> It's just like Jesus to roll the clouds away,
> It's just like Jesus to keep us night and day,
> It's just like Jesus all along the way,
> It's just like His great love.

Well, praise the Lord, these had gone, but we still had the people in the lower story dancing and drinking. I didn't know but that in their fights they would get to shooting and I asked the Lord to protect us. One woman got killed by sticking her head out of the window as some men were running by shooting. I had a little inner closet that I would most always go into and fall upon my knees and pray. Not always because I was afraid of being hit, but because I thought of what it would mean to the ones that were killed. I felt that I must pray for them. One night just as they started their carousing, husband read the Bible and said, "Let us pray." I said, "Read the Bible first." He said, "I have just read the Bible," and I said, "When did you read the Bible?" He said, "I just read it, didn't you hear me?" I said, "When did you read?" He looked at me for a minute, and then he said, "I am going to take you out of here. It is the common sense thing to do. These noises are setting you crazy." We had our prayer, then retired, he to sleep, but I to lay awake all night. It was Saturday night, next day being the Sabbath.

There was a special meeting up in the city held by two of Bud Robinson's workers. The people had expected Bud Robinson himself, but he was taken sick and couldn't come so his workers came on anyway. We rose early in the morning and went up to this tent meeting. How glad we were to get into a good place and hear the sermon. During the sermon the brother gave one of Bud Robinson's illustrations. He said Jesus was a shepherd and that a shepherd always cared for his sheep, and that we were the sheep. He said, "You know that a shepherd always shears his sheep and the fleece belongs to Him. But the trouble with us is that when Jesus begins to shear us we don't want to hold still until he takes the fleece off." That truth struck us through and through. We had gone to the Hollow and thought we would stay until the Lord said it was long enough, and He had given me the vision of the lost in the muddy stream, but I had forgotten it in the time of pressure. Now it came back to me very clearly. When this worker finished preaching he asked for testimonies and I rose and told the people of the temptation we had been through. Of how we were about to give up the struggle, but that the sermon had given us strength and that we were going right back to the place and hold still until the Lord had taken off the fleece. We knew that the Lord would bring us through more than conquerors. We went back with the burden gone and feeling like warriors. Really we shouted as we got to the top of the hill. As we came near the Mission we could see that the doors were open down stairs. Thank the Lord, our disturbers had all moved away while we were at the meeting. Hallelujah to our King! Once more He had proved to us to be a Friend that sticketh closer than a brother. We rented the vacant rooms in the lower part of the building. We had some extra Sunday-school rooms. Of course it meant much for us to have to pay the rent, but we did not tell any one of our needs. There was one brother and sister who gave us a dollar or two occasionally. We did not take up any collection, except to let the children bring their pennies to Sunday-school, as they wanted to do it. However, this was never enough to meet the expenses of their literature, but we were only too glad to pay the balance ourselves.

Husband worked this summer and the Lord helped us to get a little money ahead. This was one of the hottest summers they had had in years. People were dying all over the city from the heat. Horses were dropping on the streets. They had to cover the horses' heads. The Lord gave Brother Ray the strength to go right on with his work. He never lost a day while making a stone foundation.

Old Man Mitchell

One hot night, soon after our neighbors moved from the basement, I was awakened suddenly from a sound sleep by a conversation held at the front door of the "Greasy Front." When it was very warm, everyone sat outside. This made it easy to hear what was said. The first word that struck my ear was, "I have taken notice and I heard those people pray." Then he was interrupted by an old woman, "But they say they are sanctified." "That's all right. I have listened to them pray, and I have taken notice." "Yes, but," interrupted the old woman again, "but I have taken notice of what they say and I heard those people ask God Almighty to move sin out of that place, and I have been watching them, and now tonight they are sitting up there without a sinner in that house. They asked God Almighty to do it, see, and I have taken notice." This was old Man Mitchell who was an habitual drunkard. He had lived in the Hollow long before me moved there. He was an old bachelor and lived in one room. He worked for a

German family as porter in their saloon. The woman talking was Aunt Ellen and they were both quite drunk and having a drunken dispute over the Mission folks. At first I tried to dismiss the matter from my mind, but when I heard him say, "Move sin out of that place," I sat up for a few minutes and listened more closely to their conversation and I thought of the Scripture that says, "The Lord maketh the wrath of man to praise Him." I awakened my husband, saying, "Get up and let us thank God. Even the sinners are taking notice of the work of the Lord." We had already given the Lord thanks. Now it was our time with the drunkard to have a praise meeting.

The last winter we were there the smallpox was very prevalent all over the city and more so in this place on account of the insanitary conditions. We had plead the promises of God in the ninety-first psalm, "He that dwelleth in the secret place of the most high shall abide under the shadow of the Almighty," etc. It says that no plague shall come nigh thy dwelling. The health officers did not pay much attention to the people down there.

The children came into the Mission all broken out. When we were in the meetings in the fall several cases broke out. Brother Ray was working every day. We had saved a little bit for the winter and I felt that he should stop his work and help me in the work, but the man he worked for insisted on his taking another building so he continued his work. Then he took the smallpox. I believe that he might not have gotten it if he had kept in the secret place of the Most High, but he didn't stop. We had no idea he was affected and went right on with our mission work. He had quite a fever, and the children came and wanted to pray for him. We were glad to have them, as we had lots of confidence in their simple prayers. His fever broke right away and he got better. We had no idea that the smallpox was breaking out on him. While helping him to dress, I noticed on his neck and shoulders great red spots and I said, "Oh, you have got the smallpox." He said, "Go ahead, where is your faith." I had him look at his arms for himself, and when he saw the spots he felt pretty weak. We felt so sorry, as we had held meeting all day Sunday and had had a great many visitors, and we thought of the little children, and cried mightily to our Father to not let any of them catch it, as they had all been exposed. We sent the word around to the houses for none to come in, and sent for an officer to come and quarantine us. We quarantined ourselves. We did not go outside or let any one come in. The officers failed to come. We sent for them every day for over a week. This shows how indifferent they are with those poor neglected people. Finally they came after Brother Ray, when he was getting better. The children said, "Well, we prayed. How could he have it when we prayed." We told them he would get better, but that he already had it when they began to pray, and that he was not sick any more from that time on. For the first time I became somewhat discouraged and wished that we were in Seattle. I wondered at first why he should have the smallpox. When we were having our prayer for the night, I knelt on the floor and wept bitterly, and husband said, "Sing, don't weep." I told him I couldn't sing, that I had to cry it out. Finally we prayed again and went to bed and way in the night it seemed as though I heard a voice say, "Look to Jesus." From that moment I became reconciled. We had with us a book called, "Christian's Secret of a Happy Life." We read this book through and got such an uplift to our souls. I was a very tired woman. The children all had to stay home. We had no mission and this gave us a chance to rest, as Brother Ray was very tired himself. Our trial turned out to be a blessing and we had such sweet communion with the Lord while we were closed in. We were glad after all that it happened. We didn't know we were so tired. It was a blessing in disguise. We never needed a rest so badly in our lives. So no plague came near our dwelling. Just as Brother Ray was on his feet again and it was time for the scabs to fall off, the officers came for him and took him to the pesthouse. We had decided that if we got the smallpox we would go to the pesthouse together, but we heard of the awfully insanitary conditions there, and that they used blankets from one patient's bed for another, so I thought that as long as I did not have it I had better not go and get it. Brother Ray decided to leave me home. They took the mattress that he was on. They did that with most of the poor people as it saved the county something. After the mattresses got good and dirty they would burn them up. We only had one in the Mission, but I was glad to have him take it as I had heard how filthy it was at the pesthouse. He took some tracts with him and his Bible, also some religious papers. He said, "As I have to go, I will do all I can to be a blessing to those that are there." I tell you I felt lonesome after the ambulance was gone. I began to think a little about Seattle, but it wasn't long until I was comforted again. It was a bitter cold night, but as we had provided ourselves with plenty of fuel I built a fire. We had a lounge and I kept back one quilt so was very comfortable, and I had a good time alone with the Lord. Some of the people at the white mission heard about our affliction and sent a Christian doctor to see us, but Brother Ray had gone and he said it wasn't time for me to take it yet, but that in a few days I would possibly take it. But I had plead the promises of the Lord for myself, "No plague shall come nigh thy dwelling," and I thought that meant my bodily dwelling. I believed in divine healing. As I had the promises, I thought I would not take any medicine. Yet I did not want to have the smallpox. I didn't know what to do. The doctor said that if I took the medicine I wouldn't get it, and if I trusted the Lord I wouldn't get it. I put my Bible on a chair and put the powder the doctor gave me beside it and got down on my knees and prayed, "Dear Lord, please tell me what to do. The doctor says that if I take these, putting my hand on the powders, I won't get it; if I put my confidence in Thee I shall not be confounded. I knelt in silent prayer for a few minutes, then rose to my feet and said, "Lord, I shall take Thy word." Thank God, He was true to His promises. I did not take it. Our mission workers went right on with the meetings in one of the houses next door.

Brother Ray said he was all right at the pesthouse. Some of the inmates told him that they heard the ambulance roll up and that they heard him get out and that one of the men said to his wife, "Hello, there comes our preacher." They had been praying for a preacher and when Brother Ray came in with his Bible they called him Elder. They were glad he came. Brother Ray always says, "They gave me the name of Elder Ray at the pesthouse." There was a very sick man on one of the beds near him. He had taken cold coming, and he was dying. Brother Ray got there just in time to talk and pray for him. He sat by him all night. The man suffered intensely. Brother Ray told him to give his heart to the Lord and believed that he did. So after all it was not a plague, it was a blessing. The pesthouse was two miles from the city limits. There was a deep snow on the ground and it was very cold. After I got the house fumigated I took a basket of apples, oranges, tracts, and other things I thought he would need. I rode as far as I could on the street car and walked two miles out there. The place was fenced in with a high fence. It was like a stockade with guards on the outside of the place. I called and some colored women came and looked out the door, and I asked them if there was a Mr. Ray there and they said, "No, he died the other night." You can imagine how I felt. I said it couldn't be he, so they described him and I saw that it wasn't he. They said, "Oh, you mean Elder Ray. Elder Ray, you are called for out here." I wasn't allowed to go near where he was, but I could call to him from the distance. I hung the basket on the fence and walked away about one hundred feet. He told me he was doing fine. I thanked God and came away and praised Him all the way home for the experience. I felt that I would be a better woman, and that I would have more faith in Him after I had had such a good opportunity to prove Him out, like Job, in a time of testing and trial.

It certainly did not take long to discover that my dream was verified. Of all the dirty places I ever got into, this place was the limit, and this "Hollow" was the black stream of my dream. Our having to live among them and see their sins, and praying for them, was the swimming in the water. The Lord certainly helped us in getting some of them pulled out of the muck and mire. Many of them have moved out of the place and have lived better lives.

Jesus said, "Come ye after me and I will make you fishers of men, and straightway they forsook their nets and followed Him." We did not have a sick day and we laid up quite a little to help us through the next winter. This was the Lord's doings and it was marvelous in our sight. As we were in possession of the whole building we had no more trouble and could rest much better.

These people were all insured. The insurance agent, and the rent man were around Saturday night, and at six or seven on Sunday morning. None of them likes the idea of being buried in a potter's field, so they bury themselves. Hence it is some kind of a lodge or insurance they keep up. Not all came to us for help, but some of the parents of the children. They would often gamble and drink away the week's wages Saturday night or on Sunday, and then come to us for street-car fare to go to work on Monday. We soon saw that this would not do, so every time they came we let them have it, but we preached them a sermon. After awhile the Lord delivered us from most of them. The man who owned the house which we rented, was an influential man, and stood well in the city. He was known as a prominent church member, and yet he was around Saturday nights collecting his rents from these tenants, and the old houses were not fit to live in. He didn't seem to care. We tried to get him to reduce the rents and called the children in to sing and repeat Scripture to him. We wanted him to see what the Lord was doing. He said it was a good work. He could see the effect of it in the community, but he would not let us have the rooms any cheaper. Although he said he was very glad, we could not keep up the rent for all the vacant rooms, so we found a good moral family to take the basement, and their children, five in number, came to our Sunday-school.

The oldest daughter was a great asset to our work. She was already saved and belonged to a Baptist church. They came down there because the rents were cheaper. So our troubles were over so far as the house was concerned. One day Brother Ray met a man whom he had boarded with years before this when we were sinners. We felt he had not treated us fairly about the board, and moved out and said we would never pay him. When we left, he tried to seize our baggage for the debt. I got mad and said, "You can't take my baggage for Mr. Ray's debt. The trunk is mine. If you take it I will sue you. He has got nothing." I made the bluff stick, so the sheriff did not take the trunk. So we laughed and thought we had gained quite a victory. Later when we got saved he had moved from this place in Kansas. We did not know where he was. We had gone over our back track and settled with others, but this debt had never been settled. So this day when Brother Ray met him he told him who he was. He too had been saved since we had seen him. So they both rejoiced together and when Brother Ray offered him the board money he said, "No, you take it and use it in the Mission." We thank the Lord for a clear title to our mansion in the skies.

Experience with a Banjo Picker

There was a family living right back of us in Hick's Hollow. The man of the family was a great banjo picker, and evenings after getting about half full of beer, he would play the banjo and sing. He would make sport of our songs and every now and then would say, "Praise the Lord," and then ridicule us. One evening after work he retired early and his wife said that he had not been drinking. All of a sudden he awakened everyone in the room by saying, "Woe." He began to writhe and squirm and went into convulsions,, and began to froth at the mouth and tear himself. His wife called in some of the neighbors to help her hold him. The doctor was called, but could not give him anything to quiet him. For three days and nights it took four strong men to hold him in bed. He would gnash his teeth, and bite his tongue. They had to prop his mouth open to keep him from chewing his tongue off. This seemed to bring a hush in the whole neighborhood. We never expected the man to come out alive, but the Mission workers cried to the Lord to spare his life, until he was saved. Finally he came out a very weak man and for a day or two was so weak and sore he could hardly move. He told his wife that he thought he was sitting upon a large tank, which was up on stilts, and filled with booze, with a fire underneath, and that he was burning up. When he came out he was under deep pungent conviction. As soon as he could walk he came around to the Mission and begged the pardon of the Mission workers and said he wanted to be saved. All of the children and the workers were burdened and crying to the Lord in his behalf, and in a short time he yielded to the Lord and was made a new creature and was healed instantly and he came out a bright shining jewel. I tell you we did rejoice. His ridiculing was turned to praying and his praying to shouting. We went back there several years later and met him on the street and he told us that he was still saved and was a member of the Baptist church, for which we felt grateful to our Lord and Savior.

Testimony From Some of the Children

Little Pete, who sent us to the place where the devil was the strongest, was very much taken up with the Mission from the beginning. He carried water and helped us clean up the Mission. He was one of our first converts and was as sincere as a much older person. All the children loved to testify and felt bad if we did not give them a chance to do so. One night on the street while we had a great crowd around us, little Pete gave his testimony and these were some of his words: "I'm glad I'm saved. Some people think little boys can't be saved. They say I don't know what I'm doing, and say I'm too little; but if I'm big enough to drink beer and to play cards and shoot dice for the devil, I'm big enough to be saved and sanctified for Jesus."

We had a little boy named Dick, just four years old, who came from one of the houses next door, a rough place called the "Greasy Front," where there was a great deal of fighting. This boy's grandmother, mother, father and the whole family were fighters and bullies. He came to our day meetings and sat there listening with great interest to the testimonies. He had been saved previous to this. One day we did not pay much attention to him, as we had visitors from up town who were giving in their experiences. He went home at noon and got his lunch and said to his grandma, with tears in his eyes, "They didn't let me testify." He came back in the afternoon and still we didn't pay any attention to him. He went home that night with his heart almost broken. His grandma didn't like it although she was unsaved. She told us how the child felt and from that time until now we have always made it a point, when there is a child in the audience, to let him testify and tell of his love for Jesus.

There was a little girl named Ethel. She too was about four years old. She was a great child to pray. Mind you, these children were carrying beer when we came to this place. You wouldn't believe that they could pray the way they did unless you heard them. Sometimes we would get amused while listening to them. Some persons had been doing some stealing in the neighborhood, and the children's prayer for the thieves ran something like this, "O Lord, save these sinners. Don't let them steal. Lord, some of these niggers have been stealing around here. Please don't let them do it any more." They prayed with the earnestness of a preacher. We have often called upon them when we have had some hard cases. Perhaps a drunken man would come to the altar and would not be able to get through. I would turn to the children and say, "Now, children, pray for this man and tell Jesus to help him to see the light." It was very touching when they all took hold and held on, until light broke into the man's soul. Many instances I could tell of this kind, but space will not permit. These children also believed in divine healing as they had heard us say that Jesus could heal the body as well as the soul. There was an old grandpa in the neighborhood who was a drunkard. His daughter had to leave him during the day while she worked. The children watched over and cared for him. One day we noticed that there was a great deal of praying and noise going on in his room. On inquiring what they were praying over, we found that the people in the adjoining room had heard them, and they said the children had gone to the old man and said, "Jesus can heal you, if you will give your heart to Him. Won't you give your heart to Him? We will pray for you, if you will." The old man seemed touched and the children prayed for him and he was converted right there. Then they prayed for his healing and grandpa was immediately healed. Jesus certainly sounded a great truth when He said, "A little child shall lead them." We never shall forget our experiences there and the lessons we learned through those children. It has been twenty-three years since then, and we don't know where one of them is now. We kept track of some of them for a while after leaving, but other things have seemed to crowd them out of our lives.

What we needed then was church cooperation to take up this work and look after and care for them after they were awakened, but they did not take any action then as it was all so new to them, so they were left in a sense to struggle through life alone. We went as far as we could, not being connected with any society there that could help us. We learned right there that any work of the Lord should be organized, in order to be a success, because they get scattered and the fowls of the air with the wolves get in and destroy them. So from experience we heartily endorse organizations that are scriptural and that have fire-baptized men and women to look after the converts.

Right here I want to take time and tell you how badly we have both felt the need of an education. Here we were shut in with these poor little souls for whom Jesus died that were so eager to learn and we did not know how to teach them as we should. Brother Ray did the best he could as Sunday-school superintendent, but they needed systematic teaching. We often would pray till late at night, asking the Lord for wisdom. So when they came in to warm or to sing, for they did love to get together to sing and pray, sometimes I would get tired and say, "I shall not let them in today," but they had such a way about them, in asking, that one could not refuse, especially the small ones. One, or perhaps more, at a time would come to the door and say, "I came to have a little prayer with you." Really one could not say, "No," as we were there for this purpose. So the thought came to me, "Now don't lose any time. Teach them scripture verses." I would teach them like this. John 3:16 (calling the verse). They would repeat it, then another until they had learned many verses. Then we would sing and I would tell them Bible stories as best I could. I gave them little practical cases and that is the way we spent our time. We soon found out the need of having a church of Holy Ghost believers back of us. However, the Lord over-ruled our ignorance and helped us to do a little. In our crude way we did what we could, leaving results with Him, until the harvest time, and we are ofttimes compelled to ask, "What will the harvest be?"

Our Street Meetings

We would hold our meetings within a block or so of the Mission. In fact, all of our work was in this neighborhood. We did not have to go beyond the block to get a congregation. We usually held our meetings right between two saloons. We started out from the Mission, singing like the Army, marched down to the corner and formed a ring. By the time we got our ring formed and started to pray there would be a band of men, women, and children around us. We stayed for an hour and then marched back to the Mission. Ofttimes there were a few white people who stood listening, but usually it was all our people. Now and then one or two whites came into the Mission. The butcher from that neighborhood, an habitual drunkard, usually came out with his wife to listen to our testimonies and songs. One night he stood and wept and followed us into the Mission. He came to the altar and found the Lord. He went up into the city to the white people's Mission and told what the Lord had done for him, and was not ashamed to tell where the Lord found him.

One Saturday night as we walked down the street we started to pass the saloons and go up the street one block farther, but looked down the alley and saw a crowd of men and women standing at the side door of a saloon and drinking beer. A crap game was going on in the alley on the ground. We turned right in where they were playing dice and forming a ring, began to sing. They backed away. We sang a song and began to pray. Some one had a couple of bulldogs and they got to fighting. We kept right on with our prayer, although they were right around us. It was an exciting time for them and the onlookers. By the time we had finished praying, they were quiet. Sister Clayton, who was filled with the Holy Spirit, stepped into the ring and began to testify. It seemed to grip their attention and we had a splendid audience. The Lord helped us to tell them of their sinfulness and how badly they were bringing up their children, and that it was no wonder they were having so much trouble as a people. They believed us. We came away believing that those testimonies would have a lasting effect on those people.

There was a grocery man near-by who was a Catholic. He lived right beside the store. He would come out every night and listen to our singing and testimonies. He said he was glad we were in the neighborhood. His name was O'Brien. He said he could see the difference in the people and the children also. We talked to the people about paying their debts. We told them to go back over the back track and clean up, spirit, soul and body, and they would see what salvation would do for them. We surely produced an effect upon the grocery man himself.

Tent Meetings Held by the Holiness Bands of Our Own People in Kansas City, Kansas

Tent meetings were held every summer in Kansas City. The workers were from the different churches. We enjoyed going over with some of the workers and children. We always came away with a feeling of up-lift and with strength to go back to our labors. Some of the ministers from the different churches did the preaching, and evangelists came from Pennsylvania and Nebraska. Great good was accomplished every summer. We were often privileged to preach for them. Many of the whites visited these meetings. During these meetings I got my call to the ministry. Although I had been working for several years, I never had a definite call to preach. I knew that I was a worker and the Lord had blessed my labors; but the word "preacher" was more than I considered belonged to me. We went on with our labors and, when we were invited at different times, preached in the white mission in the city. I never could say "preach," but would say, "I'm going to talk or give a little message." It seemed too big a mouthful to say "preach." Others would say it for me, "Sister Ray is going to preach at such a place." I got into trouble over it, and I asked the Lord about it. One afternoon I was to preach at the camp meeting to a large audience. There were preachers there, educated and accomplished, and the question came up before me again, "You have never been definitely called to preach; don't say 'preach.' " I decided to fast and pray over it until time for the service. The tent meeting was near a church, and I went over in this church with my Bible, and I prayed to the Lord, "If you have called me to preach, I should know definitely. As I have never gotten any definite witness to my calling, make it plain to me this afternoon, so then I can tell the people not to call me a preacher, but just a worker for the Lord." I was intensely in earnest. The Spirit spoke to me and said, "Some are called out, some are led out, and some are thrust out." While I was praying, I broke down and began to cry, and the Spirit of the Lord fell upon me and I said, "Surely God is in this place." I began to tremble and fell on my knees with my eyes closed and with my head bowed. There came a vision before me of a bright, blazing, fiery brand, and the glory of the Lord fell upon me. I did not hear the word "preach," but I felt it through my very being. It was quite a while before I got strength to go back into the tent. I stayed in the church until time to preach, and when I went in the testimonies were being given. I could hardly sit still or hold myself until it was time for me to preach. The Lord wonderfully helped me. The altar was filled with seekers. I lost sight of everything except the souls of men. I never doubted from that day as to my calling to preach the gospel. I know that I was led out, and I am glad that the Spirit gave me this definite experience, so that the devil will never be able to tempt me along these lines. I praise Him; I praise Him; I praise Him. To Him be all the glory.

I am sorry to say that the better class of our people had no idea of the conditions as they existed among the unfortunates, as they had nothing to do with one another. I want to say right here that many of the white people think that the colored people are all alike. Human nature is the same the world over. However, there are different classes of us people the same as in other nations, and some just as refined, considering opportunities. They have their societies, churches, doctrines and ideas just as other people. The Lord gave us a few of the best colored Christian

SCHOOL IN KANSAS CITY FOR COLORED CHILDREN. MRS. LIZZIE BULLETT, TEACHER.

---

characters from the best churches to help us. As we had visited these churches and tent meetings through these we got an opportunity to lecture in a few of the churches. They were very much surprised when we told them of the conditions in the slums among our own people. I will mention here a couple of school teachers of Kansas City, Kansas, Mrs. Lizzie Bullett and Mrs. Mollie Harrison. There was also a Sister Woodford and a Sister Smith, and many others I have not space to mention. When they heard of the conditions they came down and rendered us all the assistance they could, going with us to the jails and on the streets. I will never fail to praise the Lord as long as I live for the assistance of those consecrated women, and some of the men. The first time that any of them came they said they went home and couldn't sleep of nights. Some said Reverend and Sister Ray live in hell. They didn't know there was such a place on earth. We thanked the Lord for helping us to blaze the way. By doing this work there have been great results obtained in that place today. While we did not see all that we wanted to see done, as most of their hearts were hardened, and the light was new to them, but we did see a great change. We expect to see it when the Lord calls the roll on the other side. For we know that He is a prayer-hearing God, and He answers according to our faith. Lord, I believe!

When the first year of our stay in this place was up, husband took a week off. We fasted and prayed and wanted to get the mind of the Lord about coming home. But we couldn't find any one to take our places; although it was a good work, no one wanted the job. We couldn't get the mind of the Lord, and the children were so afraid we would leave, they would ask the Father not to let us leave them, saying, "What would us little children do?" We decided to stay.

The second year conditions were much better. The policemen walked through, one at a time, and they acknowledged a great change. We prayed over it. We had stayed over two years. One day after much prayer we both seemed to feel that it was the will of the Lord that we should leave. While we felt sorry for the children, there was a Baptist preacher who said he would take the work up, and the Lord lifted the burden of them off us. We knew that our work was done and I got so blessed in thinking of what the Lord had done for us. When I knew that we were going to Seattle and that this Baptist preacher was willing to undertake the work, I said to my husband, "How do you know but what the Lord will let us go back together?" We had decided that Brother Ray should go first, as we did not have the means for both of us to leave, as we had had such a hard winter. He said, "You have faith for it and ask Him to give us the means for both of us to go." I prayed over it. There was a Christian man who was the treasurer of the Armour stock-yards, whose acquaintance we had made while there. He consented to get us half fare. We belonged to a Faith Missionary Society while there, and they also gave us a half fare apiece. The Lord gave us more than we asked for. I became so blessed thinking of it that I said one day to some of the sisters when they were saying they hated to see us leave, "I believe that the Lord has said go and I feel the go in my heart." You should have seen those poor souls as they sat around as I was packing up. I didn't have many clothes to pack up, I tell you. I had divided with them to some extent. Even the wicked mothers would come. There would be three or four in my room at once just sitting with nothing to do, watching me pack and saying, "The children will miss you."

As we were leaving, the Lord gave me the third chapter of Zechariah, especially the seventh verse, and the fourth chapter and seventh verse, assuring us that we should have open doors and opportunities to labor for Him. It looked as though we were leaving our opportunities for work behind us. We were certain we were led by the Lord to come west.

So here was our first chance to work after arriving home. With no salary, plenty of hard work, but with sufficient grace for the job, we went at it gladly, rejoicing because we were accounted worthy to labor with Him and without pay. From that day until this we have always had open doors to hold meetings, have never but once inquired for work. We wrote two letters to a certain place. We did not get the work, but we did get a rebuke in spirit because we wrote for work. This was because the Lord told us before we left that He would give us a place to walk with those that stand by and also promised to make all mountains a plain.

We have ever had open doors for work. Never from that time to this has there not been a call in our house to work, in meetings, although this promise was given to us nearly twenty-five years ago. The Spirit has led unerring to the land we hold today, and we have tried to walk in the light.

CHAPTER XIV
RETURN TO SEATTLE

We left Kansas City, Missouri, August 4, 1902. It had been two years and three months since we had left Seattle to go east. We had fulfilled our mission with our kindred, finished our work in these parts, and had done with our might what our hands found to do, and were now on our way back home with a greater love for our Savior, a deeper consecration, and a greater vision of things eternal. I had gone east alone, but on the homeward trip, husband was with me. The journey was a happy one. We sang and rejoiced together all the way back.

There was a family of Quakers on the train and when they heard us sing, they came over and got acquainted. They sat with us and we had a pleasant time clear through to Portland. We expected to stay in Portland a couple of weeks to rest. The Free Methodists were holding a camp meeting. We visited the camp for a few days, remaining over Sunday. Rev. William Pearce, now bishop, was the presiding elder, and Rev. H. V. Haslam was the pastor. Rev. Jellison and wife were the evangelists. We were delighted when we found Brother and Sister Jellison were there, as we had met them in Kansas City and they had visited our humble little Mission in the slums. They told the people about our work and said that we had lived in a regular hell, and spoke of the victory

REV. RILEY VERNON, PASTOR A. M. E. CHURCH
VERONIA, OREGON

REV. RILEY VERNON. PASTOR A. M. E. CHURCH,
VERONIA, OREGON

which the Lord had given us in that place. I preached for them one Sunday.

We also met the Rev. H. E. Kreider, who was a young man at that time, and many others of the Free Methodist preachers and saints.

In the meanwhile we had a friend, Rev. Riley Vernon, evangelist, of the African M. E. Zion Church, who at that time was away from home, but he had heard of our being in Portland. He was at a place called Veronia. He immediately sent us word to come and help him in his tent meetings. He had been in this place for over two weeks with other helpers, Brother Smith and wife, and a Brother Hess.

Brother Smith and wife could not stay any longer, so Brother Vernon wanted us to come. We prayed about it and finally decided to go. We rode about twenty miles on the train and a brother met us and took us up into the mountains about twenty-two miles. It was the loveliest trip I ever made. We had just left the Kansas City slums with their heat, noises and insanitary atmosphere. The change did us much good, especially when we opened our lungs and breathed in the good, pure mountain air and drank of the cool water. I hardly knew what to do with myself. It was a rough trip, but somehow we enjoyed it. We were riding in an express wagon with two seats and with quite a bit of merchandise packed under the seats--a can of coal-oil under the seat we were sitting on. We went over some skid-roads and the seat bumped against the coal-oil can. Sometimes I stood up and every time we came to a hill the driver told us to get out and walk. I gathered moss and pulled the beautiful ferns and just skipped along. It seemed the Lord gave me supernatural strength. The scenery was delightful. We arrived at the place just at sunset.

We had supper of some of the best milk and the sweetest vegetables I ever ate. I did not feel a bit tired. Rev. Vernon asked me if I would preach that night, and the Lord gave me unusual liberty and unction. Souls were at the altar and we closed with victory. The news seemed to spread around us that new recruits had come, and people came from twenty miles over the mountains to these meetings. The Lord graciously blessed us. There were about forty conversions. The men folks preached at the day services, and I preached nearly every night while there. It was wonderful what conviction rested upon the people. Whole families were saved. One would get through and then go back after another. We had blessed results. We went on for three weeks longer, and then we closed, thanking God for ever giving us the privilege of working with Brother Hess and Rev. Vernon.

We came back to Portland and preached in a mission. There we met a man and a woman who had come down from the country and who were stopping in Portland, believing that they were called of the Lord to go into the ministry. The husband could not read, the woman was nearly blind. They had two children. They had some means when they came, but they told us they had spent all and yet they had not found anything to do. They still believed the Lord was leading them. It was a pitiful case, and we could discern that they were deceived by the devil. One night when talking with them we found they did not have money enough for a bed. The man seemed discouraged and wondered why some one had not called them to preach for them.

Brother Ray felt it his duty to take this brother and his wife aside and talk with them. He told them that he believed that the sensible thing for them to do would be to take their children and go back to the farm, put the children in school, and wait until the Lord gave them something definite. He told them that he did not believe that the Lord would start them out in that condition and leave them confused.

At the time they did not take what he said in the right spirit. They were honest at heart, though, and thought they were right. We do not know how long they remained there. About four years later, we received a letter from them, thanking Brother Ray for giving them his advice, and stating that they had gone back to the farm; also that the Lord had given them a lesson they would never forget, and that the devil had deceived them. They said their home was happy and they were doing the Lord's will.

We were surprised to get the letter, but glad to know that the Lord led them out of their delusion.

The Lord give us wisdom, and keep us balanced along all lines.

When we arrived in Seattle we hardly knew the city, although we had been away only a short time. The streets were changed, great buildings were being constructed, and many of the residence districts had been converted into business districts. We found us a room for the night. The next day we hunted up some of our friends. We found it hard to rent a house in the city. After rooming for a week, we found a couple of little rooms between Third Avenue and Second Avenue in an old house on the alley. The rooms were up in the garret. It was all we could find. We met Reverend Faulk, pastor of the Swedish M. E. Church, now called the Swedish Temple, which is on Pine Street. He was running a large mission, called "The Stranger's Rest," at Second and Washington Streets. This place was financed by a man in Alaska for the benefit of the down-and-out Scandinavians and for any others who were helpless. It consisted of two basement rooms with a door between. Both had front entrances. One room was filled with bunks and cots, where a man could get a bed for ten or fifteen cents. The other room in the front had a large lunch counter where the men could get a cup of coffee and a piece of pie or a sandwich for five or ten cents. A curtain partition was drawn across, and back of this was the Mission. There was an organ here, and the men could come and hear the gospel. The beds and the lunch counter were an incentive to get the men inside, in order to get the gospel to them. The Mission had no evangelists at that time. Brother Faulk, with whom we were acquainted before we went east, wanted us to take the evangelistic part of the work. As this was the first open door for us in Seattle, we inquired of the Lord about it, and after we had gotten His will in the matter we started in a campaign against sin and the devil. This also was a volunteer work, especially the spiritual part.

This was a very insanitary place, as it was in the back part of the basement where the air was bad, and the tide came in under the basement. There were several holes in the walls near the floor, and under this floor there was a regular incubator for mosquitoes. We went out and had our street meetings. Quite a number of workers with whom we were acquainted before we went east came to help us. It was no trouble to pack the place full of all kinds of stranded men. Some of the men were quite drunk. You know most drunken men usually go to sleep when they sit for a while, but here the mosquitoes were so bad they worked to our advantage, keeping the men awake while we preached. Every fellow would slap his face, striking at the mosquitoes. Great were the results of those meetings. The only thing that seemed to affect me was the noise of the dishes at the counter. In preaching we would have to keep our voices at a high pitch in order that the men might hear what we said. Christian people came from all over the city and gave us a hand. There were not the number of missions then that there are now. Just those of the Volunteers of America and the Salvation Army. Much of the glory of the Spirit of the Lord accompanied every meeting. We worked there through the fall and the greater part of the winter. Some preachers came down and they said that if they had to work there the noise would tear their nerves to pieces. In the meanwhile Brother Ray worked every day at stone work on the buildings, and worked at night in the Mission. We got no salary for this mission work A collection was taken up to pay for the lights, and there wasn't anything left over. We have always been glad for our work at old "Stranger's Rest" and for the many souls that came to the altar. There was never a barren night and sometimes the place would be full clear up the steps to the sidewalk. We were so happy to do service for the Lord. Some time later this same mission hall was taken up by the Rev. C. S. McKinley and the Olive Branch Mission was organized. There were a few changes made in the room, and it was more sanitary.

CHAPTER XV
THE WAYSIDE MISSION

In the year 1897 there was a mission started at 316 Railroad Avenue, Seattle. The superintendent was a Baptist preacher, Doctor Alexander DeSoto. This was a few years after the great fire in Seattle, which burned out sixty-five acres of the business section. The city has undergone a great change since that time, and this part of Seattle is now built up with large business houses. At that time it was a part of the lowest slums. This mission was largely financed by some of the leading Christian and business men of the city. It was a splendid opportunity for doing good. Street meetings were held from ten to eleven p. m. and by that hour of night all of the rough element was coming from its hiding place to rob, steal and beg, and to hunt for a night's lodging. The men would gather around our street corner, which was in front of one of the most notorious saloons in the city, called "Billy, the Mug." The largest mug of beer was sold for five cents. There our workers sang and prayed, and told of the power in the blood that saved men from sin. This often would bring large crowds. We were each asked to take different nights, so that the workers would have set times. Ours was Tuesday night. The Lord gave us a band of helpers and we never lacked for an audience.

There was a vaudeville show-house in the basement of the building near where we stood to hold our street meeting. One night their brass band came out and lined up beside us and played. This night it was raining, and we had but few workers. Of course they gathered their crowd. When they stopped to rest, we testified, as otherwise the noise of their drums would have drowned us out. We testified and sang and the crowd would turn and listen to us and the band would start to play again, then we were compelled to keep still until they finished. We would sing such songs as "Power in the Blood" or "At the Cross." Then some one would step into the ring and testify. We felt the Lord wanted us to go on with our meetings.

The superintendent would step into the ring and say, "Men, we have a lighthouse down on Railroad Avenue. Come down and hear the gospel. If there are any sick among you, we will give you help, free of charge. If any of you are hungry, we will give you a cup of coffee and a bowl of stew. If any are without beds, we will let you stay in the mission by the fire away from the rain and cold."

We would start down the street singing and they would follow us like a drove of chickens, and oh, such a sight. There were the lame, the halt, some partly blind, dope fiends, delirious drunks, some with bruises from fights, others with putrifying sores, and quite a few hungry and naked.

This was out of the ordinary for street meetings, because they had been to Alaska and had become sick through exposure and hardships, and had made their way back to Seattle. This explains why there were so many of this kind of men. They were from every class, from an ex-judge and university professor to the most illiterate and degraded class of humanity. Our services began at eleven and lasted until twelve p. m.

The leader of the meeting would give a short talk right to the point, with scripture lesson and songs. There was one big stove in the room.

The men were in the front of the room and the workers sat facing them. There were all ages of men, but scarcely a woman. In the rear of the building, as it was quite large, there were cots in one of the rooms where the disabled were lying; in another place was a large stove with tin vessels for cooking and eating. There was a bakery that gave us its stale bread, and some of the men caught fish and other people sent in financial aid. We considered this a God-send at that time, as the poor-house was full of broken Alaska gold hunters.

There was scarcely a night that souls were not saved. It was sad to look upon their faces as we broke the bread of life to them. Most all had seen better days, but sin and greed had brought them to this place of poverty and want.

There was one man, in particular, who was an ex-judge, but drink had brought him to the mission. You could tell by his looks, by his very walk and the way he carried his hat on his arm, that he had been a gentleman. He walked like a prince. He listened very attentively at the meetings. While some around would be sound asleep and others would mutter and talk in their drunkenness, this man would look you straight in the eye, often with tears standing in his eyes. Our souls cried out to God for him as we talked. One night he was gloriously saved, and a certain Christian ex-judge and others in Seattle, who had taken an interest in him, started him in business. He sent for his wife. She was a refined, cultured lady, and they were happily reunited. The last we knew of them he was making good.

Twelve o'clock came very quickly. One night a brother who was night watchman asked if we didn't want to see the boys go to bed, and we just stepped to the doors. Some of the men had blankets, and we noticed that just as soon as the benediction was given, nearly all the men drew up around the stove as close as they could get, and when we got to the door the watchman gave the signal and said, "All right, boys," and there was just one loud thud and each fellow stretched out on the floor with his feet to the fire. They looked like sardines in a can as they lay around the stove.

The place where the mission was at that time has all been filled in by washing down the near-by hills. At that time the streets had already been regraded, with deep fills and trestle work, and the houses in this locality were left with the first story below the street. The lower stories were all empty, and here was a good rendezvous for the dope fiends and robbers. It was not long after the regrade began before all was filled in. In the spring of 1900 the mission was moved. The superintendent bought an old boat, the Idaho by name. She had plowed the waters of Puget Sound for years and was worn out and fit only for something of this kind, so she was converted into a mission hospital. She was finally moored at the foot of Jackson Street on the Sound. We were privileged to go with some Mission workers to hold the first dedication and prayer service. Later on, the boat was remodeled, cleaned and equipped for an emergency hospital, and named "The Wayside Emergency Hospital." Today it is called "The City Hospital."

Two of the patients died at this mission and their funerals were preached at the usual service hour, eleven p. m., at the close of the regular preaching. The men were given an opportunity to see the corpses. It seemed to make a deep impression on some of them. I don't know whether these two patients had been saved or not, but I know that they had a last chance and they had a Christian burial.

It was impossible to keep a bar of soap at the wash-stand, as the men would steal it all. Some have told us how they would go outside the city limits, and wash and boil up their underwear and dry it by the fire. Poor deluded souls. They were like the prodigal son; they had spent their substance in riotous living, and were now living upon the husks of this old world, when the heavenly Father had a plenty and to spare.

Thousands of mothers' boys are in this very condition today, and how badly they need to be awakened, and brought to their senses before they go down into eternal night without a Savior.

Some of the vice has been put down, and today we have a cleaner and a greater Seattle, especially since the saloon went out of business. And yet we see sin on every hand. The harvest truly is great. There are all kinds of religions, but an awful lack of vital salvation. We see infidelity, higher criticism, formalism, evolution, and false doctrines of almost every kind, and the cry of our soul is, "Oh, Lord, please send us a wave of salvation, and let it come speedily." Amen.

The Addict

We often met people we had seen in the Mission, in jails, and other places. At those times the opportunity would be given them to turn to the Lord, but they would fail to do so and the next place we would meet them would be in the hospital. There they were sorry they had not heeded when they had the opportunity.

A lady living on Queen Anne Hill requested us to search out her daughter. She had not seen her for several years. They came from the east to Seattle. Some one told her that she had a daughter that was a fiend down in the slums. We told her that we would try to do so. We hunted up some of the fiends and asked them if they knew her. They said they did, and would tell us where we could find her. There were some old dilapidated houses that had had a fire through them down on King Street near Sixth Avenue. They told us we would find her in one of the buildings, a room that the fire had not reached. I went that day to find her. I took some flowers and tracts and went to this old building, and the thought came to me, "Oh, Lord, could it be possible that she is in such a place as this?" I thought I looked the place over and went out to tell the girls I could not find her. "Oh, yes," they said, "she is there. There is one door in a certain corner that is closed; go right in there; she will be asleep; she will not hear you." I went back to this door, pulled it open, and went inside; and oh, such a sight! On an old, half-burned mattress there lay something with a little poodle dog by her side, dead to the world, under the influence of dope. I held my breath in astonishment. Once the impression came to me to drop out as I couldn't seem to be able to waken her. The room and she were very filthy. Finally I set my flowers down and took hold of her and tried to waken her. After a while, in a half-dazed tone she said, "Who is this?" and I replied, "I am a friend of your mother; she sent me to help you." I could not help but cry when I thought of the good home on Queen Anne Hill, of a loving mother and father, and that this poor girl was more satisfied in a hovel like this than in a good home under mother's care. But oh, sin is such a monster! The appetite had gripped her. I thought of how depraved a human heart can get when the devil gets in and takes possession. In a stupor she said, "Will you go over across the street and get me some dope?" I said, "No; I didn't come in to help send your soul to hell; I came to help you; your mother wants you to come home." She went off to sleep and I could get no more out of her. I went down the back alley, found an old can and filled it with water, and left my flowers and tracts and went home with my heart bleeding. I tried it again. They told me when I could probably find her awake. She would sleep there all day, and then about night, when it was dark, she would make her way out on the streets and alleys to beg money to buy some more of the drug that enslaved her. This time she was not so stupid. I tried to get her to say she would go home, but she would not. I told her father and mother where she was. They managed to get her home. They undertook to break her of the habit. They had to watch her as though she was a maniac. They did all they could for her. Finally the father died suddenly, and the mother turned her over to the police. By this time she was getting far along; she was a cocaine fiend and she used it like snuff, and it had eaten a hole up into her head and was killing her. They got her into the county hospital, and then I had a better chance to talk to her, as there they gave it to her only three times a day, in milder form. She began to fail rapidly. She knew it was only a little while until it would have the best of her. She thought that some time she would be saved, but she did not have the courage to give it up, and yet she felt as though the Lord wouldn't receive her as long as she used it. One day there came a ring on the phone and the matron of the hospital told me to come out; that the girl was dying and wanted to see me. I went as quickly as I could, but before I could get there she passed away. The matron told me that she begged her not to let her have dope. She told her, "You have got to be still then; we can't have you disturbing the other patients." The next moment she would say, "Give it to me," and then as she was about to take it she would say, "Please take it away," and she died right in that struggle with a spoon in her hand right in the act of using the dope. Oh, if she only had had courage like Lucy, the one I spoke of in a previous chapter. If she had only given it up when she had a little strength. "Procrastination, thou are the thief of time." Surely "the wages of sin is death."

A young man came to my house one day. I had met him before in the religious services. He wanted to borrow a dollar and a half. He told me he stood badly in need of it. The first impression came to me not to let him have it, but he begged so earnestly that I finally consented. I told him that I could let him have it, but it was not mine. It was the Lord's, as I usually laid aside one-tenth of the Lord's money, and if he used it for good it would be all right, and if he didn't, but went and bought whisky, it would kick back on him, as it was the Lord's money. He said that he surely would do good with it. I went to the hospital on Sunday and whom should I see but him, with a broken leg. He looked ashamed when I saw him, but he was honest enough to confess that he had used the money for whisky and had gotten drunk and met with an accident and his leg was broken. He remained in the hospital for nearly a year before that leg was healed.

"Be sure your sins will find you out." "Whatsoever a man soweth, that shall he also reap."

CHAPTER XVI
INCIDENTS
Visit of Brother Ray's Mother

In the year 1898 Mr. Ray's mother made us a visit. He had not seen her for twenty years. I had never met her. I had always wanted to see my husband's mother. When we met at the train she fairly shouted for joy. She threw her arms around his neck and thanked God for the privilege of meeting her son again. She was a real mother in spirit as well as in flesh. I enjoyed having her with us. I had my plans all set as to how I would entertain her. I thought I would have her rest, and I didn 't want her to work--I would take care of her. But I was very much disappointed in this, as she was very energetic and loved to work. She told me that I looked so thin that she wanted me to rest and let her take the kitchen. I could not think of doing such a thing. I said, "You have worked all your life, and now you can take things easy." I found that this did not lie within her nature. She said she could not sit and fold her hands. She believed that people should always have something for their hands to do even while they rested. She would do the patching and make quilts, and also do the darning, but all this did not satisfy her.

She loved to hear us pray, and she would often say these were the "readinest" and most prayerful children

MOTHER OF MR. RAY AT SIXTY-SEVEN YEARS OF AGE.
SHE LIVED TO BE NINETY-FIVE.

she had ever seen. She would join heartily in prayer and song with us. She was surprised at the kind of work we were engaged in, and would get so sorry for the people that came to us with their burdens. She began to pray for the Lord to give her something to do. She soon had her heart and hands full, and the burden became so heavy that one night while we were at family prayers she stopped praying all at once and said, "O Lord, I have asked you to give me something to do; but now, O Lord, will you please take some of it off from me?" These sights were more than she could stand. She was a real benediction to our home and when the unsaved ones came in they would call her mother and they would tell her that I did not want her to do my work, but she insisted upon doing so. I went alone to pray. Oh, my, to have my mother-in-law take charge of my home--I did not know when I consecrated myself that this was in the "unknown." She didn 't know how I felt about it and it was the hardest job of my life to sit down and let her wash the dishes. It was the first hard trial after my experience of entire sanctification. I wanted her to have the experience. I did not want my husband to know I was tried with her, and many a night as they slept I would go alone and pray until I had the victory.

One morning she went out in the back yard. It had been raining and she stepped on a wet board. She fell and broke her arm. I heard her scream and ran out. She got up, but fainted and fell again. There was no one to help me, and in my distress I called upon the Lord for help. I picked her up in my arms, carried her indoors and laid her upon the bed. I never could have done this, but the Lord gave me supernatural strength. I should judge she weighed about one hundred forty pounds. I dropped upon my knees and prayed, "Blessed be Thy name, O Lord, who giveth power to the faint, and to them that have no might, Thou increaseth strength."

I then called in the neighbors and the doctor and had her arm set. There was a brother rooming with us, and when we knelt in prayer at night, he got hold of the Lord in prayer for the healing of her arm, and from the moment he prayed she had no more trouble with it. Although she was a woman over seventy-six years of age, it healed rapidly. She seemed to think that this was the experience of sanctification, as she felt the touch of the Lord upon her arm while the brother prayed for her. She would testify to that experience. We knew that she had not received it, although she walked in all the light which the Lord let on her heart, but she did not understand. She could not read the Bible, but she knew the prayers of the righteous and the difference between right and wrong, and could tell you anything you wanted to know concerning what was right.

One day my husband said, "Mother doesn 't understand sanctification." We had told her it was possible to live without actual transgression, although we could sin if we wanted to, that the Lord could take the desire away. We told her it was impossible to live without faults and failings, but the Lord would not impute them to us as sins as long as the motives of our hearts were right. She seemed to see through it and began to ask the Lord to give her the experience. One day previous to this, husband and I were talking and he said he thought he would tell her there was a difference between healing and entire sanctification and that he believed the Lord would not want her to be mistaken. This seemed to grieve her somewhat, as she thought that he was her boy and she did not want her boy to tell her she did not have the experience. But when she saw it was true (she always believed the Bible) she went to her room feeling very bad.

The next morning she did not come down, but stayed in her room all day. By this time I began to feel very serious about her, and told my husband that I was sorry he had spoken to her about it, as she was quite old and I did not like to have her feel so bad, and she was my mother-in-law. I tried to coax her down to eat. She did not feel like coming. My husband said, "Let her alone; the Lord will teach her and she will come out all right." She stayed in her room the next day, but in the evening when he asked her to come to supper, she came down with her face all aglow, but did not say a word. We knelt in family worship, and it came her turn to pray. She lifted her head and arms to heaven and, oh, such a prayer of victory and joy and ecstasy. She said, "The Lord has sanctified my soul and I understand it now. I have received the Holy Ghost. Praise the Lord!" She thanked her son for showing her the difference and put her arms around his neck, and we three cried and rejoiced together. What a change it made in her. I was so glad the Lord held me steady, and if I had never had the experience, I am sure I would not have been willing to turn my house and the management of it over into her hands as much as I did. It was such a victory for her and it certainly paid me in the end to be patient. I had the victory and was willing for her to run the house, and she was sanctified and was willing to let me run my own house. Oh, how we loved each other, and we both saw it paid to let the Lord have His way. We worked in harmony as mother-in-law and daughter-in-law should. It seemed that the year she stayed with us was such a short one. She told me she loved me as she did her own daughter, and I loved her as I never did a mother, as I had none.

On her way back east she stopped over in Kansas City, Kansas, and there they were having a revival in the African Methodist Church, and the evangelist was preaching holiness and a great many sinners were converted; but only one or two had received the blessing of entire sanctification. Mother was visiting her daughter, who lived in the block next to the church, and one day she went in and they were having testimony. She gave her experience in Seattle and how she received the blessing. She told them she was a Baptist, and the Baptists did not believe in sanctification. They claim they receive it at death, but she is alive and knows better now. Her testimony seemed to bring conviction to many of the people. This brought a great break in the meeting, many were saved and quite a number received the experience of entire sanctification. The evangelist said that he knew the Lord had sent mother that way; and her testimony had been a blessing to the meetings. Mother's granddaughter also received the experience. After the meeting mother went to her home in Emporia, Kansas, and her children all wondered what had happened to grandmother; she was so different. She was so restful and did not worry over anything. They knew she had gotten something while she was away, although they had the greatest confidence in her religion before she left.

Mr. Ray's sister in Kansas City wrote him a letter, saying, "Mother has been here and gone, and oh, such a strange peace, a peace I can not understand. And Florence, my daughter, has been sanctified, and they both are so happy. I would give the world if I felt like them. Do pray that I may be a better Christian woman like mother."

Mother lived until she was ninety. She was a member of the Baptist Church of Emporia, and was loved and honored by all in the town, and she never failed to tell them of her experience. Before she died, they asked what they should say at her funeral, and she said that she was not concerned with what they might say after her death, as the life she had lived had preached her funeral sermon. "Blessed are the dead who die in the Lord, and their works do follow them" (Rev. 14: 13).

Our National Convention of the W. C. T. U.

In the year 1899 the National Convention of the Woman's Christian Temperance Union was held in Seattle. The city was filled with visitors from every state in the Union. It was held in the First Presbyterian Church. One of the members was Mrs. Lucy Thurman, a colored woman. She was the national organizer among the colored people. We had the privilege of entertaining her in our home. While she was here she felt that we should reorganize our W. C. T. U. among the colored women, and, when we gave the invitation, quite a few of our best women responded. They again selected me as their president. Our pastor was in favor of prohibition and encouraged us in the reorganization. This was just a year before we went east. The Lord set His seal upon the work. We labored with them until the last of April, 1900; then we resigned, as we were preparing to go east. These women did a good work for a while among our own people.

About Mother Starett

During our jail and prison work, one of my neighbors was Mrs. Starett, a white lady and a very devout Christian, and we often went to the jails together and worked among the prisoners.

She was very retiring in her manner, yet she was full of faith and love and she would always stand back as we stood in front of the prison bars. She would always stand on one side and look the prisoners in the face and pray for them. As the rest of us would testify and sing, she would take no part--only stand and listen and pray. After we were through she would speak to some of the prisoners and especially those that the others did not notice. There was one young man there that was a very hard character. He had been a safe breaker and served eleven years in the penitentiary. He was then awaiting trial on a charge of safe breaking. He would never smile and never speak to any of the workers, and seemed to be so hard and set in his manner that no one could easily approach him. This mother, as the others walked away, stuck her hands through the bars and shook hands with him, and said, "God bless you, my son," and as she did so the tears rolled down his cheeks and his heart broke up and he wept like a child. The very words "my son" spoken by an aged lady touched his heart. He told her his story, that he had been a hard customer and served eleven years in the penitentiary, but this time he was innocent of the crime. His trial was to come soon, and he didn't know whether he would get away or not. She told him she would pray for him and that God was able to deliver him. Sure enough he had his trial and was proved innocent of the crime. In the meantime she told him when he got out to come and visit her at her home. He took her at her word, and as he was hounded by the policemen, as a criminal always is when turned out of jail, and told to move on out of the city, he went to her home, and she prayed for him and there, on his knees before the Lord, he gave his heart to God and told her he had a mother in Colorado that did not know where he was, and that he had not been home since he was a boy. Now he wanted to go to her just as soon as he could, but he had not the means, and as soon as he could get the means he would go. He did not want to "beat his way" out of town because the Lord had changed his heart, so she lent him some money, but did not give it to him, as she figured too much would be a temptation for him. Sure enough he started away from her house that day with a light heart and a delivered soul, making his way home to his mother. He wrote back to the woman that he was on his way home, and again when he reached home. He got into town about nine o'clock and made his way to his mother, and when he got there she was all alone. He rapped on the door, and when she came he said would she give him a cup of coffee, and she told him it was a late hour to invite anybody in, but she had a dear boy some place in the world that might be hungry and perhaps, if she did so, some one would do the same for him. He could not stand it any longer and he broke up in tears and said, "Mother, don't you know me?" and immediately they were embraced in each other's arms and he told her the Lord had saved him and oh, you ought to have seen the aged worker as she got the news. She was a Baptist and very quiet in her manner.

She said she was so thankful that she had been of help in bringing some mother's son to God. This young man straightened up his life and later on married, and the last we heard he was living a clean life and sent the picture of his wife to this sister. Oh, the good we all might do as our days are going by! Let no one idly say there is nothing he can do, while the men of sin are dying and the Master calls for you. It was only a kind word and a smile that brought this man to the Lord. The worker was over seventy-five years old, and we feel her works will live on throughout eternity.

Our Meeting with the Beck Family

There came to Seattle two holiness evangelists named Harriman and Christy. They had with them as singing evangelist, a colored man, who was accompanied by his wife and daughter. They sang a great many jubilee songs, and it was our privilege to entertain them in our home. They traveled for several years with the Salvation Army. They were full of the Holy Ghost and fire. They sang with the Spirit and understanding, and they were wonderfully used by the Lord. They held their meetings in the old Presbyterian Church on the corner of Third and Madison Streets. While they were with us we were eager to learn about their work. We told them of our experiences with our own people, and that the preacher we had at this time was opposed to holiness and prohibition. They advised us, if we couldn't have our freedom, to go where we could. They told us that we needed a church home. They told us of meeting many who had no church home nor fellowship with any one, and whose works were scattered. They said that if we wanted our work to be permanent, we should settle down with some good holiness church. As they traveled through the country they met many people who asked, "Where do you hail from?" They said, if their answer was not very clear, they were looked upon with suspicion. Our eyes were opened and we saw that we needed Christian fellowship, and we thanked the Lord for sending the Becks our way.

Not long after this, Sister Amanda Smith came to Seattle to hold meetings in the Battery Street M. E. Church. Rev. H. D. Brown was the pastor, and we had been acquainted with him and Sister Brown for some time. They were anxious to have Sister Smith meet us in our own home. After their meetings were over they came and spent the day. We learned many things from Sister Smith. We felt glad to sit at her feet and hear her tell of the wonderful experiences she had had during her travels. We had been reading about Dr. Dowie and, as we were young and inexperienced, we thought he was all right and had never heard anything to the contrary, up to this time. She admonished us to go slow and told us that he was a fanatic. We felt surprised and sorry to hear her speak of him in this manner, but later we found out she knew what she was talking about. She told us there were many false prophets in the world, and as we were young she felt like admonishing us. We could not understand it then, but later on, as we met with all kinds of people having all kinds of ideas, we could plainly see what she was talking about, and we thanked the Lord also for sending her our way. She seemed to have a gift of discernment and was a great blessing and help to us. It was quite a while before we found it out. During her meetings at Battery Street, the Rev. Brown asked us to sing for her, and that was our first experience in doing special singing in meetings and we have been at it ever since. We were young and full of zeal and were anxious to work for the Lord. One day, after going on my errand of mercy to the hospital, as I knelt in prayer thanking the Lord for the day's work, the thought came to me, "Where are your neighbors? You have never visited them, and doesn't the Bible say that you should love your neighbor as yourself?" There were two or three families of them with whom I was acquainted, but the others were strangers to me. As I finished my prayer I thought, "If it is the will of the Lord, I will go and get acquainted with them." But the next day I thought perhaps it was just myself speaking. The next week the same impression came to me and I inquired of the Lord if it was His voice. I wanted to be sure. The next morning I got up early and I said, "I will obey; I will go and speak to them." There were a number of flats across from ours, and I knelt down and prayed before starting to visit the people there. I went to the back door of the first place and knocked on the door. The lady came to the door and I asked her to excuse me. I told her that I was a neighbor and was praying for her, and I felt the Lord wanted me to come to see her and to inquire about her soul. She looked very much surprised, but asked me to come in. After talking to her for a while and giving her some tracts, she said it was all right; that I must come again and that if more people would visit their neighbors, the world would be better. I felt relieved as I came out the door. I went to the next place and asked the same privilege. I told her my mission and she, too, invited me in, and I had a great deal more liberty than I had at the first place. She seemed very glad to have me talk with her. Her husband was a business man in the city and she asked me about my work and asked me if I ever saw many poor people who needed old clothes. She felt, too, that we should help our fellow men, and said she would be glad to help at any time. She was glad to have me pray and asked me to pray for her daughter. The folks next door were Catholics, and no one was at home. I passed on to the fourth door and asked for the lady. There was a young Swedish girl working there, and she told me that the lady was not at home, but that I could come in. I could scarcely understand her. I asked her if she knew the Lord and she said, "No," but that she wished she did and that she had been praying. I asked her if I could pray with her, and she was glad to have me do so. She said, "I pray, but Jesus won't hear me." I prayed as I came away and left her crying. I then hunted up a young Swedish Christian girl to talk with her. She went and found her and brought her to the mission, and there she found the Lord and went back to her home very happy. I was happy myself, and the thought came to me that I had better go to the mission and tell this, and then the thought came that I had better keep this to myself for, if I spoke of it, I might do some boasting. The next time I went to the mission and the testimonies were being given, I felt that I should get up and tell it. Previous to this, Brother C. M. Johnson, the superintendent, had prayed that the Lord would confound everything that was not of Him tonight, and of course I said "Amen." When I arose to testify it came to my mind, "Tell it," and then something said, "Don't do it," but before I knew it I had started to tell it, and all at once my strength left me and I fell, some thought under the power, but I knew better. I knew it was the Holy Spirit that had checked me and chastened me sorely, and that was the only time I ever lost consciousness in meetings. When I came out of this, I plead the blood of Jesus to cleanse me, but I was ashamed to tell any one about it, and it was years before I could tell any one about it, but I learned my lesson. There is a time to speak and a time to refrain from speaking. I was glad in after years that the Lord gave me this lesson. I believe that it would have ruined me in my experience for life if the Spirit had not chastened me. "Whom the Lord loveth, He chasteneth." The Lord says, "I will not give my glory to another." Many a time since I have told my experiences or some incident that happened, but never until I was sure it was the mind of the Lord. This was a great lesson He taught me. Praise His name. I never could have told this experience except for His glory and that others may watch the Spirit's check to walk softly before the Lord. I thank the Lord for this reproof.

"Have Thy way, Lord, have Thy way,
This with all my heart I say,
I'll obey Thee, come what may.
Dear Lord, have Thy way." Amen.

First Experience in Divine Healing

About this time we attended a Missionary Alliance convention. We had heard but very little of divine healing. As we listened to the testimonies from different ones, we were surprised to learn that the Lord was a healer of the body as well as of the soul today.

At this time I had a very heavy cough, for I was of a consumptive family. Several of my brothers and sisters had died with this disease, and every winter I had been coughing until spring, and sometimes throughout the summer. Then I thought to myself, "If the Lord can heal them, why can He not do so for me?" I saw that healing of the body was scriptural. An evangelist who came to our church gave me a little tract along this line, but I didn't give it much attention, yet I didn't throw it away. I put it in the dresser and thought no more about it. Ofttimes when I cleaned out the dresser drawers, I would run across this tract, and something would say, "Don't throw it away," and I would stick it in another corner.

After I went home from the meeting at night, I told my husband I believed I would take the Lord as my healer, and all at once it flashed upon me about the little tract I had had for over a year, and I began to search for it. I finally found it, and after reading it with its Scripture references, I decided I would take no more medicine. I knelt in prayer, and asked the Lord to heal me as He had healed others, and to my delight, my cough left me and my body became quite strong.

There was a friend of ours who was very sick. One morning she called us over the telephone. She wanted us to come out and see her. The Lord had laid it upon my heart to fast and pray for two days, so immediately after breakfast we went out to see her. She requested us to pray for her, not especially for her health, but for her soul. She had not been able to hold anything on her stomach for two weeks. She called a doctor and he said she had an abscess in the stomach. He wanted her to be operated upon; said he didn't promise her she would be helped, but that was her only chance. As her husband was out of the city, she would not have it done. After we prayed for her she seemed to get a little better. It had been four days already since the doctor had wanted to operate upon her, so she sent for him this morning, and he said it was too late; that blood poisoning had already set in, and when he got the word he said it wasn't necessary to come any more.

About this time there came a man to the door by the name of Con Johnson, who conducted a mission in Seattle. He asked the nurse to tell her that he had heard she was very sick, and some friends had sent him to pray for her. She said, "Oh, yes, tell him to come in and pray for me. This is my only chance to be healed." She had had some experience along this line a few years previous to this, but she had become cold and indifferent in prayer, and, as he came in he asked her if she would be willing to follow the Lord in case he prayed with her. She said, "Yes."

He read the fifth chapter of James, and told her she must confess her sins. We knelt by her bedside and prayed.

We were acquainted with this Brother Johnson, and it seemed strange that we should meet together there at this time, but it seemed to be by divine order. Brother Johnson prayed such a simple prayer, while we both held on to God with him as he anointed her with oil in the name of the Lord, according to the Scripture, and as he read, the power of God touched her and she began to shout and praise the Lord. She sat right up in bed and said, "Oh, praise the Lord, I feel I am healed."

The landlady came in and told her she must be quiet, and didn't want her to shout. She was excited and seemed very angry, but the woman said, "Oh, glorify the Lord with me; I know I am healed!" She said, "What are you cooking in the kitchen? I am so hungry. Give me some of those turnips." And Brother Johnson said, "Yes, give her anything she wants to eat." But the landlady said, "We will give you some egg-nog, but that's all you can have." She didn't want this, but the nurse made her a toast, and she ate quite heartily, and kept rejoicing, and we sang for her a song she loved so well:

"Lord, I believe; Lord, I believe;

Savior, raise my faith in Thee, till it can move a mountain;
Lord, I believe; Lord, I believe;
All my doubts are buried in the fountain."

The landlady had prevailed upon the doctor to come once more. The woman who had been sick said, "I am healed now; the Lord has done it, and I do not need a doctor." When she told the doctor, he got angry and said she would be a dead woman inside of twenty-four hours. He said, "You shall pay me for coming out," which she readily did, and he left.

As the people whom she lived with did not believe she was healed, and could not understand her case, she felt that she would not like to be left alone there, and asked me to remain with her over night and take her to my house the next day.

She slept like a child. I did not sleep much. I watched and prayed. In the morning we wakened early, as Mr. Ray was to bring a taxi out after her. When she wakened she began praising the Lord and singing, "Lord, I believe." I asked her how she felt, and she said, "I am faint, but trusting."

We sang while we put her clothes on, and she repeated Scripture. She seemed to know every promise that was appropriate for her case, as she had had some experience along this line before.

We were so glad, and really we were hilarious in the Lord, yet we were careful that we did not overdo. She went into the dining-room and ate her breakfast. Soon Brother Ray came after us. She lived on Twenty-first Avenue in the Madrona addition. That was considered quite a long way out at that time, and as we started, the neighbors were all very much interested and thought we must be crazy. I propped some pillows on each side of her and put my arms around her and we began to sing and praise the Lord. The cab was an old-fashioned one, drawn by horses. Mr. Ray rode on the outside with the driver.

It all seemed to be so wonderful to me, and I believed with all my heart the Lord was bringing her out of it. When we arrived home, our neighbors were all looking out of the windows, as the news had spread that she was dying. When we got inside we knelt in prayer and thanked God that He had brought us through thus far, and then a stream of people began to come and see her. Every one was very curious, but we kept constantly in prayer. I never realized what the power of unbelief could do, although I had read in the Bible where Jesus could not do many miracles on account of their unbelief. She said that when some one who doubted would come, she would feel that she was getting weaker. When others who would pray, came in, she would feel stronger and she would say, "The Lord has undertaken for me."

She kept getting better and people kept coming in and wondering. Some by this time had begun to believe. They would tell others and they, too, would come to see.

Her husband was a porter on the railroad, and they had telegraphed him to come. He was a good Christian man, and was a preacher in the African Methodist Church, but was not in the regular service, as she objected to going with him. He arrived on the third night. We awakened in the morning, had break-fast as usual, and she was still improving. We had our prayers, and all at once her husband came to the door and called us to come quick. We ran in and looked upon her. Her eyes were glassy and she was straightened out stiff, and she said, "Sister Ray, it's no use; I am dying." Her husband knelt beside her bed crying, but I could not feel that the Lord would let her die after giving us such a manifestation of His power. Quickly I said, "Look to Jesus," and began to sing, "Lord, I believe. Savior, raise my faith in Thee, till it can move a mountain," and she sat right up in bed and said to death, "I shall not die. I command you in the name of Jesus Christ to depart. I shall live, because the Lord has promised me." We all began to sing, and that was the only hard test she had. She was able to be up and around the house then. She said she believed the reason she had this test of faith was that she neglected to trust and leaned upon her husband's prayers and presence. She was able to go to church on Sunday and gave testimony to the power of God to heal the body as well as the soul. She lived for a few years afterwards and bore witness to her divine healing.

Seeming Defeat

In February, 1902, while working in the "Stranger's Rest," we were called to help in a meeting at the Free Methodist Church in Pleasant Valley, Washington, by the pastor, Mrs. Hattie Teegarden. We secured Rev. Moore of Portland, Oregon, to take our places in the Mission while we were away. We labored at Pleasant Valley for one month with apparently small results. The class was small and the place new. There was a shingle mill in the community that employed quite a number of young men and boys. There were quite a few young people in the neighborhood. Almost all turned out to the meetings. They were bright, talented young people, and good singers and full of mischief. We had taken with us quite a number of new books, which we invited them to take and help with the singing. This they did very readily. It was a cold winter and there came a deep snow. The people came from Mountain View and Blaine, Washington, in their sleighs, a distance of five miles. We were staying with a devout old Englishman and his wife and son. They helped us in our praying and in carrying the burden for those souls. This old father was a man of great faith. He never seemed to tire of prayer and of waiting upon the Lord. He would oftentimes say, while praying, "Father, Thou hast said that they that wait upon the Lord should not be confounded, and I believe it." The young people seemed very much unconcerned. While we prayed at night the boys would throw shingle nails across the room and keep up a disturbance. Several times we found some of Brother Ray's books torn half-in-two. It seemed as if they did everything they could to make us mad.

The song, "Will There be Any Stars in My Crown?" was new in those parts and they would ask for this song to be sung every night. It seemed as though the devil helped them to sing it, and the devil seemed to say, "They are mocking you in this song," and I got to the place where I wished they would not call for it.

We would have become discouraged and given up, had we not believed in the possibilities of God's Word to bring things to pass, and we gave ourselves over to the Holy Spirit in prevailing prayer. We looked into these faces night after night and coveted their souls for the Lord. We had no purpose in being there than to see them saved. We remembered the command Jesus gave when He said, "Go, preach the gospel to every creature," so we plead His promise, "Lo, I am with you alway."

We had a song of our own that we called "All Right." These people would come and go singing it. Reverend Carmichael, a Menonnite preacher, helped us one night. It really looked from a human point of view that the meetings were a failure. A young man, however, came through there giving temperance lectures. He stopped at the home where we were, over night. He had a knowledge of salvation. He went to the meeting with us on Saturday night and on the Sabbath he heard us preach on sanctification. He sought until the Holy Spirit came upon him, baptizing him with Himself. He left there a very happy man. He came to Seattle. Dr. Carradine was holding meetings on East Pine Street at the Methodist Protestant Church. This young man testified and told his experience while over in the Valley, and then went back east. A few months later he gave up temperance lecturing and joined the M. E. Conference and was given a charge. Later he called for us to come and help him in his meetings. This encouraged us.

The last night of the meeting the young people became very quiet and attentive, and also serious, but as we closed and made the altar call there was no break. There was weeping and some of the young people said they would go to the altar, but that their parents would not let them, as they felt prejudiced towards the church. We felt some good had been done, but we did not know how far-reaching it was.

We came back to Seattle. I was a very tired woman. I had contracted some cold, so we did not take up our regular work in the Stranger's Rest. We worked after this, only once or twice a week, as my health was so impaired from the hard battle we had had in the valley.

CHAPTER XVII
HOW THE LORD GAVE US A NEW HOME

In 1903 I received a letter from my father stating that he wanted to come and bring his wife, my step-mother, and live with us. We had just sixty dollars that was given us in meetings. When husband worked, he earned good wages, but it was impossible for us in this mission work to save a cent. The place we were living in was insanitary and inconvenient, but up to this time we had never given a thought to owning our own home. However, it was impossible to rent a decent place. Brother Ray went out to Green Lake, a suburb of Seattle, through the persuasion of a friend and bought a couple of lots, paid thirty dollars down, and began to plan to build.

There was an old shed next door to where we lived, full of old doors and windows, and the man who owned them told Brother Ray that he might have anything he wanted, if he would clean up the yard and take care of the rubbish. To our surprise there were doors and windows, also frames enough of every kind to build a seven-room house. Husband worked a few days and then went out on Saturday and worked on the ground, getting ready for the basement. Some of the mission men volunteered to help him dig the basement. As he was a stone mason, he said to me, "I believe I will build a stone house." I did not want him to do this, as I could not see the possibility of it, but he said, "The Lord has plenty of stone lying here and there in the streets, and He put them there for my benefit." There was a man who had gathered a great many of them out of his strawberry patch, and he told Brother Ray he did not want them. At one place where they were grading the streets, they told him he could have the large boulders; and if he would split them up they would haul them to him. In this way he had stone enough to build. We had the doors and windows and the lot. We knelt in prayer and thanked the Lord for this much towards a home. There was a woman in the vicinity who had had a well dug. The soil was all sand. She gave Brother Ray the sand if he would haul it away. There was an old building that had to be taken down and replaced by a larger one. They gave Brother Ray several wagon loads of this lumber, just for taking it away. This was all the Lord's doings. Each Saturday and on rainy days husband worked on the home, and within three months, with the help of a carpenter, we had a nice little four-room stone bungalow, plastered, finished all but plumbing, and ready to move into. It was wonderful; when the Lord got ready for us to have a home, how quickly it was done. A little later we sent for my father and his wife. In the meantime Brother Ray built a little cottage on another lot for them to live in. Within two years my step-mother became dissatisfied, as she was sick so much of the time, and we had to send them back east. This caused us to part with the home in order to have money to meet expenses. We sold the home very cheap and sent them back home and had just money enough left to buy a lot and to start in again. We got the ground and within three years from the time we moved to our new home we had built us a five-room modern bungalow and furnished it. This is the home we have lived in for nearly twenty years. It was all done through the mercy of God and we believed we were blessed for our faithfulness while back east and other places where the battle was hard. Does He not say, "Blessed are the merciful, for they shall obtain mercy"? We praise the Lord for verifying His word.

Song

There's a little wheel a-rolling in my heart,

There's a little wheel a-rolling in my heart,
There's a little wheel a-rolling in my heart,
Oh, surely my Jesus must be true.

I feel the fire burning in my heart,
I feel the fire burning in my heart,
I feel the fire burning in my heart,
Oh, surely my Jesus must be true.

It is the love of Jesus in my heart,
It is the love of Jesus in my heart,
It is the love of Jesus in my heart,
Oh, surely my Jesus must be true.

During the spring and summer we went to the camp meetings and other places, wherever the Lord led us. Husband would lay aside his tools, and would always respond to the Holy Spirit's Macedonian cry, "Come over and help us."

The Lord gave him enough work. He made him his own boss, so he was left free to follow the Lord. In missions, when at home, at camp meetings and revivvals, wherever the Spirit has led, we have gladly followed.

RESIDENCE OF MR. AND MRS. L. P. RAY AT 7526 SUNNYSIDE AVENUE,
SEATTLE, WASH.

CHAPTER XVIII
MY TRIP TO OREGON

A short time after we were settled in our new home, Rev. Purcell and wife, Mennonite evangelists, requested us to go to Oregon and help them in a revival meeting. Brother Ray could not very well go at the time, so I went alone. The place was away up in the mountains some distance from Sweet Home, Oregon. There was a logging camp there with a saw-mill. We labored there for three weeks. It was almost entirely an infidel community except one family. Even the children were infidels.

The family I stayed with had a granddaughter or niece visiting them from Seattle, and they asked me to bring her with me on my return as far as Portland, as the evangelist and his wife were not going that way. We left there by stage in the morning at four o'clock. We rode twenty-two miles and then got the train for Portland. The girl's uncle was to meet her in Portland, and she was to stop over there for a few days and visit them. We were late in arriving at Portland, but her uncle met her and took her home with him. I planned to stop over for a day or two and visit some friends. I did not know where to find them at the time, so thought I would get a room and look them up the next day. Now began a tug of war with me to see where I could get a proper place for the night. There was a colored boy working in the depot, and as I knew it wasn't every place that a colored person could stop, I did not dare venture out until I knew some place where I could go. I inquired of this colored boy for a place where they would accommodate colored people.

He told me to take a bus outside for a certain hotel, as they would take in colored people. When I reached the bus, the driver was calling "omnibus" for this certain hotel. I offered him my valise and started to step in. He didn't respond, but beckoned me aside, and went on calling "omnibus." It was pouring rain. I wondered where to go. I was perplexed. A cab man came up and said, "Hack for any place in the city." I told him that I wanted a decent place to sleep and asked him if he knew of a place where a colored woman could get a place for the night. He said, "Yes." I gave him my valise and he drove me to a hotel up in the city, but after my other experience I was afraid to get out, and I asked him if he would go in and see if they would take me, as I didn't want to be left outside in a strange city. He came back pretty soon and said they were full. He went to another place and came back with the same reply, and then to another, and then I noticed by the lights and the location that we were getting down towards the slum district. I called to him and asked him if we were not in the slum district. I told him I did not want to stay all night in a place of that kind. Then it came to me that there was a mission somewhere near and that I was acquainted with some of the mission workers, and I thought if I could find them I could find a place for the night. He drove me to the mission hall, but they had moved out a few days previous. I knew it would be an expense to have the driver take me farther, so I decided to walk and find the mission, as I did not know what else to do. I had my umbrella, valise, and a Christmas cactus plant in a basket I was bringing home. I struck out down the street, inquiring as I went, for the mission hall. One person would say, "Go two blocks and then turn the corner," and the next person would send me back in the other direction. I walked until I was cold and tired. Then I met a man who knew where they had moved, but when I got inside, there was no one there I knew. A lady came up and asked me if I could give them a song. I told her I couldn't sing now until I knew where I was going to stop for the night, and asked if she knew a place.

She told me of a widow who kept roomers, and who lived about four blocks away. I left my flower there and went down the street looking for this place. I would go up one flight of stairs and would be in the wrong place. I would come down and go up the next place. Sometimes I would go up four flights of stairs to be refused. I was so tired. I asked another lady if she would let me have a room for the night, but her rooms were all full. I could see readily that she did not want to accommodate me. I came down and went across the street to where it said "Hotel and Lodging." I noticed that it said office on a door. When I went into the office, I found myself in a saloon, but I thought I would take a chance anyway. The man said he had one room left upstairs with two beds and that he was expecting some one else to take one of the beds unless I would pay for both of them. This made me suspicious of the place and my heart failed me. I went around the corner, and it said "Furnished rooms for rent upstairs." I began my tiresome climb up to the third floor. This was not the place I was hunting, but I asked for a room. As I turned away I felt like crying, and I began to pray for help. I put my valise down and got right down on my knees in the hallway and asked the Lord to help me find a place for the night. I went to another place. There was a lady standing in the hall looking over the banister. When she saw me coming up the steps she said, "Come on up, I'm your friend." And I thought, "Thank the Lord for a friend." As I got to the top of the steps I saw that she had been drinking, but by this time I was very tired and weak. I asked for a room with a stove, as my clothing was wet through. She said she had one, and gave me a very nice corner room, well ventilated, clean, and fresh. She said, "Your friend can come and stay with you, if you have one."

I told her that I had no one that I wanted to stay with me; that I was an evangelist. This gave me a chance to talk with her. I told her that I had been down in the country helping in a revival. When she discovered that I was a Christian she was anxious to talk with me. She told me her tale of woe and it was a sad one. The thought came to me that this must be the place the Lord wanted me to come to. She was very kind and listened very attentively to all that I said to her. She seemed to be hungry for the Lord and tired of the life she was living, although she was drinking some. As I sat there and found out where I was, I became disgusted with Portland and asked her what time the train left in the morning. I went back to see if the mission was open. I found it was and I got my basket and plant. The landlady said she would see me when I came back, as she wanted to continue the conversation, but she seemed to have other business on hand. I saw her no more until the next morning as I was going away. I had hoped to be able to pray with her that night. Before going to bed I dried my clothing and prayed the Lord that in some way He would save this poor soul. She had a kind and tender heart.

While I meditated over this experience, the Holy Spirit whispered to me and said, "Jesus was born in a manger because there was no room in the inn. He had nowhere to lay His head. He was despised and rejected of men. Are you any better than He?" Again He said, "The harlot Rahab took in the two spies who went over to Canaan to spy out the land, and lodged them. Did not the Lord save her and her house when the children of Israel destroyed the city?" I was glad then that I had passed through that way and trusted that this woman and all her house would be saved. It was an earnest prayer that I offered to God for her soul that night.

I went away in a hurry the next morning. The train was late in arriving in Seattle, and I got home just at twilight. I looked through the window and saw husband sitting by the table reading, and right there I looked up to heaven and thanked God for a HOME. I have been to Portland several times since, and have been entertained in some of the best and finest homes in the city. It all comes through the guidance of the Holy Spirit. Teach me Thy way, O Lord, and lead me in a plain path.

CHAPTER XIX
REVIVAL IN A. M. E. CHURCH, SEATTLE

Rev. Donohoo, pastor of the A. M. E. Church on Fourteenth Avenue, Seattle, called us over the telephone and told us that there was much need of a revival at his church, that the mortgage on the church had been paid off, everything was out of the way, and that they wanted our help in a meeting. We were glad of the opportunity, as here was where we were converted. We told him we would pray and consider it, as we never went to any place without first taking it to the Lord in prayer. We afterwards called up and told him we could come, that we preached sanctification and a full gospel, and requested him to give us our liberty in running the meeting as the Spirit directed us. He told us all right, that sanctification was a Methodist doctrine, and that he endorsed it.

We began on the next Sunday. The first week we had holiness meetings in the afternoon, which were continued throughout the revival. As the meetings progressed, two or three of the members there confessed that they had never been converted, and some said that they were backsliders in heart. Others sought the experience of entire sanctification. The Lord gave us a good wholesome meeting. Two of the officers, Brothers Allen and Clemens, were sanctified later through the baptism of the Holy Ghost and fire, and also two or three others were saved in the old-fashioned way. Rev. Donohoo and his wife did all they could to make this meeting a success. He occasionally preached to give us a rest. The result was that Brothers Allen and Clemens got their call to the ministry, which they fulfilled faithfully until they were called home. Brother Allen passed away a few months ago, and Brother Clemens about two years ago.

After these meetings closed some of the sisters were ordained as deaconesses. There was a good attendance afterwards, especially good at prayer meetings, and the church was in good working order. The conference convened soon afterwards, and as Rev. Donohoo's time was out, he was removed to another field of labor. We deemed this occurrence unfortunate, as we hoped to see him enjoy the fruits of his labors.

A Sister Hayes, who was sanctified in the meetings, was quite a blessing to the church. She was slightly stricken with paralysis and thus hindered from attending. It was a great trial to her at the time, but the Lord put it in her heart to pray for lost souls, and she really had the gift of prevailing prayer. She said, "If I can't go to the church, I will have a part in all the souls that are saved by praying for them." I asked her to pray for us at the mission meetings. Sunday nights, while we were preaching, she was upon her knees at home doing her share, pleading for the conversion of the lost. Monday morning she would call me up and say, "How was the meeting last night? I watched the clock, and when it was time for preaching service I held on to the Lord for conviction in the meetings." When I would tell her how some one was converted and how the meeting went, she would say, "I knew it. I felt it." The Lord certainly answered her prayers.

She continued to grow weaker and the devil tempted her through her weakness, by telling her that she would finally go crazy and blaspheme God. Sometimes the pressure was so great that she would call me up over the telephone and tell me of her sore temptation. I would tell her to stop right there and look up while I prayed, and I would pray for her over the telephone and resist the devil. She would say, "Good-bye, I am helped. Praise the Lord." In a little while the devil left her for good along this line. She grew weaker, and finally one morning she had another light stroke. I went out to see her and she had a peaceful look on her face. She could not speak a word. This lasted for a day or two, then one day, while a sister and I were sitting by her bed, all at once her voice came back and she spoke distinctly, "Oh! praise the Lord. Oh! praise the Lord. I am drinking at the fountain." It seemed as if the glory of the Lord filled the room, and our souls were blessed. I don't think she spoke another word. She went home to glory the next day. Instead of blaspheming God, as the devil tried to make her believe she would, she passed away with victory over the sting of death, and went sweeping through the gates in triumph.

Several years have elapsed since this revival. We have had the opportunity of preaching in this church for Rev. Osborne, Rev. Graham and others at different times. We have been led to preach in the highways and hedges, and over thirty years have been spent in slum work, with the exception of some occasional evangelistic work. We have always kept in mind the day when our choice was fixed and we said, "Yes" to Jesus. In August, 1924, Bishop Lee, of the A. M. E. Church, passed through Seattle. He spoke at this church. We went to hear him, as we had not seen him since I was converted. He said that meeting was the most evangelistic one he had ever held. I felt like shouting "Glory," because I was converted at that time. He said, "This is the last year that I will preside, as I expect to superannuate this year." I was glad to shake hands with him, and tell him that I was one of the converts in that meeting, and that the Lord had kept me true ever since. My husband was converted a year later, and I felt it would please him and glorify God for me to tell him about it. He was glad to hear it. He had a remarkable memory for a man of his age. There was only a small society when he was here first, not over twenty, I believe, and mostly middle-aged people. The meeting was held in a small dwelling house with partitions out. It was the first A. M. E. conference on Puget Sound. A great change has come now. There is a large modern brick chapel with a membership of four hundred, and a Sunday-school of three hundred, with some of the brightest boys and girls, intellectually, I have met in any community. The pastor tells us that quite a few of the older ones are still members of the church. It did my heart good to see such a turnout to Sunday-school. Rev. Jones, the pastor, is an able preacher. May the Lord bless and prosper this work in every way, and may many precious souls be saved and filled with the Holy Spirit is our earnest prayer. Amen.

CHAPTER XX
OUR WORK IN THE OLIVE BRANCH MISSION

In the fall of 1903 the Olive Branch Mission was organized by Rev. C. S. McKinley, then pastor of the Free Methodist Church on Pine Street near Eighth, in Seattle, Washington.

Reverend McKinley secured the mission room in the "Stranger's Rest Hall," in the same place we had labored the year before. Some changes were made in the hall. It was a little more sanitary. However, the same class of men came. He had a fine band of consecrated workers with him, and a Mrs. Annie Walker was his assistant superintendent. There he pitched battle anew against sin and the devil, and he had some of the most marvelous conversions I ever saw.

There was an Englishman by the name of E. Burke who came to the Mission. He had seen better days, was a well educated man, and held positions of honor under the queen's dominion, and had been an officer in the British navy. He was an English gentleman, but through the continued habit of using strong drink he was brought low. His health and hope gone, he, after having several spells of delirium tremens when he had to be put in a padded cell and in a straight jacket, finally came to the Mission. He seemed a hopeless case, nervous and sick with abscess on the liver. The doctors told him to get his

MRS. RUEY WITTEMAN, SUPERINTENDENT OLIVE
BRANCH MISSION, SEATTLE, WASHINGTON

business all settled as he had only a short time to live. He was a moral and physical wreck. He fell at the feet of Jesus and cried for mercy. The Reverend McKinley and his workers knelt around him, praying. He was graciously and miraculously saved and healed. He came out a new creature, a new-born soul. He has been an active worker in Olive Branch Mission ever since, nearly twenty years. He has a special gift of song, and sings with the spirit and understanding. Scores of souls have been brought to the Lord through his songs and testimonies, both in the Mission and on the streets. He was one of the first converts of the Mission. Rev. McKinley appointed Mr. Ray and myself to take charge of the Sunday night services, which appointment we have held ever since, except the times when we were sick or out in evangelistic work. Different workers had their special night, except when revival meetings were being held by other evangelists. Preachers from the several Free Methodist churches in Seattle usually preached the Sunday afternoon sermons.

We had spent nine years in the slum work before the Olive Branch Mission was organized. We enjoyed our labors under the leadership of Rev. McKinley, who later changed work, coming to Green Lake as pastor of the Free Methodist Church.

Mrs. Ruey Witteman then took the superintendency with Rev. Charles Witteman, her husband, Mr. Burke and others as assistants. We were permitted to continue our Sunday night services as before. Here we have labored, watched and prayed under her leadership for nearly twenty years.

The Mission doors have always been kept open every night in the week. Souls have been brought to the Lord during all these years. Many miraculous healings and deliverances from sin of all kinds have occurred. Homes have been made happy, families which had been separated through sin have been reunited, girls rescued from lives of shame, and others before entering into sin. Some have been saved while stopping over night in passing through the city. On hearing the singing, they came into the Mission and were saved, and then went on their way rejoicing. The Mission is also a home for Christian sailors when they come into port. Some have been saved from temptation, who were on the verge of falling. You will find every nation represented.

We praise the Lord for giving us one service a night in Olive Branch Mission. On Friday afternoons there is a Mission prayer meeting, Sunday afternoon we attend, and Sunday night we hold the service. We go on these days regularly, except when out of the city. We spend the whole day Sunday at services; in the morning at our home church at Green Lake, and the rest of the day at the Mission. Occasionally we give special services at the Mission, lasting a month. Quite a few of our own race have heard us on the street and have followed us into the hall. The Lord has saved some and purified their hearts by faith.

One night the grandson of Chief Seattle (for whom Seattle was named), the son of Princess Angeline, came into the Mission. He had been drinking. He was an elderly man, I should judge of about fifty years. He had been given a fair education, but was a drunkard. He prayed just as earnestly as others, for he realized his lost condition. He had a godly sorrow for sin and seemed willing to forsake it. He arose to his feet with a new light in his face and he praised the Lord with a new joy that he had never felt before. We did not know at the time that he was Chief Seattle's grandson, but he told us in his testimony. We have seen him but twice since then. He lives across the Sound at one of the seaports.

Rev. Charles Witteman, the husband of the late Mrs. Ruey Witteman, superintendent of Olive Branch Mission, began his labors in Olive Branch Mission, together with his wife, twenty years ago. He is a man of faith and prayer, and while he has not made himself prominent, he has been the power behind the throne. He has done the unseen things that made it possible for the superintendent to carry on her work. He is father to the Mission workers. We have heard some of the workers tell of his godly advice given to them in times when they were in need of a friend to tell their secrets to. He is a man of deep discernment and a man whom God uses to lift in song and prayer when the spiritual tide turns low in meetings. Our souls have been blessed while we have listened to his preaching. We are glad that we met him. May the Lord give him many more souls as his reward.

The Converted Tramp

Many tramps came to our house in those days, as we constantly met them in the jails, and in the missions and hospitals. Ofttimes my husband met them on the streets where they were begging, and in order to have a chance to talk salvation to them, he brought them home with him and gave them something to eat. Then he would ask them where they came from, and when was the last time they had written to their mother. Finally we became acquainted with so many that they knew us from Frisco to New York, and also to Seattle, and would tell the others where they could get a hand-out, so we never were without a visitor.

One morning, after Mr. Ray had gone to his work, there came a very hard-looking customer to our door and asked for a cup of coffee and something to eat. He said he was very hungry and was willing to cut wood, split kindling, or do anything. I let him split the kindling while I got him some coffee, and then I invited him in and as he ate I began to ask him about his mother and his past life. I told him the Lord had something better for him than to be tramping over the world, and I asked him when he had written to his mother, and he told me he had none, but he had been tramping from place to place for over two years. His home was in the east. He said that he was restless; could not be satisfied in any place. He said that he had seen better days, that he had had a praying mother, that his father had died while he was young, and afterwards his mother died and he fell heir to fifty thousand dollars. He immediately began to drink and sport, and he said that he could not drink it up fast enough, but would give it away; spend five or six hundred dollars a night treating, drinking and carousing, and inside of two or three years he had not a cent and had become an habitual drunkard. So he was not able and did not want to work.

He had one sister who was ashamed of him, and when his money was all gone, his friends forsook him and he began to go from town to town. He would strike one town and it would not suit him, and he would go to another. He would ride on the brake-beams and would go to sleep there and ride for hours that way, sometimes drunk. He did not see why he was never killed. I told him it was his mother's prayers that had kept him safe. Tears came into his eyes. He said he was sorry his life was such, but it was too late now. He never expected to be any better. He had made up his mind that morning before coming in our home to try just this one more place for something to eat, and if he did not get it, he was going to have it any way. He had never committed an outbreaking crime, but he felt desperate and hungry and tired of life. If he did not get something here, he would murder the next one who refused him. I asked him why he didn't give his heart to God. He said he could not stop roving or quit drinking. I told him the Lord was able to take the habit away from him. I had seen Him do it for others, that He could stop him from roving and, as he was young, he could be a man yet. The tears were in his eyes, and he said, "I'll think it over." I asked him if he would come back in the evening when my husband was there. I prayed with him and gave him some tracts to read, and he promised he would come back. I told him I believed I could trust him, and sure enough, in the evening he came. At this time we could see that he was under conviction and had been thinking seriously. We asked him if he would let us pray with him again. He said, "Yes, I want you to." We three knelt in prayer, and after my husband had prayed and I had prayed, we asked him to pray. He said he did not know how. We told him to talk to Jesus just as he would to his mother, and tell Him just how he felt. He began to pray and he broke all up, his heart became soft, he prayed until his burden of sin was taken away. He said, "I feel better and I know I am saved." We sang for him and afterwards we asked him to stay all night. We immediately put on a boiler of water. He took a bath and we gave him some clean clothes, as we had quite a few old clothes given to us for that purpose. After taking a bath, he looked much better. The next morning we gave him some money and told him that we would trust him to go and get shaved. We had him sit down and write a letter to his sister, as we believed he was telling us the truth. When he came back all shaved and clean, he looked like a different person altogether; he did not look so old.

He stayed with us for a few days. Finally he got a letter from his sister, who was so glad to know he was saved. She had written a letter to a friend of hers who was in Seattle at the time, and asked him to help her brother out. This was during the Alaska boom, so the friend took him to Alaska. He came back a year later as best I can remember, still saved and a bright, intelligent young man. He went east in a couple of years and I did not hear from him any more.

> "Down in the human heart, crushed by the tempter,
> Feelings lie buried that grace can restore;
> Touched by a loving heart, wakened by kindness,
> Chords that were broken will vibrate once more."

A Colored Tramp

While we were visited by many tramps, we scarcely ever had a colored one. One morning there was a rap at the door, and when I opened it there stood a cripple, apparently. He handed us a paper which stated that he was paralyzed, having been struck while working in the field, and because someone threw cold water out on him, it left him in this condition. He had a father and mother and was trying to get money enough to take him home, and anything we could do to help him would be appreciated. It was properly signed.

Of course we were glad to invite him in and felt sorry for him as he was one of our own people. He seemed so crippled that he could hardly get to a chair and could scarcely make himself understood. I hurried and gave him his breakfast and talked to him while he ate, and asked him if he had ever been saved. He seemed surprised when I talked salvation to him, and looked a little strange. I thought he was getting under conviction. I believe that the Lord was talking to him. When he had finished eating, we went to prayer. He had a terrible time getting on his knees and I felt so sorry for him that I helped him, and when I did so he seemed embarrassed. I thought to myself, Now the Lord is talking to him. I gave him some tracts and then I made him pull off the old coat he had on and gave him a nice one. He did not want the coat. The more I talked to him about salvation, the more nervous he became. I thought he felt nervous because I was so good to him. And then I ran and got him a hat. He said he did not want it--I had done enough, and I said, "You must take it; needy people are coming to us all the time, and these clothes are given us to give to them." He said, "You have done enough." I gave him some money and got him fixed up nicely, and gave him all the advice I could, and I felt so broken up that I could hardly talk. The sadder I felt the more nervous he became. I thought sure it was conviction. I helped him out to the door, and I prayed as he went.

When my husband came home that night, I told him a poor colored man had been there and that I had been feeling bad all day about it. The next day a friend of mine came and said, "Sister Ray, did you see that paralyzed man that was around begging?" and I said, "Yes, poor man, I helped him all I could," and she said, "So did I, but he is nothing but a fake." I could hardly believe it, such contortions as he went through, and his hands were drawn and his limbs twisted. I did not see how anybody could get himself into such a shape. I said, "Surely you must be mistaken." "No, I am not," she replied. "I saw him going down the street and he had straightened up and was walking as brisk as any one, with his cane under his arm, and whistling."

In the afternoon we went to a sister's who lived near-by, and she said, "A poor colored man was here today and I gave him money, and several of my roomers gave him money to help him to his mother. Several of them saw him afterwards on the street. He was a fake and a gambler." I don't know when I felt so small, and I felt like praying for his soul. My husband laughed at me, but I was glad that my motives were right, if my discernment was poor. Since then I have prayed the Lord to give me discernment. We have had many deceive us, but never any that we had taken into our house from the jails in our prison work.

The tramps began to be so numerous that I would ask them not to send any one else, if I fed them. I said the boys took advantage of us. While I did not refuse one, after a while they began to drop off one by one until, before we left to go east, there was not one who came. This was the Lord's work. It was all done not unto tramps, or hoboes, or drunks, but unto the Lord. "Inasmuch as ye have done it unto these, ye have done it unto me." He surely was in the right church when he came to our house to fake, but he felt himself in the wrong pew, and if he could have backed out after he discovered he was dealing with a Christian, I believe he would have done so; but he was in a hot box and he was compelled to carry out his game or else he would have been found out.

I shall always believe that this experience was the means of awakening him. The Bible says, "My word shall not return unto me void, but it shall accomplish that which I please, and it shall prosper whereunto I send it" (Isaiah 55:11).

CHAPTER XXI
MR. AND MRS. RAY JOIN THE FREE METHODIST CHURCH

We attended the Pine Street Free Methodist Church. Rev. C. E. McReynolds was pastor. We were very much impressed by the sermon that he preached at that time, and we came away feeling that we had been feasting from the Word of God. We went to our friends and told them about the sermon and invited them to go with us to the meetings. We considered him one of the best exponents of the Scriptures we had ever listened to. The lessons we learned through his ministry have never left us.

After serving out his time at First Church, he was followed by Rev. A. N. West. He, too, was an inspiration to us. These godly men and their wives visited in our homes. They did all they could to encourage us on our way. Brother Ray asked Rev. West for one of the church Disciplines. We read it over carefully and we told Brother West of our intention to join the church. We told him that we wanted to be free to work in the slums. He told us that he wished more people felt that way.

On the following Sunday the district meeting was held. Rev. C. E. McReynolds was back again, this time as district elder, and we united with the church. We felt sure that we were led by the Lord. We went east soon after and were away nearly two-and-a-half years. It was not long after we came back from the east that the First Church property was sold, as the city was growing rapidly, and many of the members had moved out to the suburbs, near the Second Church, others to Green Lake. Rev. McReynolds was the pastor, so we joined the Green Lake society, and we had three more years of feasting upon the Word, for which we are very grateful.

CHAPTER XXII
BROTHER AND SISTER JONES' CONVERSION

Brother Jones was a converted drunkard. One rainy night on the corner of Washington Street and Second Avenue, while a band of Christian workers was standing singing, there staggered out of a saloon a drunken man. He stopped and began to mutter some words, but the workers kept on with their testimonies. Finally he stepped out into the ring where they were standing and began to talk. Two of the brethren put their arms around him and asked him to go to the Mission with them. They led him down to the foot of Washington Street into a basement near First Avenue and gave him a seat. The superintendent and a brother sat down beside him. In the meantime the services went on. His wife had sent some neighbors to look for him. He had been away from home for eight days. When he left home he had taken his daughter, a little girl eleven years old, with him, but left her standing on the corner of the street while he went into a saloon. He got drunk and forgot all about her. She stood there until she became cold, and when he did not come she became alarmed, but one of their neighbors passed by and saw her and put her on the car and sent her home. As Brother Jones did not come home for several days, his wife got the neighbors to hunt him up. They happened to see him, as he went into the ring with the Olive Branch Mission workers. They watched the workers lead him off to the Mission. Of course they did not know the difference, but telephoned and told his wife to come quick; that they had located him and that he was with the Salvation Army workers. She hastened into town. It did not take her long, as she lived in Georgetown. She met her neighbors on the corner and they took her to the Mission. When she went down into the Mission she said she thought that it was one of the worst places she had ever seen, but she was glad to find her husband and went over and sat down beside him. He was talking out loud, but Sister Witteman told her to let him alone; that the Lord would save him. She thought he was too drunk to be saved, yet she said that if she thought they could do anything with him, they might do so. She watched him as they led him to the altar and all began to pray for him. As they prayed, he began to sober up and finally began to pray for himself. He kept it up until he prayed through to victory. Mrs. Jones said it astonished her as she saw the light break in his face, and he rose up from the altar. His face was so changed that she thought he looked like an angel. They told her he was converted. She said she knew that something miraculous had taken place in his life. He shouted for joy. Then as he started for home, he remembered going into the saloon and leaving his daughter on the corner. He had had a valise with him which he had left in the saloon. He told them that he wanted to go by and get it. Brother Burke, one of the Mission's faithful workers, told him he would go with him. Brother Jones went into the saloon shouting for joy and told the saloon-keeper what had come over him, and that he never expected to come into the saloon again. His wife said he spoke tenderly to her and when he got home he just kept praising the Lord. The next morning the little daughter was surprised at him. He was driving some nails and struck his finger. She ran into the house and said, "O mamma, papa struck his finger, and did not swear."

Their home was a typical drunkard's home. Some of the windows had never been put in, as it was a new house and he had never finished it. They went back to the Mission soon after. She said she did not know what to think of the people, but she was glad to have a change in her husband. She did not think of herself, but wanted to encourage him. She found out she had never been converted herself, although she had belonged to a church, and said she had been baptized, but she longed to have the same experience he had. Mrs. Witteman, the superintendent, stuck to her and visited her often, and one day she gave her heart to the Lord, she and her little daughter, Margaret. Margaret was a natural musician. She was playing the violin at that time, although she was but a little girl. Mr. Jones himself is a musician. This is a family of no small talents. He began to build up his home, and he sent his daughter to school at Seattle Pacific College. The whole family was sanctified and filled with the Holy Spirit, and it was a benediction to any one to go into their home. They all became Mission workers. The daughter went to Bellingham Normal and finished her education, and expected to be a school teacher. Later on she married a young minister, James Bishop by name, a very devout man filled with the Holy Ghost. They took a charge at Sunnydale, Washington, and soon after received their call as missionaries to China. Now they are in China preaching the gospel to the heathen. They have two beautiful children, and they write to the mother and to others and say that they enjoy their work. The Lord is prospering them in teaching and in bringing souls to Christ.

Brother and Sister Jones are both evangelists and the blessing of the Lord is upon their labors.

CHAPTER XXIII
MR. SETTERLIND'S ACCOUNT OF HIS CONVERSION

A young Swedish man followed us into the Mission from a street meeting one night and sat down in the rear of the room. I noticed that he was not accustomed to being in the Mission. I can nearly always tell whether or not the men have come for the first time. He seemed to take in everything.

After his conversion he attended Seattle Pacific College, at that time Seattle Seminary. He worked his way through school. He has since married and is an honorable Christian citizen of Seattle. Hear his own testimony. He has never been a down and out, although he stood just as much in need of a change of heart, which the Lord graciously granted to him.

362 Emerson St.,
Seattle, Washington.
Easter Sunday, 1925.

Dear Readers:--In trying to tell of my conversion in the Olive Branch Mission in Seattle in 1907 it may be well to state a few facts: First, I realize my shortcomings in writing, especially in trying to condense a matter and still bring out the cardinal points in the story so as to retain the life that belongs to it. Again, I realize the difficulty of the reader who knows nothing of the moral conditions which existed in this part of the city at that time, for the mission worker of that day and of this has entirely different conditions to contend with. These conditions, if I tried to incorporate them into my story to make a perfect whole, would make the story too lengthy, so I hope the reader will kindly practise some clemency. So to the story:

One evening in the fall of 1907, I, a young lad of twenty-two summers, found myself listening to a band of religious workers on a downtown street in Seattle, Washington. They had chosen their place in front of the "Oregon House," a cheap rooming house, at the crossing of Second Avenue and Second Avenue South, where I had just sought temporary quarters because of limited means, and also because of its being close to my new work at the Great Northern freight office at the foot of Second Avenue South and King Street.

The captain of a band of Volunteers of America was talking. He was pleading for five dollars for a poor widow with five or six children, who was sick, and without the means to pay the rent that was past due, and to buy the necessary fuel and food to keep the family together. He took up a collection for her, but failed to reach the amount by twenty-five cents. Seeing this I said to myself, "Well, the poor widow is worse off than I am; I might as well give it to her." So reasoning, I left the gathering for the room on the second floor to get the money. Returning I found the Volunteers just entering their mission hall across the street. Bent on fulfilling my purpose in giving the quarter, I was obliged to go into the hall too. I took a rear seat. The meeting opened with song and music, the soldiers on the platform seemed free and at ease, as they walked to and fro while singing and playing. The collection plate was passed around. I dropped the quarter on the plate. Soon I heard the leader say something which I took for an invitation to the penitent bench. Ashamed of myself I hurried out, stumbling up the stairway to the street. While gaining my balance and continuing up and out, I heard the captain saying, ". . .The wicked flee seven ways when none pursueth." A few minutes later I found myself on my knees in my room praying. I knew without a shadow of a doubt that God wanted to save me. I felt a distinct call. There was no room left for argument about it, so I made up my mind to see it through.

The following evening I took a bath and then put on my best clothes, figuring that if God was going to clean me up on the inside I might as well clean myself up on the outside. As I stepped out on the street and headed for the Volunteers of America hall, I faced their band, and at once this obstacle presented itself to my mind: "Well, now you know they are mad at you for stumbling in the stairway and making a noise; you had better not go down there to get saved; they won't help you." So I passed them by and came to the corner of Second Avenue South and Washington Street, where I stopped and asked God where I might go to get the needed help.

While I was praying and looking around, I saw another band in front of the "O. K." Loan Office on Washington Street. One of them, Mrs. Ray, was talking loudly to make herself heard by the large crowd listening and also to prevail over the din of the noises of the street. While watching them from my vantage point the Lord said to me, "You follow them and you will be safe." So I remained on the corner until I saw them break up, pass by and walk into their hall underneath a saloon on the southeast corner of Washington and Second Avenue South.

I followed. When I had descended the stairway I was met by a man of middle age, Brother Burke, who handed me a song book and led me to the second row of seats in front. Naturally I sized up everything and everybody that came under my observation. Those on the platform came under my special scrutiny, for I could see them face to face, see them sing and talk and act. "This one here seems pretty good, and that one, and that one there not so bad; but this one looks kind of doubtful, and that one--but he may be all right." And so I philosophized to myself while listening and watching intently to see what was going on. Certainly God's children were there together, united for the one purpose of bringing the gospel to the down-trodden and the outcasts. That was plain. Even the rats must have realized something of that sort, for while the meeting was in session I saw almost directly above me a good-sized rat taking its time walking up a trough leading from the saloon above and receiving the slop from the drinking glasses. The trough being defective, a pail had been put underneath on the floor to receive the drippings. And so, with the pail on the floor before me, the rat and its associates above, the saints on the platform and the audience sprinkled with saints and sinners, I saw for a few hours a fierce war going on between two forces contending for the souls of men. And shortly I was to become an object in this warfare, for at the close of the meeting an invitation was given to those who so desired to come up to the altar and be prayed for.

The time had come for me to decide. I was not willing to go without a personal invitation, however, but told the Lord that if He would send one of them to give me one, I'd go. The minutes I waited praying for that invitation seemed like hours, and I was almost discouraged when a gentle-faced man with a quiet and unassuming disposition, Brother Percy Mann, touched me gently with his hand preparatory to a hand-shake and salutation. To his question, "Brother, are you a Christian?" I answered, "No." "Would you like to be one?" "Yes! But what guarantee have you that I can be one? That I can be one tonight? What proof have you?" To this his answer, "If you will ask God to forgive you, and ask Him with all your heart, He will do it." "All right, I'll put you to the test," and so saying I went with him to the altar where, for fully one hour and a half, the saints prayed and pleaded with God and fought for the salvation of one whom they had never before seen and whom they knew nothing about save that he acknowledged himself a sinner and expressed a desire to be saved. While they were praying, God also was dealing directly with me. Something was taking place within me which I recognized to be of divine doing. In fact, I was being made a new creature in Christ Jesus. That night I found the guilt of sin had departed. On the following day, while performing my routine work with the freight bills, the Lord wanted me to call up a friend of mine over the 'phone and cancel an engagement I had with him, that I might fulfil the desire of the superintendent of the Mission to be there next evening. But I put it off and put it off until too late to do so, the result being that I felt my peaceful relationship to the Lord strained and severed.

I went to the street meeting, however, ignoring the date I had with my friend. While I was standing with the others in the ring, Brother Percy Mann came down and asked me if I was saved. Being answered in the affirmative, he asked me to testify to the men on the street. But this I refused to do, knowing I was not on the square with the Lord. Instead, a few minutes later I hurried to my room where I again went on my knees, asking God to help me become a real Christian. The real conflict had begun and I determined to see it through. Accordingly, the night after I went to the Olive Branch Mission again. That night Mrs. Ray was leading the testimony meeting. Her request came to me to testify. I was obliged to say I felt I wasn't saved yet, but desired a second chance to be prayed for. And when the meeting closed the battle for this soul of mine was renewed with a vigor and vehemence that only real, seasoned soldiers of the cross understand and know anything about. For another full hour and a half the battle raged.

While this was going on men were coming in from the street to find out what the noise was all about. One of the workers told them that God was at work redeeming a soul from sin. And sure enough He was. When I arose I was again at peace. But a new problem presented itself to me and to them when they asked me if I felt I was saved--felt I was saved. No, I did not **feel** that I was saved. I had no witness to that effect. Then came the difficulty to them to explain to me that I must believe--have faith that God had done the thing which I had asked Him to do. After much endeavor in explaining faith (a word I had never heard before), Mrs. Ray finally brought the Bible and had me read the ninth and tenth verses of the tenth chapter of Romans. This cleared the situation and I walked home that night practising faith, saying to myself, "Well, Lord, you do save me now." "Well, devil, the Lord does save me now." "Well, I know the Lord saves me now." Reaching my room I went to bed and slept as sound as a baby, a thing I had not done for many years. At six o'clock the following morning I awoke. My first thought was to thank God for salvation, and as I did so He gave me the witness to that fact.

A few days after this, the Olive Branch Mission moved to a hall in the basement at the southeast corner of Main Street and First Avenue South. While they were moving I thought it was best for me to write home to my parents in Gothenburg, and to relatives I had lived with in Jamtland, Sweden, and also to my fiancee in Norway. My oldest sister in her letters sent me this news, that mother cried for joy in reading about my conversion, and that she carried the letter in her skirt-pocket. Shortly afterwards she took sick and died, but while on her death-bed she read and reread the letter. She died with faith in God and according to my sister's statement, her face seemed twenty years younger; a look of happiness on her face such as they had never seen before was there when she died. Then I wrote to an uncle with whom I had resided for two and a half years. I received a letter from him that both he and his wife wept for joy in reading that letter. My third letter was to the girl I left behind, telling her the same news also. Her answer, would you know? "If ever I loved you, Axel, I love you now," was her staunch reply.

Nearly eighteen years have rolled their course since then. The work began in 1907 still stands. But the powers which fought a losing fight then are still fighting to defeat, if possible, the work God has performed in my soul. Why? Simply this: Read Eph. 2: 10, "For we are His

workmanship, created in Christ Jesus unto good works, which God hath before ordained that we should walk in them." "Created . . unto good works"--this is His purpose in saving my soul and this is the earnest of my soul to work out. My spirit seems to groan to get out on the foreign mission field. Should any one of you readers feel like joining with me in prayers that this may come to pass in divine order, I invite you to do so. Praise the Lord.
Yours in Christ,

A. V. Setterlind.

CHAPTER XXIV
INCIDENTS IN MISSION WORK
A Miracle Through an Accident

One night, while giving an exhortation in the Olive Branch Mission, I felt very much impressed to warn the people to prepare for sudden death, as they did not know when they might be killed in an accident. I said, "Some of us may be overtaken before we get home tonight, as there is danger lurking on every street corner." I did not know but that I was preaching to myself also, as we scarcely go to town without a narrow escape. After we had left the meeting and were nearing home, as we turned a corner on Green Lake Boulevard, where there was a cement wall, a large auto came right towards us. It came on the wrong side and before we could think, it was right upon us. As quick as a flash Brother Ray swerved the machine, but they struck us a kind of a side blow, and just before they struck us I cried, "O Lord," and then came the crash. They turned our car right around. It skidded about twenty feet back towards town, and their machine back the other way. We stopped with a crash. Our front wheel was smashed, the windshield shattered, the fender turned up against the machine, the seat I was sitting on crushed underneath me, the top torn off, and the floor broken out where my feet were. As we crawled out and looked around, we found the top in shreds, as if a blast had been exploded under it, and the bows on one side broken off. It was a miracle we were not killed outright. Husband asked me if I was hurt. I had felt something strike me on the head, but never did know just what it was.

As quickly as possible we went to the other machine to see if any one was hurt. To our surprise there were four men in the car, all under the influence of moonshine. It was a fine, large car and the windshield was broken all to pieces. The two men in the front seat were bleeding, and the two in the back seat didn't know what had happened. Finally one roused himself enough to ask, "What's the matter?" A piece of glass had struck the driver in the mouth and had split the end of his tongue. He said to us, "You were on the wrong side." I called up the police station and reported the accident. When the police came, the men tried to put the blame on us, but as it had started to rain just before the accident we could prove by the tracks and also by the broken glass that we were on our own side of the street. It might have gone hard with us if we had not had this proof. They told Brother Ray at the police station that these men had been there before; that they were bootleggers, and that the driver had had several such accidents. Brother Ray went to see him the next day and he told him that he was insured for $10,000 and that he would make good his car, and he did. About a month later, this same man, under the influence of liquor, killed an old lady on her way home from church. About a month after that he turned the machine over on himself and was instantly killed.

On my way home, as I began to get over the shock, to my surprise a song kept running through my mind. The song did not leave me, and I began to wonder what it was. I did not know it. I called up one of my friends and gave her the tune, but couldn't repeat the words. She had heard the song and remembered the air, but couldn't remember the words. Then I called up my pastor, Reverend Wilson, but he couldn't remember it. Then I called my class leader, Sister Sutton. She had heard the air, but couldn't place the song. It stayed with me that night and up to the next day. Finally I went to the home of Brother and Sister Morgan and hummed the tune for them. They told me the words. I was so glad when I found out that the song was one of the promises of the Bible. It certainly let me see that the Lord delivered me at that time. I praise His name for it all. This is the song:

Under His Wings

In God I have found a retreat,
Where I can securely abide;
No refuge or rest so complete;
And here I intend to reside.

CHORUS
Oh, what comfort it brings,
As my soul sweetly sings;
I am safe from all danger
While under His wings.

I dread not the terror by night,
No arrow can harm me by day,
His shadow has covered me quite,
My fears He has driven away.

The pestilence walking about,
When darkness has settled abroad,
Can never compel me to doubt
The presence and power of God.

The wasting destruction at noon
No fearful foreboding can bring;
With Jesus my soul doth commune,
His perfect salvation I sing.

A thousand may fall at my side,
And ten thousand at my right hand;
Above me His wings are spread wide,
Beneath them in safety I stand.

The Drunken Man

One night at one of the missions there came a man into the meeting. He had been drinking and talked all the time the preaching was going on. He kept saying, "I wonder if the Lord could save me; I did not mean to do it."

After the preaching was over, some of the workers asked him if he would come to the altar to be prayed for. He said, "Yes, but I know I can't be saved." As he came, he cried, and told us the following story. At first we thought it was just a drunken man's statement, but as we tarried with him, we found out that he was sincere.

He said that he had been out of the penitentiary but a short time and that he had killed his best friend in a drunken brawl, and had been sent to the penitentiary for his crime. He said, "I didn't mean to do it; I was drunk." He said, "I have prayed while in my little cell in the penitentiary, all night at times, but there did not seem to be forgiveness for me." This was as far as he would go. He was very dirty and was pitiful to look upon. At that time there was no place for the drunkard; there was a home for fallen girls, but not for the men. We believed that if he had a chance, the Lord could do something for him, and as at the close of the meeting no one seemed to give him a bed or to care for him, my husband looked at me and said, "Shall we take him home with us?" We decided to do so.

After we reached home we put on the coffee pot and a boiler of water, and spread down a sheet on the floor. My husband had him take off his clothes and gave him a bath and a change of clothing. He then gave him strong coffee. He was too nervous to hold the cup in his hand, but splashed the coffee all over himself. My husband steadied his hand and helped him to get the coffee down. After he had eaten and had a good bath, we said, "Now we will finish our prayer." We each prayed and told him to pray again. He readily did so. He seemed to appreciate our kindness to him. He had a godly sorrow for his sins, but all seemed dark to him. Afterwards we sat up and read the Bible. He could not believe that Jesus would save him. In his four by six cell he had often prayed, but got no relief. As we read the Word to him, fourteenth chapter of Saint John, first to eleventh verse, we got to the verse where it says, "Believe me for the very works' sake."

By this time he was quite sober, and all at once the light flashed through his heart, and he said, "My, wasn't that strange they didn't believe," and we said, "Yes, and that's the way with you." He began to say, "I do believe; oh, I do believe; now I see," and he sprang to his feet and began to praise the Lord, and said, "Oh! it has been dark so long; why could not I see it, why could not I see it?" And we sang to him and he joined with us--he had a beautiful voice--until it wakened the neighbors. And the next morning we could see them talking to each other over the fence, and they knew someone had been saved, and they rejoiced with us. We let this man stay a few days and he found work. The last we knew of him he was serving the Lord in a mission. He went to California to work, later on. After the Lord saved him he went forth trying to save others.

We did not have any coat for him, and I had to wash his old coat as it was so full of vermin. As I rubbed I sang:

> "The grace of God, it is so sweet;
> The grace of God, it is so sweet;
> The grace, the grace, the grace of God."

By the time I had gotten to the chorus, I was blessed in my soul, and it was one of the greatest blessings that I ever received. He stood watching me and helping me get water, and tears came into his eyes as I sang and rubbed. Years after he seemed very grateful, and could never forget what the Lord had wrought in his heart.

A Drunken Sailor Saved

At one of our street meetings there was a young sailor standing on the sidewalk, under the influence of liquor. He seemed to be looking for something and as we stood and sang the Gospel his eyes fell on me. He began to laugh, and talk loud, and call me names, and say things about us all. He would answer those that were speaking and he became very noisy, while others stood by and encouraged him to go on. As for myself I felt so sorry for him and prayed and said, "Lord, forgive him, for he knows not what he is doing. It is some poor mother's boy." All at once he stopped and walked away two or three blocks, stopped and listened and came back. We were just starting into the Mission, and he said to us, "Something struck me." The Lord spoke to him and his countenance seemed to suddenly change and he was in great soul agony. He said, "I am sorry for the way I talked, and I want you folks to pray for me. I made fun of that old colored woman. I want her to pray for me. I want you all to pray for me." How glad we all were to pray for him. We had no trouble to get him to pray for himself and confess his sins to God. It was astonishing how the Spirit had sobered him up and let him see himself as God sees him. He shed bitter tears of repentance, and the burden of his sin rolled away. He rose to his feet a happy boy, and what a transformation! His face just beamed with the glory of the Lord, and my own soul was made to rejoice with the others. He was sorry he had ridiculed us and, because a sinner had come home, we all were happy to see and hear him glorifying our God.

There are many people who say we are too bold, and many others declare we are after gold, but they are all mistaken. We are hardly bold enough to rescue poor lost sinners, those diamonds in the rough.

> "The day will soon be over,
> When digging will be done,
> And no more gems we'll gather,
> So let us still press on.
> The dying love of Jesus
> Will make you love the tough;
> Remember, please remember,
> They are diamonds in the rough."

This was a real diamond, polished and made to shine for the Lord.

Conversion of Two Colored Girls

A burden was on our hearts for the people and especially for the girls in the cabarets and places of sin. The Lord had put it into our hearts to pray almost all night that He would bring some of those poor souls out of their prison-houses into the Mission. Sure enough, this night the Lord answered our prayer by bringing in two octoroon girls. One was married and the other single. We kept our eyes on them all through the meeting, praying that the Lord would restrain them and not let them go out as they do sometimes when they are under conviction. They seemed serious and listened to the sermon attentively, and to the singing. After the preaching, Sister Witteman went and had a talk with them. One had begun to cry as she came into the room. We could see that they were not accustomed to going to church. Finally one consented to come to the altar. She was almost overcome with godly sorrow for her sins. She leaned upon Sister Witteman's arm and wept as she prayed. After kneeling for a while she seemed to see the light and was gloriously saved. While they were praying with her, I went back and talked with the other one. She acknowledged that it was the thing to do and said that she had seen better days, but had come west and gotten away from home influences and gone down in sin; that she would be glad to come herself, but knew if she came she couldn't live the life she was in. When the other one arose to her feet, she said, "I wonder if she has got it? I hope she has the real thing, as she has had so much trouble. Nothing but the real thing will keep her." When the girl turned around so her face was seen, she said, "I believe she has really gotten it." I said, "Don't you do anything to discourage her," and she promised she wouldn't. The next night they were back again. It was quite a while before the second one gave up, as there was a great deal in her life she knew she couldn't hold on to, if she changed, but finally she died out to it all and was graciously saved. The two of them took the way of the cross with all that it means.

They told us, when we were talking to them, that the first night they came they had been sitting in a movie, very unhappy, but not knowing where to go for peace. They finally decided to get out and walk down the street, and the Lord led them right to the Mission. They came to the Mission for a while afterwards, and then moved away, one going one direction and the other back east.

One of our brothers, who had been on a trip to England, stopped over at a town in the middle west and met the latter at a religious gathering. She told him who she was and sent her regards to us. She was married and in the work of the Lord, having married a preacher.

Revival at Yakima

The following short account of our revival meeting in Yakima was written by Ray Langworthy. He took an active interest in these services and added much to their success:

The two revival meetings, held by Brother and Sister Ray at Yakima, were conducted during the winter months of the years 1920 and 1921, while Rev. John A. Logan was pastor of the church and the writer was superintendent of the Sunday-school.

During the first meeting the house was filled from the beginning, and at times crowded. God's Spirit moved on the people and a number of old, hardened sinners sought and found the Lord. The church was greatly helped and stirred, but the best part of all was the number of children who sought the Lord and gave themselves definitely to Him. The altar was lined with children a number of times, many of whom received real help. About fifteen of these joined the church, with several older persons, and many of them remain plain and stalwart Christians to this day.

The following winter the question was heard from all sides, "Are those colored people coming back again?" The children, especially, looked forward with great pleasure to hearing them sing. As before, the house was quite often well filled and the Spirit of God troubled the waters so that a number found Him to the salvation of their souls. Often since that time the same question has been asked by outsiders, "Are those people coming back again?" Unsaved persons have expressed their approval of the way in which Brother and Sister Ray conducted their meetings, acknowledging that they liked them, and would like to have the kind of religion they preached.

If we do not see them back at Yakima again, we hope to meet them on the golden streets of the New Jerusalem, where we may all offer our tribute of praise to Jesus Christ, the King of Glory, for all He has done for us.

L. Ray Langworthy.

Olive Branch Mission

We finished up our campaign and came back to Seattle in the early spring. In the meantime the workers at the Olive Branch Mission had been very busy. It was one of their first winters in ministering to the poor. They had been accustomed to help at Christmas and Thanksgiving every winter, but this winter they had commenced in the early part of the season, giving one meal a day to the down-and-outs. When we visited the Mission at their meal time, it was packed to its capacity. They had been feeding 350 to 450 every night. There were people of every nationality, except the Japanese and the Chinese, and about one hundred white people to every colored person. We have seen times when we have had to have police to hold the men in line, but this time they seemed very orderly.

When the speakers took their places on the platform, the seats were all filled, and also the standing room in the back. It was the most pitiful sight I ever beheld. There were young men and old--all kinds of talented men, and all hungry.

The Mission doors were kept open all day, so that the men could go in and read and keep out of the rain. Before the feeding the workers preached for a short time, while the tables were being prepared. Those in the front filed from their seats to the table and all the front seats were emptied. Then those in the back moved forward and filled up the chairs and waited their turn. This was the old Mission on Washington Street and Second Avenue. They have better accommodations now, having a larger place and a separate dining-room.

That year they had Bible readings and some of the workers talked to the men through the day, and quite a number were saved. From among them, the superintendent got her cook and waiters to serve the others.

In the meeting there were some of the brightest testimonies that I have ever heard. There was one man in particular who had a very striking experience. His name was Kirk. He had tramped over the country all summer, in fact he never worked. He was an I. W. W. and a speaker for them and held street meetings in the different cities over the United States. He was converted one day in the Olive Branch Mission, and was among those we met when we came back. He was traveling with a band of tramps and went into a little city near Seattle. They canvassed the town for food and then met in the suburbs and cooked their meals together. He happened to visit the home of a lady who was a Christian. She gave him something to eat and some tracts to read. One of these she asked him to think about. The title was, "Is Life Worth Living?" When he went back to his comrades, he said, "I have some junk to make fires with, but the lady asked me to read the papers before I destroyed them and, as she was kind to me and gave me food, I will read just this one." As he did so the words, "Is life worth living?" struck his eye. They got upon his mind, and he tried to get them off, but could not. The more he tried to put off the thoughts, the more he thought about them. The tramps made their next beat to Seattle. He went to the Mission, although he was not accustomed to it. The words, "Is Life Worth Living?" kept ringing in his ears. He listened to the prayers and the exhortations and thought he would look into the matter and see what there was in it. As he got on his knees he surrendered to the Lord. That morning he was saved. He had a tatoo on his arm, "No God, no boss, no country." He proved to be a very bright man intellectually, and accepted the Lord Jesus as his God, and he wanted to work as other people. He would testify on the streets to the confusion and dissatisfaction of his comrades. He told them he had found the Lord and of the change He had wrought in his life. He was a good speaker and went around to the churches and different places, just telling of what the Lord had done for him. A year later there was a man found dead on the streets of Seattle. The newspaper said that he was unknown, but had a tatoo on his arm, "No God, no boss, no country." He had been away for a while and had just come back to Seattle. Our superintendent went to the morgue and identified him. He had been in the Mission previous to this, telling how the Lord had kept him saved. He was thought to have been run over by an automobile, but it was never known just how he was killed.

We have never been able to find out who the woman was who gave him the tracts, and perhaps she will never know, until the books are opened, the blessings she brought to this man.

Last Revival Meeting in Olive Branch Mission

In the year 1920 we held our last special meeting in the Olive Branch Mission, and after that took up evangelistic work for three or four months during the winters. We were getting much older and felt that we were unable to work on the streets in the rain every night before the services, as we had done during the previous years, and that the Lord wished us to go out and evangelize during the winter. Previous to this we had held but one revival during the entire winter and had put in the rest of our time in home work.

Somehow it never entered our minds to keep a diary, but the first of the year 1920 I thought I would try it. Time and space will not permit my telling all of it. I kept it for four months, and then my sister came to visit us and I stopped. In reading it over I notice that almost every Sunday night there was some one at the altar. If there happened to be two Sunday nights in succession that no one was saved, we would get down on our knees humbly before the Lord and examine our hearts and plead the promises for souls and we would nearly always see results afterwards. We give Him all the glory.

In the regular Mission meetings, Saturday night is the Seattle Pacific College students' night, and we asked them to continue their night with us as they were on fire for souls. It is customary for the workers to take up their night, when there is a special meeting on hand, leaving the evangelists free to labor. We began the 18th of January and the meetings lasted over four Sundays. Here is an account from the diary, as it was written during this special meeting.

Sunday night, January 18. Text, Isaiah 3. "I have loved you with an everlasting love." Sister Ray preached. One man sanctified, one saved, three girls at the altar.

19th. Brother Ray preached. One at the altar.

20th. Proverbs 1 : 18. One man, an Indian, at the altar.

21st. One man at the altar. Brother Ray preached.

22nd. Brother Ray preached. No visible victory. Text, "Sirs, I believe God."

23rd. Friday, a day of fasting and prayer. A Sunday-school teacher reclaimed, a little girl saved; a good meeting. A large crowd followed us off the street. Lots of conviction. We expect more results later.

24th. Saturday night. Seattle Pacific College students with us. Two at the altar. A young Philippino saved. He was a student at University of Washington.

25th. Sabbath. Text, "Holiness becometh Thy house, O Lord." Sister Ray preached. Big crowd. One preacher's wife and a young lady out for holiness, one Seventh-day Advent girl who had never been saved, and others.

26th. One sailor boy saved. Brother Ray preached.

27th. One at the altar. Brother Ray preached.

28th. Brother Ray preached. One at the altar, came through well. Good audience.

29th. One at the altar.

30th. Great night. Glory to His name. Several seekers at the altar. Some prayed through to victory.

31st. Meeting in charge of students from Seattle Pacific College. Good sermon with conviction. No one forward. Good audience.

February 1. Sunday. Souls at altar afternoon and night. Successful altar service. Throughout the weeks souls were at the altar every night, and the week ended with great victory. Near the end of this special meeting the flu epidemic broke out, and in our neighborhood a night or two before we closed, the lady living the next door above us was stricken. One of the neighbors across the street came over while I was talking with my next door neighbor, from the porch, and asked us if we knew the neighbor above us was dead. She said the lady did not realize she was dying. It was the first we had heard of it.

At the first of the week I began to come down with it myself, and about this same time the neighbor across the street, who told us of the first neighbor's death, passed away. When she was coming down with the influenza she went to the next door neighbor's to 'phone for the doctor, and by using the telephone after her this neighbor took the disease, and in a very few days was gone. Later, a fourth neighbor took it, but although quite sick, did not die.

When I heard the ambulance carrying my neighbors away so rapidly, I thought my time had come, as I was so weak from the strenuous work in the Mission. We prayed that it might be the will of the Lord that I be spared. I took a turn for the better, but had a stubborn cough, and I notice in my diary that I plead the promises of God and said, "My cough is stubborn, but I am trusting Thee for victory, and I believe I have it." The Lord graciously delivered me.

These revival meetings were good, but were not up to the average on account of the flu epidemic throughout the city, but we were graciously blessed through it all, and the glory is all the Lord's.

Thus ended our special meeting in Olive Branch Mission, and we haven't held a special meeting since. Two weeks later we were back at Olive Branch on Sunday night at our regular post of duty. We want to say to the glory of God that we never had a special meeting at Olive Branch but there have been converts, and others sanctified through the baptism of the Holy Ghost.

An Answered Prayer for a Fisherman

Early one morning while doing my work, a fisherman came to the door and wanted to sell me some fish. I had already ordered my meat for dinner and told him that I didn't want any fish that day. I noticed that his countenance was sad, and I said to him, "I'm sorry; some other day." He said, "My horse hasn't had his feed today, and I have gone from house to house today and no one wants to buy fish." He then began to swear, and I said to him, "Don't swear; it is wrong to take the name of God in vain. Trust in the Lord, and He will help you out." This enraged him more than ever. It made me feel bad to hear him blaspheme, because I had tried the Lord and knew what He would do for those who put their trust in Him. I said, "Bring me some fish. I will take some, although I do not need them." When he brought the fish, he said, "There is no God. Do you think a God would allow a man to go half the day without feeding his horse? My horse goes hungry. There is no God." That made me feel so bad that before I knew it I grabbed his hand and began to pray. I said, "O Lord, sell these fish for this man." He stood and looked at me as I prayed, and when I had finished he said, "Thank you." I said, "The Lord will sell the fish for you. I know He will." After he was gone I was astonished at myself and yet I felt sure the Lord would sell the fish. When my husband came home I told him about it, and he thought it was strange that I would do such a thing. I couldn't help but think of the fisherman the rest of the week, and one day, as my husband and I were going up the hill, I spoke of the fisherman, and to my surprise I turned the corner and walked right up to him, and I said, "Here he is. Didn't you sell the fish?" He said, "I did." And I said, "Praise the Lord." On Sunday night who should come to the Mission but the fisherman. He had a strange look on his face. He had given his heart to the Lord. I rejoiced to hear him testify, and I was sure that the Lord had put it in my mind to buy the fish and to pray for the man in his infidelity.

CHAPTER XXV
PROHIBITION CAMPAIGN IN WASHINGTON, 1914

When the State of Washington adopted prohibition we were exultant. We had long prayed that we might live to see the saloons closed and old John Barleycorn voted out. We will never forget the time when this took place, or the joy we experienced in our hearts as we watched the saloon doors close.

Previous to this we had a great rally in Seattle, and this also was a memorable day. There was a call for every prohibitionist to meet at a certain place in the morning and take part in a parade. For once most all sects of religion answered the call and came together, and with them a great number of unbelievers. There were men, women, children, young people, old people, and cripples; the feeble ones that could not ride mustered up strength and marched, all with the determination that John Barleycorn must go. "In union there is strength." There were floats of every description, and almost every person had a banner. Some of the banners read, "John Barleycorn must go," "He robbed me of my father," "He killed my brother," "He broke up my home," and such like. We started at the North End and marched down First Avenue. Part way down First Avenue we looked back towards Pike Street and it was a beautiful sight to see those banners and flags floating in the breeze. It reminded us of the Scripture in the Song of Solomon, when he was speaking of the church, and asked, "Who is she that looketh forth as the morning, as fair as the moon, and as clear as the sun, and as terrible as an army with banners."

We noticed how this demonstration struck terror to the hearts of the saloon-keepers. As they stood in the doors of their saloons, or on the walks, and watched, we could tell by their faces that they, too, believed that we would gain the victory.

I had witnessed such a sight once before when but a child, and that was when the Negro race celebrated its first national independence. I felt just such a thrill then as I did when in the parade. Every one that could walk marched in the parade. Mothers with small children holding on to their skirts, and with babies in their arms, some of the returned soldiers from the war, and old ex-slave men.

We had no paved streets to march on at that time, but dirty rock roads, but we expressed the gladness in our hearts that we were free. Abraham Lincoln, under God, had set us free.

This same joy of freedom was in the hearts of some of the men in the prohibition parade. Had not they, too, been slaves, and had not the Lord delivered them? As we marched we sang,

> "The fight is on, the trumpet sound is ringing out,
> The cry 'To arms' is heard afar and near;
> The Lord of hosts is marching on to victory,
> The triumph of the Christ will soon appear.
>
> CHORUS
> "The fight is on, O Christian soldier,
> And face to face in stern array,
> With armor gleaming, and colors streaming,
> The right and wrong engage today!

The fight is on, but be not weary;
Be strong, and in His might hold fast;
If God be for us, His banner o'er us,
We'll sing the victor's song at last!

"The Lord is leading on to certain victory;
The bow of promise spans the eastern sky;
His glorious name in every land shall honored be;
The morn will break, the dawn of peace is nigh."

The superintendent of the Olive Branch Mission and her co-workers were in this parade. As we marched down the street four abreast, we were privileged to march beside one Brother Collins and wife. Brother Collins had been wonderfully saved from drink in the Mission. He had been associated with most of the men in the slum district. They had heard him give his testimony on the street and had seen what a radical change had been wrought in his life. They called him "Scotty." He had left his home when he was but a lad. He had been partly raised by a pious old grandmother, as his father and mother were dead. He was a sailor, and when he came into port he would spend his earnings for drink. He was about forty years old when he was saved. At this time he was a logger.

His old comrades wept as he testified. As we passed by them as they stood in front of some of his old haunts with pale faces, they paid strict attention, and some saluted us. Brother Collins was a very pious man. He was honored by all who knew him. The Lord gave him a Christian wife. Since that time he has been called to heaven, to be forever with the Lord. His widow is still left to continue her labors of love to the poor and needy.

The parade was about two miles long, and as we closed it we had the feeling that God would give us a dry state.

Later we had the election. The state went dry, as we expected, and then came the last night that the saloons were permitted to be open. Such a night of drunkenness and debauchery. Many were angry because the state had gone dry. Some of the business men in the slum district put up signs, "We're going out of business," "Seattle is dead--Prohibition has killed her," in their windows. The men began to drink early in the morning. The saloon doors were wide open, and the men were almost two deep in some places at the bars. Some sat near the saloon doors asleep, some around the corners and in the alleys. They were all trying to drink all they could, because it was their last opportunity for open drunkenness.

There was an advertisement on the roof on the corner of Second Avenue and Yesler Way. It was a large beer bottle about eight feet long. I had long prayed for the time to come when it would come down, because it had been a terrible instrument in calling the men into the saloons to drink. It was worked by electricity. The bottle was standing up with the red ale near to the neck and the foam running over the top as if the cork had just been drawn and a glass was sitting near. The sign would first flash, "Rainier Beer," then the bottle would automatically turn the beer into the glass with the white foam on top. Many a man on the street who would have gone home to his wife and children with his week's earnings, could not resist walking into the saloon to get one drink, and then spending all he had.

We watched the men until twelve o'clock when the saloon doors were to close. Men were in from the logging camps and every place else to get their last drink from open saloons. They would stand in bunches and reel and put their arms around one another and scream and yell while the old bottle in the sign did its work in advertising, and the bartenders did their part in handing the beer over the counter. But, thank God, there comes an end to all things some time, and, while this drink is not put away entirely, it paid to vote prohibition. We stood and watched the mug houses close their doors. When the clock struck twelve, the old bottle poured the beer into the glass for the last time, and we shouted, "Hallelujah" and "Amen."

We who have had the chance to watch the after effects, to look into some of the places that were once saloons, and into places where houses had gone out of business, remember the saying, "Seattle is dead because she went dry." We find that there is not a building but that is filled, and most of them with legitimate business.

Most of the men who inhabit this part of the city wear decent looking clothes. They come into the Mission even if they are broke. Some have been drinking moonshine, but they cannot get as much as formerly or as easily as they did with open saloons. The temptations are not so great. While the saying of the Lord is still true that the poor we have always with us, we realize that the devil is not dead, and unbelief and sin are still rampant. When we see it demonstrated upon our streets we faint in heart, but the Holy Spirit whispers to our soul the precious words of the Bible, "Ye shall reap in due season if ye faint not." I am reminded right here of how, when children, we used to kill joint snakes. There were many in our locality. When we would strike one, he would break up and the pieces would scatter through the brush and rocks and we could not find them, but if you could hit the snake on the head you could destroy him. Now we have some of the serpent's "joints" scattered here and there. Prohibition has struck the head a hard blow, and by the help of the Lord we are going right after the joints with our prayers and faith. We will keep at it until victory is achieved through Christ our Lord.

There is a degree of common decency and morality existing which we did not see before the dry law went into effect, and men have a better chance to resist the temptations which were so prevalent everywhere they went. Yes, thank the Lord, it pays in this life and in the life eternal.

The next day after the saloons were closed there were heartaches and heart-breaks, and an intense thirst for drink. Many drank pure alcohol to quench their thirst. Some became blind, some died, and this was our chance for a revival. So we started a special meeting in the Mission. The Lord gave us a full house. There were no saloons for the men to sit around in, and they did not know where else to go, and they could not get their drink as before. They gradually began to wake up to their terrible condition. On one occasion there was a party that had a quart of wood-alcohol, and some of its victims died, but two came into the Mission, one with his eyesight almost destroyed, but the other recovered and was converted.

We had a great revival and many were saved, others besides the drinkers. A man and wife by the name of Johnson were converted in these meetings. She was a backslider, but he had never been saved. As a result of these meetings the Lord put it in her heart to start a little Sunday-school in her home on Eastlake Boulevard. She went around the neighborhood and gathered up all the children she could get from the boat-houses, and made her front room into a Sunday-school room. After her carpets were all worn out and her furniture about destroyed from the wear and tear of the children, the Lord put it into her heart to solicit money enough to build a place for the Sunday-school. That was several years ago, and this Sunday-school is still in existence today. Eternity alone will tell of the good results of the special meetings we held right after the saloons were closed. Soon after the building was finished, Sister Johnson resigned from the superintendency of the school, on account of poor health, but the work is still being carried on by workers from the Free Methodist Church. The Lord is wonderfully blessing the work.

CHAPTER XXVI
THE POWER OF TESTIMONY

In one of our revivals, Brother Ray, while preaching, was led to tell how the Lord delivered him from drink, although the devil always said, "Don't tell that. People will think you are a pretty good man, if you don't tell." He said, "There may be some one here tonight in the same bondage that I was." I, myself, felt ashamed to have him tell it, but when I thought of the others who might be in the same condition, I could say, "Amen, Lord; anything, just so some one is helped and you get the glory for it."

There was a man in the audience, with his wife, daughter, and little boy, and just as soon as Brother Ray finished preaching the man rushed to the altar, followed by his family. All four bowed at the altar and surrendered to the Lord. The father, mother, and little boy had never been saved, but I think the daughter had once belonged to some church. This made quite a stir in the neighborhood. They were a very happy family.

In giving his testimony, he told us that back east while he was working on a barge running on the Missouri River, he stopped in a little town. There he heard a sermon that brought him under deep, pungent conviction, so much so that he trembled, but he would not yield to the Spirit's wooings. The conviction left him and it had been twenty years from that time to this night, when he surrendered to the Lord. He was not in the habit of going to church, but came with his family out of curiosity, and heard Brother Ray's testimony. He had lived only a few blocks away from this church for a number of years. He had no use for the Christians, and didn't know why. He would always pass down on the other side of the street, and had often done so while under the influence of liquor, but this was the night of all nights. His wife's experience had been somewhat like mine. Oh! how it pays to obey the Lord. He saves us that we may be instrumental in helping to save others. We are ashamed of our evil life, but if God can in some way reach some one who has had a like experience, we are glad to tell what He has redeemed us from.

In this meeting there was a man who told of how he and a Catholic man stole a hog from a neighbor, and how, when he sought the Lord for pardon, the thought of this hog came before him. The burden of his sin was so heavy upon him that he had no peace until he was willing to make restitution by paying for the hog. He said that he went to the neighbor and confessed and paid for the hog himself, rather than bring the Catholic into it. The Lord pardoned him and blessed him in his soul, so much so that he could hardly testify without mentioning it.

There was another man in the audience who had stolen some money from his employer. It was such a large amount that he was afraid that if he confessed it he might be sent to the penitentiary, and he did not want this to happen on account of his family. This was ever before him. He had promised the Lord that if He would save him, he would pay the money back, but afterwards he backed down and this had been a burden on his heart for years. The testimony he heard brought such agony to his soul that he finally decided he would have to make good, regardless of consequences. He said that while praying about it in his store, some man heard and thought he must be sick. He finally decided to put himself in the hands of the Lord and to go and see the man who he hoped would not be in. He found him at his place of business and went right up to him and told him he had a confession to make, and threw himself on his mercy. The man said, "I certainly will forgive you. I knew all the time that you took the money, and I am glad the Lord put it in your heart to confess." He came to the meeting the next night happy in the Lord. He afterwards sought for the experience of a clean heart, and the Lord baptized him with the Holy Ghost and fire. The day we left he came to see us. His face was shining and his testimony was clear. He told us that he was glad that the Lord had sent us that way.

A young lady, a good Christian, came to us at this same meeting. She invited us to her house for lunch. She said her mother had been saved in a meeting previous to this, but that her father was an infidel. She wanted us to meet her father, thinking we could talk with him and get him to change his views. He was very angry because the girl and her mother were Christians. Their home was very unhappy.

This invitation seemed to appeal to us, so we accepted. Her father treated us with courtesy until the conversation drifted to salvation, and then at once he was in a rage. He said that he did not believe in religion and that he was an infidel. He quoted Ingersoll, Payne, and others. He was so set in his belief that it was hard to approach him. We asked him if he would not prefer to have his daughter a Christian than to have her a wayward girl and a heart-break to his life. We wondered what harm he could see in her serving the Lord. We begged him not to discourage her. We asked him to come to the meetings, and also asked him to let us pray for him. This request he granted and then we left. When we got outside there came a great pressure on my mind. I said to husband, "I wonder if we have made a mistake by going?"

In a night or two he came to the meeting. While inviting souls to the altar I shook hands with him. I asked the young lady how he was after this meeting, and she said, "He is worse than ever. It makes it so hard for mother and me to live our religion." We told her to keep praying. To our surprise, he came the next night. We were not led to speak to him, and I don't think anyone spoke to him. We could see a change in his countenance. The next day he told his wife that he wished we had spoken to him, that no one seemed to notice him. We began to feel new faith for him. We held on in prayer and fasting day and night. Sunday morning he was back again, and right while I was preaching he sprang to his feet and ran to the altar. He wept like a child, shook with emotion, and cried to God for mercy. He confessed his infidelity and was gloriously saved. This occurred four years ago. The last we heard, he was sanctified and an officer in the church, and the mother and daughter were very happy.

All who came to Jesus during this meeting were not hardened sinners. There were scores of children, some of whom were the Sunday-school scholars who attended from the beginning. They came for several blocks away. Rev. Logan told us that he had faith for a large audience, that he expected to see the Sunday-school rooms opened up and the house filled. These rooms were opened up the second night. People started to come in at six-thirty o'clock, and by seven the place was filled and extra seats borrowed from the neighboring church. The children caught the spirit of the songs, and it was an inspiration to hear them sing, especially after they were saved.

The Lord graciously blessed these meetings in a special way. Influenza was raging, but the interest of the meetings held good. The influenza was especially bad the second winter. (We were with them two winters in succession.) Both young and old, hardened men, with women and children, glorified the Lord by yielding themselves to Jesus.

CHAPTER XXVII
MR. RAY'S SICKNESS AND HEALING

We arrived home from eastern Washington after a series of evangelistic meetings lasting about five months.

Mr. Ray was offered a few days' work, which he accepted. The work was very heavy, and in the exposure he contracted a severe cold, which developed into acute inflammatory rheumatism with rheumatic fever.

For several days we prayed for healing, but he continued to grow worse. We called in Brother Crook to anoint him and to pray. At first he seemed to be helped, but soon relapsed to his former state.

His condition became very serious. After fasting and much prayer, we decided to call a physician. When he came he pronounced Mr. Ray a very sick man and ordered perfect quiet and rest. No visitors were to be allowed in the room. Several days elapsed and husband still failed. The doctor told us he could do no more, and desired another doctor for consultation. They gave me no hope of recovery and thought the end was very near.

In the meantime husband lay with his mouth open and eyes set. He could move neither hand nor foot, and was perfectly helpless.

I had prayed until it seemed I could not say another word. It seemed as though the deep waters were up to my chin and I was trying to hold my head above them and trust in the Lord.

Some friends wanted me to take him to a healer who was in town; others wanted the healer to come to the house. I was in a close place. He had already been anointed and no visible results.

I had had very little sleep and both mind and body were worn. I was persuaded to take rest while my friends would care for Mr. Ray.

I went into a room to be alone, but one of the friends came in and said, "Now, which will you take, wintergreen or God?" Wintergreen was the only medicine we had used. I told her I did not want to call in a healer, and she left me.

I thought of Job's comforters, and went into Brother Ray's room to be by him. When I came out, they had all gone.

There was a young man boarding with us and going to school. He, with others, offered to sit up nights and let me rest, but I said, "If I need you I will call you." I wanted to be alone.

We had already talked over our business affairs. He had told me what undertaker to call, and said, "All is well."

> "The soul that on Jesus has leaned for repose,
> I will not, I will not desert to its foes;
> That soul, though all hell should endeavor to shake,
> I'll never, no, never, no, never forsake."

I prayed the Lord to give me fortitude for the crucial hour. I stayed by his side until four o'clock a. m. I went into another room and tried to pray. But I was impressed to sing. I began to sing, "How firm a foundation," and without feeling I sang, When I reached these last words a flood of tears streamed down my face, and the very depths of my soul broke up. I said, "Thank God, He has come. He has come." I must have stood there some time weeping tears of joy, when I was reminded that I ought to go into Brother Ray's room. I felt as though I had been out in a storm on the deep sea and a big man-of-war had slipped up by my side and rescued me. I dried my tears and stepped out into the hall, and to my surprise Mr. Ray was sleeping as normally as could be. I worshiped Jehovah God. As soon as Mr. Ray began to waken, I stepped to his side and sang softly, "How firm a foundation, ye saints of the Lord," and to my surprise he began to sing with me. We both wept and praised the Lord, saying, "Glory be to God, He is here."

Gradually he regained the use of his limbs and wanted to get up, but through the advice of the physician he was cautious not to overdo. In a short time he was able to sit up and get about the house.

After Dealings of Providence

After his healing, Brother Ray had to learn to walk, as he was as weak as a baby. It was surprising how fast he gained strength. He had been on a diet. He could drink only a little milk and for a while the doctor took that away, and he had only a little water for three or four days. The first thing he wanted to eat was chicken broth. The doctor advised us not to give him any dark meat. A Sister Morgan brought him down some chicken. His appetite was immense. He called me and asked if there was any more broth, and I told him he had eaten it all. He told me to crack the bones and boil them again, but I laughed and said we would buy him a chicken. I was going to telephone the grocer for one, but the door-bell rang just then. I opened the door and, lo, and behold, there was a chicken that had come right on schedule time all the way from Grandview, nearly two hundred miles distant, from a Brother and Sister Branch. We both rejoiced, because we both thought it came direct from the Lord. He had promised to supply all our needs.

The Lord has also promised to make our beds in sickness. He does not say that you will not be sick, but that He will make your bed. Some one has said that He can make a dying pillow soft. Now the test was on. Watch the results.

After a long, weary night, with pain and inflammation that was racking Brother Ray's body, I thought about our finances and the doctor's bill, and the devil said, "Now, how will you get along? You can't eat your home, and what will you do? Don't you wish you had not given out your money so liberally when you were solicited for different things? Don't you wish you had been insured? You could be drawing some aid now. If you had belonged to some kind of a lodge, or union, you would not be in such straits." We had brought some money home with us, as the people had given liberally; but we found our taxes due, and we paid our full fare over the railroad, and in fact we found many a place to use our money, and this sickness had come on us suddenly. We had some money left, but wanted to hold on to it, as we did not know what the end would be. We had left all to follow the Lord and had Him alone to depend on for everything we needed. The devil said, "You are in an awful strait," but I thought, "We have not spent all yet, and we will hold still and trust, and He will see us through." For a few minutes this would bring a cloud, but I did not want husband to know how I felt, so would go away by myself and pray and always get the victory. I would sing and try to keep him cheerful.

One day I thought of the lilies of the valley that were in the yard. Most every spring I would take some of them to a florist and sell. I got a friend to stay with husband and gathered quite a few of the flowers. I had almost always sold them for two or three cents apiece, especially near Mother's Day, and had made as much as eight dollars. This was Saturday. I had been up so much at night that I was tired and footsore. No one wanted the flowers, but I thought, "I must sell them." I went down Second Avenue and up Third for eight or ten blocks, trying all the florists' shops with no success. Finally I tried selling them to individuals on the streets. I met a German boy whom husband had helped to get work, and who was just in from a logging camp. He had a new suit on and told me how well he had gotten along. I thought perhaps he would buy a quarter's worth and I could make my fare home, but he didn't. At last I went to the public market and a woman at one of the flower stands offered me two dollars. I gave them to her, did some trading, and as I came home I thought, "By the help of the Lord I won't let the devil kill me. This is no time to get discouraged." I heard a preacher say, "If you become discouraged, you are whipped already." I began to sing, not because I felt so good, but just because the Lord had promised never to leave or forsake us. The next day someone gave me five dollars, then another and still another. On Monday we received forty dollars in all from the Green Lake society, Rev. Marsh pastor. Then came seventeen dollars at one time from Yakima, and I think fifteen dollars from Grandview. Later on our brother-in-law and sister sent us fifteen dollars, and a little later the brother-in-law sent five dollars more, writing, "I send you five dollars more to clear my conscience. If I had obeyed my mind, I should have sent it at first."

We have tested, tried and proven the Lord many times in our financial troubles, and He has always come to our rescue and I believe He will for every soul who puts trust in Him. I am reminded now of something that came to us last spring.

One Sunday night a Porto Rican boy came into the Mission. He was very filthy and ragged. He couldn't understand our language, but there was a man in the audience by the name of Rev. Stayt, who had been a missionary to Porto Rico. I looked upon the boy in his debauchery and my heart was moved in compassion for him. I asked him if he wanted to get saved. He didn't clearly understand, but said, "Yes." I invited him to come to the altar. He was a Catholic. We called Brother Stayt to talk and pray with him. He told the boy that Jesus could save him and that he might pray to the Lord himself. He seemed to break up in his heart and to get some help from the Lord. When I came home I began to pray that the Lord would give me some clothes for him. We have some friends by the names of Woods and Robinson, who have always come to our rescue when we have found some person in need of help. We called them up and asked them if they had anything they could give us for this boy. They told us they would see, but as we didn't hear from them for a few days we called up some of our friends in the church, and they helped us out. We had everything but a coat for him. Brother Ray had a coat that he wore by day after work, which I gave to the boy. When husband came home that night he said, "You shouldn't have given that coat away, as I will have to put on my next best coat." I told him the Lord would give him another one, but he couldn't see where it would come from, as Mrs. Woods had not responded. She didn't have one at the time, but later got one from a friend. She called me up and told me she had a suit at last. I told her the boy had gone, that I expected he had gotten work, as he was talking about going on a boat. She said that if I didn't find any one who wanted the suit, it might do Brother Ray some good. We brought it home, and it was just his fit and a great deal better than the coat he gave away. We had it cleaned and when he put it on, every one thought he had a new suit. One Sunday at the camp meeting he changed and put on his best suit, and some one said, "Brother Ray has put on his Sunday suit, but the other one looks better." Every one was saying how good his new suit looked.

This is the Lord's doings and it is marvelous in our sight. He tells us to give and it will be given to us again in a good measure, pressed down, shaken together, and running over.

In a few days the Free Methodist conference convened in our city and Brother Ray, although very thin yet, was able to attend. About the last of July there was a camp meeting also in this district, which we attended. Brother Ray was still getting stronger. On the 17th of August, 1922, he was strong enough to go to Chewelah, Washington, to sing in a tent meeting with the Rev. Logan. The tent was pitched in a Catholic community. There was a Catholic school and church adjoining the lot on which the tent was pitched. Some feared this would be a hindrance to the meetings, but it was not so. It was very hot weather and the people sat out on their porches and listened to the sermons. One of the brethren was surprised one night to find one or two of the people who lived in the house next to the Catholic church, close up to the tent on the outside, taking in the sermon. The children came up to the tent on the outside, but not many came in. The Lord certainly helped Brother Logan in preaching the truth, and we believe that they got something from the Lord that they will not be able to throw off.

There was one family of Catholics who sent in provisions from their farm to the parsonage. People came from twenty miles around to the meetings. When we arrived there, Brother Logan told the pastor he thought the tent was too small, and it was, as it was filled to its capacity the first night. The next day the pastor, Rev. Coats, drove one hundred miles to get an addition for the tent. The next night it was filled to its capacity again, and there were lots of people listening on the outside. This meeting, I think, was something new to this community. There was conviction from the very start, but few came to the altar. It was a good meeting and there was good interest. We made a mistake by not holding on longer, but as the meetings had run their scheduled time, and home duties were calling the evangelist, we closed the meeting with good interest and deep conviction upon the people. Two school teachers were at the altar the last night of the meeting, with several others, and eternity alone will tell the results of the meeting.

We bought the few clothes we needed, that is, everything but shoes. Our faith had gone up considerably. We prayed for shoes, but they didn't come then, so I had my shoes patched. Our fare to Chewelah was given to us. Later we went to Daisy. A Sister Maxwell had sent away for a pair of shoes for herself. She noticed my shoes while I was kneeling on the platform. The Lord said to her, "Give Sister Ray those shoes." She asked some one my number. When the meetings were over, she took us in the mountains twelve miles to rest while waiting to go to the next revival. She gave me the shoes. The Lord knew my size, for they were just my fit and have lasted me for three years. They are the most comfortable shoes I ever wore. This is one of the many ways the Lord has helped us out. We did not tell any one our needs. The enemy said, "You are begging," but we were not. The Lord just sent them to us. He sent all our fruit ready canned, and vegetables for the winter.

CHAPTER XXVIII
REVIVAL MEETINGS AT WANETA, WASHINGTON

During the winters of 1920, 1921 and 1922 we held several revival services, the first being at Waneta. Mrs. E. L. Roloff, in the following letter, gives her impressions of the meetings at Waneta:

Waneta, Washington.

Brother and Sister Ray have been a great help in the Waneta community, which is situated between Sunnyside and Grandview in the Yakima Valley, Washington. A few pilgrims had been holding Sunday-school in the Waneta schoolhouse and having cottage prayer meetings. They saw the great need of a revival in the community. It was decided, if possible, to secure Brother and Sister Ray to hold a meeting in the schoolhouse. Our dear brother and sister came in the winter of 1919-1920. The people in the neighborhood responded and attended the meetings. Outsiders came. God's people got down before the Lord in earnest prayer and souls were saved. Oh! that was a great meeting. Nearly all of the converts are now real old-fashioned pilgrims, rejoicing on their way to heaven. There was a colored family in the community by the name of Pollard, with several young men in it. They were all gifted and talented. They were building a fine new home and had planned to give a big dance when it was finished. But the Lord got hold of them. One of the boys was converted a week or so before the revival, and during the meeting the others turned to the Lord. What a happy home now! Instead of the dance, a gracious prayer meeting took place in the home. About seventy people were there and best of all, the Lord was present. Can it ever be forgotten? Brother and Sister Ray built up the work and started it going.

A strong class was organized and now it is branching out into other fields.

These dear souls are dearly loved by the saints, and we pray that many more may be won to Christ through their instrumentality.

Mrs. E. L. Roloff.

In the month of December, 1920, during a series of meetings held by Brother and Sister Ray at the Waneta schoolhouse, near Grandview, Washington, we were wonderfully saved. We had never before attended meetings held by our own race in which a full salvation was preached--the deliverance from sin. After a special prayer meeting which was held in our behalf, it was not long until we were convinced of our need of a Savior.

We are enjoying salvation full and free and today, through the agency of these two pilgrims, we are able to tell the world around of the peace that He alone can give.
Yours in His cause,

Harry and Isaiah Pollard.

I had been saved a few months previous to the meetings in which my brothers were converted, but it was during these same meetings that I received a definite call to preach the gospel. Since then I have had the privilege of living with Brother and Sister Ray in their home while attending Seattle Pacific College, where I studied for the work of the ministry.

My life has been greatly blessed in my association with them while the love of Christ places them as a father and mother to me. May God speed them on their mission of spreading the gospel.

Yours in Christ,

Allen Pollard.

CHAPTER XXIX
REVIVAL MEETINGS
Revival at Blaine, Washington

Our next place was at Blaine, where we went after resting at home for a few weeks. Rev. Rozella Douglas was pastor of the church. There was a small class, nearly all old people, and the most of them living quite a distance from the church. Pastor Douglas would take out her car and bring them to the church, then take them home after the meetings.

The Whatcom County Holiness Association held its all-day monthly meeting there the first day, and afterwards the revival commenced. It began to rain right away and kept it up, with wind and snow, nearly every night of the meetings. It was the most stormy experience we ever had. There were two people who seemed to get definite help; one was a backslider and the other had never been converted. Rev. Mower, a superannuated preacher, belonged to this class. He said he wanted to work as though this was the last revival he would ever be in. He went from house to house, praying and inviting the people out to the meetings. He also carried a burden for souls. There was a good spirit in the meetings and the members all took on new inspiration and quite a bit of conviction was upon the people on the outside. We felt that the meetings were much hindered by the heavy rain. We came home feeling that we had done what we could, with the help of the Lord. Rev. Mower died very suddenly a short time afterwards.

Revival at Burlington, Washington

Our next meeting was at Burlington, Washington. There was a larger membership and the weather more favorable. There we held on for four weeks with good interest and good results. Quite a number of young people prayed through to victory; also a number of adults. We had great liberty in preaching, and several were sanctified through the baptism of the Holy Ghost. One night while we were having an all-night prayer meeting, a young lady arose to her feet and said she had a definite call as a missionary to a foreign field.

This meeting also started in with the Whatcom County Holiness Association all-day meeting. Several ministers were there from the different churches throughout the county. Among them was a Rev. Schultz, pastor of the Methodist Episcopal Church in Burlington. While speaking in the meeting, he told of how he had met us nearly twenty-five years before in services held with a fire-baptized minister and wife by the name of Carmichael.

At that time there were many who came from the logging camps and other places throughout the country to these meetings, and Rev. Carmichael was a fearless preacher who dared to stand for the truth. One night he announced that he was going to preach on the popular sins of the day and invited every one out to hear him. We were surprised at the number of people that were present from every walk of life. The Holy Spirit helped him to uncover sin. Some of the people turned white in the face, others were red. Some spoke out in the meetings. Some arose to their feet and asked permission to speak. Others arose and attempted to speak, but he kept preaching. He sprang from the rostrum to the seeker's bench. As one man arose and started to contradict him, he said, "You sit down," and down he sat, almost as quickly as he got up. He went right on preaching as though nothing had happened. Another and then another arose and he would order them down, and they obeyed. It seemed that they had no power to resist the Word as he preached it with authority. I said, "Lord help us." I thought that we would not be able to get a soul out that night. He gave an altar call, and to our surprise several came forward. He dismissed the audience, while some of the workers stayed. Those that didn't go forward, went away. They were angry. Some stayed outside and talked loudly. Some climbed up to the windows. The crowd looked very threatening and they acted as though they were watching to catch us as we came out. We sang and prayed, while others worked with souls at the altar. The altar service ran late. After a while the crowd began to thin out. One after another left until finally all was quiet. This calls to my mind the time when Paul and Silas prayed and sang in the Philippian jail until their chains fell off and they said to the frightened jailer, "We are all here. Do thyself no harm." No wonder the devil was so angry and made such a fuss. A preacher was born in that meeting and God was glorified.

Rev. Schultz got under conviction for salvation in these meetings, and one night was saved. He came back a week later and was sanctified. He asked us if we remembered him, but as there were quite a few at the altar in this meeting, and as many years had elapsed since then, we had forgotten the incident. However, we were glad to meet one who had been saved so long, who was now preaching full salvation, and was pastor in the town where we were holding the revival meetings. There were times that the church was full and we had to borrow seats from the Methodist Episcopal Church. The pastor and his wife worked faithfully and every one of the members lifted and helped to make the meeting what it was.

The Experience Right After Our Meeting at
Burlington

We closed at Burlington the first of April. This ended the campaign that had begun August 17, 1922. Husband worked through most of the summer, and we went to two camp meetings. The last one was at Burlington and, on the last night of this meeting, we had a heavy rain and we stayed in the tent over a day after the camp meeting closed. We did not want to break up camp in the rain, as we were not coming back home. We had planned to go to White Rock to rest in a little cottage belonging to a friend, but after coming to the camp meeting we received word that it was already rented. This changed our plans, so we stayed over night on the camp grounds, after all the saints had gone home, and of all the places that ever I was at this really seemed the loneliest. After the shouts, hallelujahs, amens, and songs of Zion throughout the week this night, with everything dark, foggy, and quiet, except for the flapping of the tents when the wind stirred them, was like being in a ghoul yard. It made me think of what it will be like to be left alone in this world after the Lord has caught away His saints. I will say that I don't want to be left here after the saints are taken away. It was a long night, for I could not sleep, and as it was damp in the tent and our little oil stove was out of order, I took cold. The next morning as we started away, Rev. A. E. Warren, the presiding elder, came on the grounds to look after the tents and told me I looked so happy. Indeed I was happy to get off those grounds now that the saints were gone. We went from there to Whidby Island and camped for two weeks and preached on Sundays.

My cold had developed into neuralgia, but did not hinder me from working. We were making our plans now for our winter revivals. One night, on the 28th of September, I awakened and my face was very stiff and I felt strange. I thought I was paralyzed at the time, but as I was very tired I rubbed my face a little and, as there was no pain in it, I turned on my side and went to sleep. I had been working very hard and some of the saints had been to visit us from over the district. I didn't realize my condition. This was Wednesday night. I was busy up until Saturday and didn't have time to look in the glass at my face. Sunday morning I hurried off to church. There we heard that Sister Marsh was sick, so went by after services and sang for her. Her daughter said she noticed my face looked strange, but she didn't say anything at the time. I hurried on, ate my lunch and, while I was preparing to go to the Mission in the afternoon, I noticed Brother Ray looking at me so strangely that I asked him what he was looking at. He said, "One of your eyes is larger than the other." I told him I had neuralgia and that Wednesday night I thought I had a stroke. He said that I didn't appear to be suffering; he would let me go on with the day's work. We were in the Sunday afternoon meeting in the Mission and that night were out on the street singing. One of the sisters said, "Sister Ray, your face looks strange." I told her I thought I had had a stroke the week before, but guessed it was just neuralgia. I gave the message that night. There were two souls at the altar. We stayed quite late laboring with them. While on my way home the tears began to run from my eyes in a continual stream. I undertook to close one eye and it seemed as though the lid was dead. Then I remembered how my face felt on Wednesday night. I said, "I believe I am paralyzed." Husband said, "We will see when we get home." I came in, walked right to the dresser and picked up a little hand glass and my face was a sight to be seen. I said, "I'm sure it is paralysis." My mouth was twisted to one side and one eye was crossed, but I couldn't help but smile and I said to my companion, "Somehow I don't feel bad about it." Now I know that a stroke of paralysis is of a more serious nature than I felt it was at the time. I had a doctor's book in the house, so I looked up paralysis and the first thing I saw was facial paralysis, and it gave my symptoms exactly. I remarked again, "Somehow I can't feel bad about it. Better people than I have had paralysis, and why should I complain? I believe the Lord will deliver me." I had no pain, only a kind of stunned feeling, as though I had had a slap in the face. The next day I got up and did my work, as it did not affect me any place except in the face. I went up to a neighbor's, and the moment she saw me coming she said, "Sister Ray, what is the matter? You are sick." She felt quite excited over it. I said, "O Sister Morgan, don't frighten me. I don't feel bad about it, but I have had a stroke of paralysis. I have lived for this day and I can't feel bad about it. I will leave my healing to the will of the Lord."

Rev. John Logan came out and prayed for my healing, and Rev. McReynolds also came out and gave me a tonic which I took, feeling that it was the Lord's will that I do so. This was the first time I had called a doctor for over thirty years. I had almost always taken the Lord as my healer without any remedies. When I was younger I thought I would never have a doctor for myself, but as I had watched others and especially some divine healers with whom I was acquainted and heard their decisions at death, I had learned a lesson that was a help to me at this hour. The Lord does not want us to set our wills in anything. There was one healer who told us that the Lord did not want us to be ironclad, so I had learned through experience a good lesson. I felt that I was unwise along this line. Brother McReynolds told me I would be all right shortly, that I needed a rest. He also prayed with us, and as I prayed for myself I saw His will in it. I said, "The will of the Lord be done." Then I said, "Lord, if it is not Thy will to straighten my face, please put on the glory," and as I prayed for the glory the cross of wearing a crooked face disappeared, and I began to laugh and shout glory. And the glory fell upon me as I was kneeling. It seemed the glory filled the room. I was blessed. I took his advice, used the tonic, took some chiropractic treatments. Inside of two weeks my face was straight, my will was pliable, and my soul was restful, and I learned that the Lord has more ways than one to heal the body.

Revival at Grandview, Washington

"The wilderness and the solitary place shall be glad for them; and the desert shall rejoice, and blossom as the rose." Surely God has poured out His Spirit most abundantly upon us here in Grandview, and in Waneta. Rev. L. P. Ray and wife have been with us. Beginning about the first week of November, at Sunnyside, Washington, for a month the Lord helped them to preach His gospel, and as a result the church was greatly strengthened and helped. After that Brother and Sister Ray held a one-week meeting at Waneta. Seven were wonderfully saved and sanctified, and our work has had another mighty uplift at that new appointment. Beginning at Grandview, December 27th, and continuing until January 22nd, one of the most blessed meetings was held that the writer has ever witnessed. From the very beginning God began to bless Brother and Sister Ray with unusual liberty and freedom, the church catching the vision of their part in the work. Immediately they began to fast and pray, some taking only one meal a day while the meetings lasted, and nearly all fasting a part of the time. God honored this sacrifice, and began to send out His convicting Spirit, until, as in the days of Finney, men and women about us could neither eat nor sleep. Several came to the parsonage, crying under dreadful conviction, so that when we began to pray with them, they would soon break through and be saved. One bachelor, who has for years lived across the street from the parsonage, got under such conviction that he could not sleep and was wonderfully saved, and to hear this man pray and testify in the meeting is beyond anything words can describe. Some twenty-five or thirty were clearly saved, about sixty were definitely helped, a large number were sanctified and several healed. Twenty-five have already united with the church and many more will follow. Well, we have had an OLD-FASHIONED REVIVAL. Brethren, do not say we can not have such revivals as they had years ago. We can when we pay the price. Brother and Sister Ray assumed great responsibilities. They fasted and prayed day and night. The church did likewise. At different times we had to turn folks away who could not get inside the doors. The Holy Ghost came, and we were all filled with the Spirit. Well, the effect of this wonderful meeting will go on and on. We do not expect it to ever end. The people of Grandview love Brother and Sister Ray. We had them in the parsonage, and we shall ever feel that this place is more sacred because these holy people have been here. Never have we seen such mighty demonstrations in praying, preaching and singing of God's blessed gospel.

Rev. E. H. Harmer.

CHAPTER XXX
TRIBUTES TO MR. AND MRS. L. P. RAY
Testimonial from Brother Witteman

My acquaintance with Brother Lloyd and Sister Emma Ray dates back about twenty years when I first met them in the missions and the street meetings in Seattle, Washington.

They were singing and preaching the old-time religion to the crowds which were attracted by the melody and pathos of holy song. Singing with the Spirit, and with the understanding also, has been a prominent part of their ministry of the Gospel of Christ. A great many of their songs are peculiarly their own. They also possess great liberty and power in testimony, telling of their rescue from the bondage of sin.

How often I have seen the men on the street listening with tears running down their grimy faces, as Emma Ray told them of a mighty Lord who is standing with outstretched arms to lift them up and save them. She is mighty in the Scriptures, too, while preaching. I remember one occasion when she was preaching (a number of preachers being present in the congregation) and urging the necessity of living religion as well as professing it, she suddenly said with great emphasis, "Come out into the open! Come out into the open! Practise what you preach!" I have seen that a prominent part of their work for God is living their religion in the home. Sometimes they have taken a boy or a man that was in need of everything in the way of food and clothing. After getting him cleaned up, and fed up for a few days and doing a lot of praying with and for him, they clothed him from head to foot and brought him down to the Mission looking like a respectable gentleman.

Emma Ray is especially one of the Lord's anointed in prayer. How often have I felt the very powers of darkness give way and heaven come down as she prayed for lost sinners.

Brother and Sister Ray have been a great encouragement to me in the Mission, especially in the testing times, and dealing with those who walked disorderly and had to be reproved and dealt with; yes, in warning the unruly and comforting the feebleminded, and in supporting the weak. It takes deep piety to do this, and they have that kind.

We say of some people that if they were gone, it would be difficult to fill their places. This is true of Brother and Sister Ray.

I hope they may long remain active in the service of the Master, in their God-appointed place and mission.

C. H. Witteman.

Rev. and Mrs. L. P. Ray are among our most estimable workers in the Olive Branch Mission, having worked for nearly twenty years in the battle against sin and crime.

They have been among our best spiritual advisers in times of important phases and conditions of the work of the Mission. They have carried the burden longer, and faced the issues, as they came in our work, longer than any other workers.

We heartily recommend them to the gospel work anywhere.

Mrs. R. G. Witteman.

To Whom it May Concern:--

Having had the services of Brother and Sister Ray in special revivals in churches over which I was pastor, it affords me great pleasure to commend the blessed and efficient evangelistic work they are doing under God.

For nineteen years I have known Brother and Sister Ray. I have never known or heard of them other than as most worthy Christians and as ardent, faithful evangelists. Truly, Brother and Sister Ray belong to that class of whom Saint Paul speaks in Eph. 4: 11-16.

Their work, which is peculiarly fitted to themselves, as evangelists, with their influence in the quickened spiritual life of the churches and in the large number of additions, will be felt for many years to come in the communities in which they minister.

May it please God to cause this book to be a blessing to all who read it, and may it be the cause of much inspiration to the Christian Church.

I can truthfully say that sectarianism, commercialism, and sensationalism are never made prominent in their revival meetings. They seek to save lost souls, to edify and establish professed Christians. Any financial income to them from the sale of their book will be well deserved, and appreciated when they can by reason of old age or sickness do little or no evangelistic work.

Sincerely in His name,

Rev. F. L. Donohoo,

Minister African M. E. Church,
April 22, 1925. Bremerton, Wash.

Mrs. Morgan's Testimony

In the fall of 1902 we were first privileged to meet our Brother and Sister L. P. Ray.

At that time they were conducting holiness meetings. During the following winter they had charge of the services in the "Strangers' Rest Mission." The untiring efforts of Brother and Sister Ray as they stood on the streets night after night, and also in the Mission hall, telling the "old, old story," won many souls to Christ.

The congregations were composed largely of drinking and debauched men and women. One evening during the service we were greatly startled as a poor drunken man fell down the steps into the hall. Kind hands helped him to his feet, and led him to a seat near the front. The truth penetrated his poor soul, and after an hour of earnest prayer he was instantly sobered, was saved, and glorified God.

Night after night Brother and Sister Ray told what God had done for them, never seeming to tire.

While the writer was helping in a tabernacle meeting at Blaine, in the summer of 1903, we were requested to accompany a band of workers to hold a series of meetings at Pleasant Valley, about eight miles distant, and imagine our surprise when we learned that this was the place where Brother and Sister Ray had worked so hard. The community far and near was ripe for a revival, but still no one seemed to have the courage to make a start until one night a young man, W. R. Grout, deliberately left his seat and knelt at the altar.

Now came the fruition of Brother and Sister Ray's labors. Oh, the days that followed! Wrongs were righted, confessions were made, and the young people who had tried to sing Brother and Sister Ray's songs in derision, now could be heard a mile away or more, singing their new-found joy.

There were many remarkable conversions, and a great company was saved and sanctified, and several went into the work.

One remarkable conversion was that of a young man, Oscar Ray. He had many times said in sport that he was a full brother to Brother Ray. Now he was a brother in the Lord. While amusing his young friends, he sometimes took a text and preached. More than once he became convicted and rushed from the room. Eventually he came to the meetings and fell at the altar. After struggling for several nights, God came with pardoning love to his soul. He rejoiced for over an hour, then preached such a remarkable sermon on hell and the judgment that souls rushed to the altar, many falling in the aisles, while others prayed, all crying for mercy. Several were saved that night, among them my husband.

I cannot refrain from telling of one very remarkable case of deliverance from demon possession, through the prayers and faith of Sister Ray.

A young lady, who had become so mentally depressed over the death of her mother, had been advised by her physician to try a change of place by travel, was visiting with her sister in Seattle. Hearing about the camp meeting at Ferndale, she decided to attend and was placed in our care.

The tents being overcrowded, one night it became necessary to let this young lady tent with another Christian young woman. In the early morning we were aroused by the startling news that the young lady had gotten up and gone to the river to drown herself. Several ran in different directions, and after going about eight miles, Sister Ray and I found her.

While men in a near-by mill were shouting in derision, "Hallelujah, praise the Lord," Sister Ray raised her hands and shouted back with all her might, "Yes, glory to God!" Sister Ray then requested the friends who had gathered to put the poor girl into the buggy, but she resisted with all her strength. Finally after getting her into the buggy, Sister Ray laid her hands on the young woman's head and commanded the demon in Jesus' name to come out. Instantly the devil left her and she became perfectly quiet and restored. She found perfect deliverance. She was well educated and had been a school teacher up to the time of her affliction.

We telephoned to her sister at Seattle. She came up immediately, saw her sister calm, blessed, and in her right mind. She, too, sought the Lord and was born again. They did not have to travel any more. They joined the church. The afflicted one went to teaching again. She lived a few years and died triumphantly in the faith.

Cascade Tunnel, Washington,
February 4, 1916.

Dear Sister Ray:--

Just a line to-day to let you all know I am still in the mountains, snowed in. A train has not moved from here since last Monday night. We have had a fearful storm here; no accidents that I can find out, but plenty of snow. We have had over thirty-seven feet of snow up here this winter. It is clear and cold to-day. I wish you could get a glimpse of the scenery up here. It's just grand. If I can I will send you a few photos of it. Some of the boys have cameras, and I will try to get a few views of snow-slides, etc. I am still on the "Rock" and praising God every day, and asking His help, and praying for all the folk in Seattle. Some of the boys up here look at me strangely when they hear me singing "On the Rock" and "Yield Not to Temptation." A lot of them have whisky and wine and have offered it to me, but I have explained what I did in Seattle, and they all know just how I stand, and don't even drink or have it around where I am now. I haven't found one real converted man since I came up here, but they are all like the men that came into the Mission and sat in the back seats. All say the same thing when I ask them if they are right with God--always the same, "As near as we can be." I have some pretty good facts to put up to them in my case, and cases of others I know, and I tell them about it, too.

And I am setting the example, or practising what I preach, and they watch me pretty close, and some have changed and a lot of them are under conviction, I know. One lad asked me to let him see my Bible, and he has read aloud a number of times to some of the fellows right here in the office. I have a song book Mr. Ray gave me, and we are learning the songs. They are all railroad men, and as a rule fine fellows personally, but don't get much chance to get to church or even to read a Bible. Sunday, if I am here, I am going to have a real old mission meeting. I've got the only Bible I know of in camp, so I guess I'll have to do the reading of it, as I don't know much about preaching. We can praise God and sing and pray so, if we get that far along, I know that God will be with us and bless and help us in our struggles. Will let you know in my next letter just how we make out and try and get every one thinking about his soul. God bless you and Brother Ray and each and every one of the Mission workers. Please give my best regards to them all. Would love to write each one of them, but know how it is, and my stamps are limited--two left. If you get a chance, drop me a line here, and if I'm not here they will forward it to me. Tell Sister Richey I dreamed that she had joined the Red Cross Society and I saw her plainly getting on board a steamship. I lost track of the dream. Hope you are all well, and that I'll keep right with God. God bless you all.
From your isolated friend,

E. E.

Warren, Ohio,
November 18, 1917.

Dear Brother and Sister Ray:--

Just a line to let you know I haven't forgotten you, even if I never have written you. I lost your address and am taking a chance on your getting this letter. This is Sunday, and I have been to church here. We surely had a grand sermon. I wish I could see you personally and tell you, Brother Ray, that I am still saved. I am working for the Postal Telegraph Company here and am doing well. We have the old-time religion here in Warren, as you folks have in Seattle. I often think of you all there and wonder if the little Olive Branch Mission is still saving men as it was when I was there--saving them to keep saved. It is wonderful what you folks did for me, and I never cease to pray for you. How are all the brothers and sisters there, especially Mrs. Witteman? She is a grand old lady. I have been to Italy and England since I saw you last, but in all my travels I have never forgotten the teaching I learned of God while I was in Seattle. Praise God! Well, Brother Ray, I have a thousand things I want to write you, but am going to postpone them while waiting to see if this letter reaches you O. K. When I hear from you, I will write you again, telling you lots of little things that I know you will like to hear. So I am going to say good-bye for this time. Write me soon and kindly let me have your address and Sister Witteman's address. I hope this will find you well, also Sister Ray and all the Mission workers. Give them all my best regards. Tell them I am still on the Rock. You remember my favorite song, "On the Rock at Last." Write when you can find time.
Your friend,

E. E.

It was in July, 1902, at a camp meeting held in Sellwood, a suburb of Portland, Oregon, where I first met Brother and Sister Ray. They were returning from the South, where they had been visiting and doing missionary work among their people. They stopped over a few days in Portland, and attended the meeting in which they were a valuable asset. Sister Ray preached one of her characteristic and soul-stirring sermons, and their singing was a blessing and inspiration to all.

I was reminded of a discussion I had with a fair-faced man from southern Missouri. He was of the opinion that the Negro did not have a soul. If he had been present and had seen Brother and Sister Ray, and had heard them sing, testify, preach and pray, under the blessing of God, he would have been thoroughly convinced that the Negro had a soul in which God deigned to dwell.

Later, while attending our school in Seattle (known then as Seattle Seminary, but now as Seattle Pacific College), I was delighted to meet Brother and Sister Ray again. They were conducting a mission in the slum districts of Seattle. The name of the mission was "Strangers' Rest," and truly it was made a place of rest to many heavy-burdened and weary souls.

Brother and Sister Ray were full of faith and the Holy Spirit, and consequently they were filled with the love of God. They believed that Christ died for all men, even the lowest of the low, and that the grace of God was equal to any case. Such love and faith caused them to labor tirelessly but hopefully, and their labors were rewarded. Many diamonds were dug out of the rough and brightly polished--"made meet for the Master's use."

We had opportunity to put in our bit of strength in fighting the great enemy of righteousness, who in those days was so deeply entrenched in the slum district of Seattle. Seattle was an open town. Saloons, gambling houses and other places of vice were thronged. It was common for the mission worker to be persecuted. Rough men were capable of doing rough and wicked acts. We remember one street meeting when the mission workers were a target and eggs were ammunition. The leaders of the mission, Brother and Sister Ray, were unmoved, and rejoiced that they were counted worthy to receive persecution for Jesus' sake.

They have proven themselves capable, under the grace of God, of rescuing precious souls from the cesspool of sin in the slums. Their ability and adaptability to labor for the salvation of all men make them successful evangelists to all classes.

Sister Ray has been and is a stirring preacher. She believes it to be the duty of a preacher to stir the people to action. Her definition of a preacher is to the point: "Preachers are God's stirring spoons to stir the people up." Many preachers would not go amiss if they put that definition into practise.

They have labored extensively and successfully as evangelists throughout the Northwest. Many souls have been added to the church through their labors. Certainly they will not have starless crowns. They have not labored in vain. God has blessed them with that wisdom which makes men soul-winners. They will be among that class which shines as declared in Scriptures, "And they that be wise shall shine as the brightness of the firmament; and they that turn many to righteousness as the stars for ever and ever."

The years of tireless labors have drawn on the physical powers of Brother and Sister Ray and they cannot be as active as in the past, but their love for souls has not waned. They are sending out this book, which is a record of the Lord's gracious dealings with them, and of the powerful manifestations of God's power in the salvation of souls.

We join with them in prayer that the book may bring glory to Jesus Christ our Savior, and be a great blessing to its readers.

Rev. Harry E. Kreider,
District Elder, Seattle-Tacoma District,
Washington Conference.

In 1899 we were assigned the pastorate of Seattle First Free Methodist Church, where we met Brother and Sister Ray, and had the privilege of receiving them into the church. Having been associated with them also in several revival meetings, and believing that the time to commend others is while they are still with us, we gladly contribute a few words of commendation.

During the first years of our acquaintance with them, we were impressed by their godly lives and deep spirituality; their loyalty to the church, and unswerving fidelity to the Lord. During the intervening years this impression has been deepened, and in all our association with them we have never known them to speak or act in any way unbecoming children of God.

We have always felt ourselves very fortunate when we were able to secure them for revival services. Their preaching, exhortations, and singing have always been inspiring, and under God they have been very successful in winning souls to Christ.

Brother and Sister Ray are endowed with an unusual insight into spiritual things, and quick to detect error in the various new religious movements with which they have been brought in contact during these years. While many older in experience have been carried away by the various winds of doctrine, they have never been moved.

They abide under the shadow of the Almighty, and His blessing falls upon them again and again in testimony and in song. We know that life has been made better by our acquaintance with them.

They have been abundant in labor for the Master, and we are sure that when their journey is over the Lord will say, "Well done." Many who have been saved through their efforts will welcome them into realms of the blest.

Rev. A. N. West.

Dear Brother and Sister Ray:--

Perhaps it may prove an encouragement to you to know that you were instrumental in my eternal salvation, which has meant so much to me.

During your evangelistic compaign at Pleasant Valley, Washington, I was living with my parents about one mile from the church in which you preached and sang the gospel. When the news spread through the community that "colored preachers" were going to tell "white folks" where they were going, the frolicking crowd of young people (of whom I was one) planned a time of great fun. No doubt you remember how the young folk swarmed into the church, chewing gum, cracking peanuts, lighting matches, etc., but, Sister Ray, we knew not what we were doing. Your patience and kindness and love for us young folk, demonstrated from the pulpit, began to be felt, and Holy Ghost conviction seized the crowd, until one young person after another said he didn't know what was wrong with him, but he didn't feel like disturbing the meeting any more.

Your labors at Pleasant Valley will have their reward in heaven, for the seed was sown for a great harvest, which came just a short time afterward, in which about sixty people were converted, over thirty sanctified, and about twelve called into the ministry. To God be all the glory for sending you our way.

E. W. Wilder.

To Brother and Sister Ray:

It is really a great pleasure to me to speak and write a word for dear Brother Ray and his wife.

In the early part of 1890, when in a great battle with the devil and his host, it was my pleasant privilege to meet Brother and Sister L. P. Ray in the slums of Kansas City, Missouri, in my mission, then called Union Mission, located at Eighteenth and McGee streets. Brother Ray and his wife often attended the meetings and took an active part, and gave their splendid testimonies as to what God had done for them and, when not in our Mission meetings, they were in different missions and churches among their own people, telling the wonderful story, how Jesus had come into their lives, and how gloriously they were kept by the Holy Spirit.

Whenever they came to our meetings, they were on fire for God, and they surely made it hot for the old devil. I was glad to see them come into our meetings and hear them give out the Word of God to a dying people.

They were true and loyal, and faithful in the discharge of their duties. They did much good in Kansas City, and many precious souls were saved under their ministry. I have always found them ready to go at a moment's notice, ready to pray, ready to sing, ever ready to take an active part when called upon.

Their labor among us and the different missions and churches made an impression for good, and the influence was felt whenever they appeared before an audience. God blessed them in their earnest efforts and appeals. Their good work will never be forgotten. I trust and pray that God will pour out His Holy Spirit upon them and make them a great blessing to many hungry souls. Wherever they go, they have my prayers and the prayers of my faithful workers. Such Spirit-filled, holy, sanctified people as Brother Ray and his wife bring happiness to other lives. God grant that they may yet do much good.

C. F. Ferguson,
Superintendent and Pastor of Union Mission,
Eighteenth and McGee Streets, Kansas
City, Missouri.

In the year 1902, Brother and Sister L. P. Ray came to our neighborhood and began a meeting in a little church near-by. I, being a young man of nineteen years, and always curious about any new thing, went to the meeting for the entertainment, and as Brother and Sister Ray seemed honest and so earnest in song, prayer, and preaching, I couldn't help admiring them for it. They sang, I remember now after twenty-two years, "Oh, the downward road is crowded with unbelieving souls." My hair would rise when they sang it, for I knew it was the truth and that I was on the road. And then they would pray and tell the Lord that the people were lost and how they wanted to see them saved, and would ask the Lord to convict them of sin.

I could see they were interested in me and I began to feel uneasy. The preaching was of such a nature that anyone could understand it, and it brought up my past life and revealed the future so clearly that I decided to seek the Lord at the altar of prayer. The evening I made the decision, when the invitation was given, a neighbor, seeing my misery, came to me at the first opportunity to urge me to seek the Lord. Stubbornness arose in my heart and I told the most dangerous lie of my life. I said, "I don't believe there is anything in it," and I continued to say that, and within a few hours the conviction was gone, and I was as hard as before the meeting began. Never since has conviction come to me as strong as at that time and I believe I almost went too far.

The following year, on September 22, I was saved in a tent meeting and have enjoyed companionship with the Lord for nearly twenty-two years, and my testimony to-day is, "The Christian life is man's greatest privilege on earth." Brother and Sister Ray have a very warm place in my affections, as well as all others who were instrumental in my conversion. I would say to all who read these lines, "Be patient; do not give up. Our Lord has said, 'Be thou faithful unto death, and I will give you a crown of life.' "

Yours in patient waiting,

W. R. Grout.

2716 Woodland Ave.,
Kansas City, Mo.

In the year 1900 Brother and Sister Ray came to Kansas City, Missouri, to visit us and it pleased God to have them pitch battle against sin in a certain portion of Kansas City called Hick's Hollow. The people were very wicked and would drink, fight, shoot and kill. It was a very rough place.

One day they were looking for a house for their Mission, and they made the remark that they wanted to get into the place where the devil was the strongest. The Scripture says, "A little child shall lead them." So a little boy who lived down there heard them and he said, "Oh, I can show you where the devil is the strongest." He took them to a corner, 590 Lydia Street, and there they opened the first mission in the place. They suffered many hardships and worked among these people, who never gave them a cent to help support the work, but who begged for help from them. Brother Ray worked in the daytime and preached the gospel at night on the streets. My sister was like faithful Aaron, ever holding up his hands. They also carried the first band of colored workers to the county jail to preach to the prisoners of their own race. Many were saved and came to see the error of their ways, and to-day, after twenty years, the work is still going on. I can truthfully say that their work was a success, and their labors will never be forgotten.

In accordance with Sister Ray's request, my husband and I have made an investigation of Hick's Hollow, and I can see that the moral and spiritual conditions are now much improved over what they were when they were here. There is not much improvement in the buildings. The old mission has been changed into a duplex house. The mission that Brother A. B. Ross ran is a Baptist Church mission now. There is a very good school in the locality, the same one that was here when they were here, but much improved. In the old O'Brien grocery store is another mission hall, and altogether there are ten churches and missions.

Many of the people here have immigrated from the South. There are not many white people, and few foreigners. The people in general are more spiritual than in many of our better class churches.

From your loving sister,

Mrs. M. D. Ross.

Dear Sister Ray:--

I am glad the Lord has put it on your heart to write a book telling of your life and work. I praise the Lord for what He has done for you and for the many souls you have brought to the Lord. There is no one happier over your work than I am just to see what God has done. Seeing you when you knelt at the altar, and when you said "Yes" to the Lord that night in James Street African M. E. Church.

I am thankful that you stuck to the faith and that you have been the instrument in His hands of saving souls.

May the book bring the blessings that your life has brought to others.

Mrs. Lucretia Roy,

Byrn Mawr, Washington.
Seattle, Washington,
December 15, 1924.

Dear Brother and Sister Ray:--

    I remember the time, now more than twenty years ago, when you attended our meetings in old Battery Street M. E. Church. About that time we also had Sister Amanda Smith for a meeting. I was attracted by your singing, as were others. I invited both of you to come out and sing before the congregation. The people were delighted with your singing, and the public soon became acquainted with you. From that time you have been in great demand and the Lord has used you in many places to accomplish a glorious work. I know that many souls have been blessed by your singing and, I trust, many have been led into the kingdom. Go on with your singing for Him until you shall take up the "new song" in the land beyond the river.

As ever your brother and friend,

H. D. Brown.

CHAPTER XXXI
FAVORITE SONGS

Among the many songs we sing, the Lord has put His special endorsement on the song entitled, "The Old-time Religion." Although we have sung it upon the streets for nearly thirty years, it has never grown old to us. It has inspired and helped us to call up an audience the same as the ringing of a church bell. When it has been rainy, and no one has cared to stop and listen, it has always helped out. At times when some unwise worker has talked too long, and his testimony has become dry and void of the Spirit, and our crowd has left us; when some soap-box infidel has been speaking across the street, ridiculing the Bible and the Christian workers, calling them sky-pilots, burlesquing their songs by singing the same tune with words of blasphemy, the Spirit has suggested that we sing "The Old-time Religion" song. Then the crowds came from far and near and gathered around us and listened, some with tears in their eyes. We have watched its effect on the people and the Lord has especially honored and blessed this song to us. After the singing has drawn the crowds, we preach to them the way of salvation.

At one time a man stepped up to me while I was singing on the streets and asked if I thought the Lord would hear a colored woman's prayer. He made me think of a cartoon drawn by an artist, Mr. Beard, and which appeared in a little prohibition paper called "The Ram's Horn."

There was a poor, faint and thirsty man, almost starved for water. He was creeping through a hot, sandy desert and suddenly came upon a large rock, from which water was streaming. Under its drippings sat all kinds of labeled cups to drink from, such as Baptist, Methodist, Presbyterian, and all kinds of sects.

Underneath the picture were these words, "Never mind the vessel; it's the water you want." Poor man, his eyes were upon the vessel instead of the water.

Jesus has promised to be in us a well of water, giving us eternal life, by taking away the curse of sin that is destroying the souls of men. "The Spirit and the bride say, Come. And let him that heareth say, Come. And let him that is athirst come. And whosoever will let him take of the water of life freely."

That poor man needed a Savior.

The Old-time Religion

Give me the old-time religion,
Give me the old-time religion,
Give me the old-time religion,
It's good enough for me.

It was good for our mothers,
It was good for our mothers,
It was good for our mothers,
It's good enough for me.

It makes soul and body happy,
It makes soul and body happy,

It makes soul and body happy,
It's good enough for me.

It was tried in the fiery furnace,
It was tried in the fiery furnace,
It was tried in the fiery furnace,
It's good enough for me.

It will be good when you are dying,
It will be good when you are dying,
It will be good when you are dying,
It's good enough for me.

It will be good when the world's on fire,
It will be good when the world's on fire,
It will be good when the world's on fire,
It's good enough for me.

It will take you home to heaven,
It will take you home to heaven,
It will take you home to heaven,
It's good enough for me.

Just give me the old-time religion,
Just give me the old-time religion,
Just give me the old-time religion,
It's good enough for me.

The Submarine Song

God's command came unto Jonah, telling him where to go,
When he learned 'twas that great city, Nineveh, he said
"No."
He from Joppa sailed to Tarshish, feeling so awfully mean,
God "prepared" a fish to take him, riding in a submarine.

CHORUS
Never take a submarine trip, let us take a flying airship,
Meet Christ in the sky.
Submarines for all backsliders, aeroplanes for higher riders;
Meet Him way up on high.

Underneath the deep blue ocean Jonah began to pray,
Submarines may suit some people, Jonah didn't like that
way;

When this prophet pledged his service to Nineveh he would
go,
Then his submarine got orders, landed him upon the shore.
There are some who doubt the Bible, saying, "How could
it be
That a fish could swallow Jonah, carry him through the
sea?"
Submarines are hard to locate, specially if you're blind,
But if one comes along to get you, you are not hard to find.

Many folks are often captured, taken in a lower stream,
All because of disobeying Jesus, the Nazarene.
While the stormy winds are rising, manage your aeroplane
right,
If a U-boat tries to find you, never can it reach your height.

Christian Prospect

O come, all ye scattered race,
And the Savior's love embrace;
You may see His smiling face yet with care.
He is on the giving hand,
Will you come at His command?
And you'll with the angels stand, over there.

CHORUS
Over there, over there,
There's a land of pure delight, over there;
We will lay our burdens down,
And at Jesus' side sit down,
And we'll wear a starry crown, over there.

We are going through the land,
As a missionary band,
Leading sinners by the hand to Christ's care.

That salvation He may give,
And they turn to Him and live,
In the pretty world of light, over there.

Oh, consider our stand
When He took us by the hand,
From that dreadful bar of sand to His care.
And He placed us on the rock,

And He owns us for His flock,
And we're marching to His fold, over there.

Yes, He went to Calvary,
And they nailed Him on the tree,
That poor sinners such as we He might spare
From the bitter pangs of death;
He did with His dying breath,
Seal us everlasting life over there.

By the Savior's gentle hand
Gospel flows from land to land,
Through the missionary band in His care;
And they feel the precious truth,
While the harvest is so great,
And the joys it will create, over there.

When I Was a Sinner I Heard the People Say

When I was a sinner I heard the people say,
If you want to be converted you had better pray;
I trusted in them, for they had known the Lord,
And He had promised them a sure reward.

CHORUS
Jesus says, "You go, and I'll go with you;
You preach the gospel, and I'll preach through you."
Lord, if I go and tell them what you say,
They must believe on Thee.

When I started out to pray,
Let me tell you what the Spirit said to me;
"Come unto me, I am the way,
And I will teach you to watch and pray."

My hands were tied, my feet were bound,
The elements opened and the love came down;
The voice I heard sounded so sweet,
Love ran down to the soles of my feet.

"I am He whom you seek to find,
I am He who turned the water to wine."
He's taken my feet out of the miry clay,
And placed them on the rock of eternal ages.

CHORUS
Oh, He's taken my feet out of the miry clay,
Placed them on the rock of eternal ages.
For Jesus is coming after His own,
And we shall dwell around the dazzling throne.

But I left old hell in a mighty uproar,
I never expect to go back any more.
Before I'd lie in hell one day
I'd sing and pray myself away.

--Author Unknown.

Lead Me On

Traveling to the better land,
O'er the desert's scorching sand,
Father, you may grasp my hand
To lead me on.

CHORUS
Lead me on, lead me on,
Father, you may grasp my hand
To lead me on.

When at Marah, parched with heat,
I the sparkling fountains greet,
Make the bitter waters sweet;
Lead me on.

When the wilderness is near,
Show me Elim palms grow near,
And her wells as crystal clear;
Lead me on.

Through the water, through the fire,
Never let me fall or tire,
Every step brings Canaan nigher.
Lead me on.

Bid me stand on Nebo's height,
Gazing on the land of light,
Then transported with the sight;
Lead me on.

When I stand on Jordan's brink,
Never let me fear nor shrink;
Hold me, Father, lest I sink;
Lead me on.

When the victory is won,
And eternal life's begun,
Up to glory we will run;
Lead me on.

I'm On the Rock at Last

My little bark was tempest-tossed, and drifting with the
tide;
I had no chart or compass true, no pilot for my guide;
A life-boat came to rescue me when hope was almost past;
I entered, and now I can sing, I'm on the rock at last.

CHORUS
I'm on the rock at last, I'm on the rock at last,
No more I sail a stormy sea, my wanderings are past;
I stepped into the life-boat, and now my anchor's cast,
Oh, hallelujah, praise the Lord, I'm on the rock at last.

I built my house upon the sand which could not stand the
test,
For when the storms of life swept o'er, my heart was sore
distressed;
I called on Christ to save me from the fury of the blast;
I've found the sure foundation now, I'm on the rock at last.

When Satan comes to buffet now, when fiercely beats the
tide,
I do not fear the angry gale, but in the rock I hide.
And there I sing with trusting heart, tho' clouds may over-
cast;
I'm safely hidden in the Cleft, I'm on the rock at last.

And here upon the rock I'll stay, till Jesus comes again,
And catches up His waiting bride a thousand years to reign;
And then I'll sing this song anew with all earth's sorrows
past;
All glory be to Calvary's Lamb, I'm on the rock at last.

Up-to-date Religion

Creeds there are unnumbered everywhere we go,
And new-fangled theories pass to and fro;
But since Jesus wonderfully saves, I find
That up-to-date religion is the old-time kind.

CHORUS
Up-to-date religion is the old time kind,
That which makes anew the heart and gives us peace of
mind;
Every soul that comes to Jesus soon will find
That the up-to-date religion is the old time kind.

Many seem to think that these enlightened years
Have no place for Calvary with its blood and tears;
All we need to do is to improve the mind,
But up-to-date religion is the old-time kind.

Some would have us think that Christ was not divine;
Others say His life was but a light to shine;
But they are at least two thousand years behind,
For up-to-date religion is the old-time kind.

Sin is just as black as in the days of yore,
Hearts are just as broken as they were before;
Calvary's cross is still the hope of all mankind,
And up-to-date religion is the old-time kind.
Copyrighted by Lillenas Pub. Co.

Mustard-seed Faith

This mustard-seed faith, hear Paul make it plain,
Turn over to the Hebrews, there he'll explain;
And in the eleventh chapter at the first you'll read
It's "substance of the things unseen."

CHORUS
Oh, this old-time religion and the mustard-seed faith,
It sanctifies wholly by a second work of grace;
It helps us on to glory on a satisfied line;
With this old-time religion we are feeling mighty fine.

This mustard-seed faith grows well in the soil,
Though planted any time of year 'twill never spoil,

It blossoms out in holiness and bears pure love;
This special seed comes from above.

This mustard-seed faith won't mix with the world,
Which makes it mighty fine for the boys and girls,
The older folks, the middle aged, the rich and poor.
This is the faith that will endure.

This mustard-seed faith bears fruit the year round,
And every time the tree's seen it's loaded down;
The fruit it bears is gentleness and peace and joy,
There is no law that can destroy.
Copyrighted by W. P. Jay.

CHAPTER XXXII
DIVINE GUIDANCE

Now as we are nearing the end of our allotted time and as we take a retrospect of the leadings of the Lord, we can see the plain path all the way down the line. The nearer we get to our heavenly home, the clearer the mission. There were some things that we could not understand at first, that stand out as clear and as plain as the noon-day sun today. Some have mocked us and thought we were beside ourselves in taking the way that the Lord has led us, but we could hear a voice behind us saying, "This is the way, walk ye in it." I have often recalled the Scriptures, saying, "A voice behind you"; also the passage saying, "Goodness and mercy shall follow me all the days of my life." The Lord not only leads, but He follows.

I got a lesson one winter here in Seattle. It had been snowing for several days. The snow became deeper all the time, and traffic was almost at a standstill. One night it looked as though it would lighten up, so we ventured out to the Mission in the city. When we came out late that night, to our surprise we found that there were about two feet of snow. After waiting a long time a street-car came. We lived about seven miles out in the suburbs of the city. When we had gotten about half way home, the car came to a standstill. It was snow-bound. Finally the passengers began to get off to walk home. The snow had greatly increased in depth. The paths on the walks and streets were all filled in, and the best place for us to walk was on the car track. We started out on our three-and-one-half mile journey. It was still snowing. The great flakes looked like falling feathers. We prayed as we walked. I kept slipping, as there were places on the track between the ties where there were deep holes. We couldn't see them and would step upon the snow and go down. My husband got behind me and, as I would start to slip, he would take hold and help me to move on, catching me before I could go down. Just so the Lord, in the person of the Holy Spirit, has been as a voice behind us, saying, "This is the way, walk ye in it." He has ever kept us on the track. Although the way has been sometimes rugged, His grace has upheld us, and has kept our feet from slipping.

We were so glad to find His way. When we were saved the world with its attractions and pleasures lost its hold on us. Some of the things that are legitimate and that others can do and enjoy, we have no desire for. There has always been so much to be done and we enjoy doing the Master's will, and we are both longing for a closer walk with God. We never have seen the place where we could go out just to have a good time or have been inclined to go over a city sight-seeing, while a battle has been on for souls. In fact we have gone to many places to work and, when we left could not tell what the town looked like any further than what was seen on the way to the train, or passed when in our car. While we were in the east some of our friends wanted to give us a good time, but there were so many who were unsaved, especially our own kindred, that we couldn't find time to go, as our time there was so short. While a revival is on we feel it is necessary to abstain from any visiting unless it is visiting or praying with the sick, or someone who needs help. Some have thought us strange and criticized us, but we never have time to stop and explain as we have to keep pace with the Spirit, as He leads us on. We love to take outings, and have taken a few just to rest our nerves and minds and to get quiet before the Lord. However, there have been very few times when we have not been given something to do while resting. We don't need to look for it as we have a ready mind, and this is what the Lord has given us through the baptism of the Holy Ghost. This has satisfied and settled us, and we have gladly turned away from worldly pleasures and let Him use us as He will.

Through the study of the Word of God and with the experience of my own heart I have become thoroughly convinced that the baptism of the Holy Ghost and fire, which purifies the heart by faith and causes it to overflow with the love of God to our fellow man, is the only thing that will give boldness in the day of judgment, and make us to be as He is in this world. God is love and He has set forth the command that we should love Him with all our heart, soul, and mind; also that we should love our neighbors as ourselves. On these two commandments hang all the law and the prophets. This is just what the world, with its infidelity, modernism, sin, and crime on every hand, is gasping for with its last breath. The love of many has waxed cold and there are those who have lost their first love. I pray the Lord to give to His people the love that never faileth. Many a heart is failing today over the things that are coming upon this earth. God is love; love never faileth. If we watch, pray, keep humble before Him, and ever trust in the shed blood of His Son, He can not, nor will He, deny Himself. We will have boldness because our sins have gone on before us to the judgment by the way of Calvary, and we can gladly meet the one who gave His life for us, just because He loved us, and loved first. Oh, glory, hallelujah! My heart is on fire now as I write and I must stop to sing a verse:

> Judgment, judgment, judgment day is rolling around,
> Judgment, judgment, oh, how I long to go.
> King Jesus is a sitting in heaven I know,
> How I long to go there.
> King Jesus is a sitting in heaven I know,
> Oh, how I long to go.

There is no fear in love. Perfect love casteth out fear. Fear hath torment. With this hope burning in our souls we hate sin with a godly hatred. There will be times when we will have need to reprove and rebuke sin with long-suffering and with kindness, and at the same time love, pity, and feel for the sinner the same as any faithful mother or father does for their wayward boy who because they love him chasten him. This love is not the sentimental and soft kind that compromises with sin, but is the love that purifies the heart and prepares us to meet our God. Nothing can take its place.

CHAPTER XXXIII
PERFECT LOVE DEMONSTRATED THROUGH TWO MISSIONARIES TO THE FOREIGN FIELD

Some years ago there was a young married couple, Rev. Jules Ryff and wife, who left Seattle for New York, to sail across the ocean to the shores of dark Africa. They were sent out through the Free Methodist Missionary Board. How happy they were that they were called to carry the gospel to these people. They remained seven years. After that they came home for a furlough. As we were acquainted with them before they left, in fact before they were married, we were anxious to talk with them about Africa. One day the opportunity came when I could have a talk with Sister Ryff.

She told me how the Lord had put His love in her heart for these souls and how she longed to help them to the light. She said that when she was quite a child she went to a missionary meeting at her home church and heard the missionary tell of their needs. That night she had a dream in which she saw these dark people in a strange land. There was a great river between her and them, and they were sitting under a great tree looking across to her and saying, "Come over here. Come over here." She said she could never get away from that vision. Later on she had her call to go to Africa as a missionary. She married this young man who also had the call. After training for a certain length of time, they sailed. We saw them when they bade farewell. Their faces were beaming with joy and expectation. She said after arriving at their destination they took a rest for a few days, then went to the people they were to teach and that as they neared the place she saw the same faces, same people, and same scenery as she had seen in her dream. She was at the end of her vision.

They remained home until they were fully restored to health and then they went back to Africa, as their hearts were in the work and they loved the people they had left behind. The morning they left we went to see them off. Mrs. Ryff's father had very poor health and as he bade them farewell, he said, "I will never see you any more." They were there for a few years when she took sick and died, and her remains lie today far away from her home and native land to stay until the resurrection.

This was love demonstrated. The Word of God says, "Greater love hath no man than this, that he lay down his life for a friend."

While we were back east in our mission work in the slums a Christian gentleman visited us and requested that a lady missionary from Africa be permitted to come to the Mission and give us a talk. She had been sent out from some place in Canada to Africa with her young husband after they had been married but a short time. She told us how they bade farewell to home and loved ones and left with great anticipation. After they reached their port across the sea they were met at the docks by some of the natives who were to carry them into the interior to their destination. There was quite a caravan, with just one white man besides her husband.

She swung for seventy-two days in a hammock carried on the shoulders of four men. She spoke of the careful manner in which they carried her across the logs and cataracts and how still she lay as she heard them say, "Steady, now," as one misstep would have proved fatal. At the last camp they were very tired and in great anxiety to see the people they were to spend their time with. The next day as they arrived at the village, they came to a standstill and there was something ran out of the woods. As she raised up and looked, she said, "What is it?" It was an African woman. They told her that the African woman said, as she saw her for the first time,

"What is it?" in her own tongue. She said these natives looked so much different from the ones who had carried her to this place. Her carriers were more civilized. The first thing she said was, "Please pitch my tent as quickly as possible." Her husband was at the rear end of the caravan, and when he came up she saw he had been crying also. She went into her tent and wouldn't show herself until the next day. She said she looked upon them with abhorrence. She found out that she didn't have the perfect love that is necessary for a missionary or one who labors with any people. She said she cried to the Lord until He filled her heart with perfect love. In a few days the carriers and the white man left and she and her husband were alone with those people, not to look upon another white face for one year. They had not learned the language and had to just watch the people and guess their words the best they could. In the course of time they learned the language. They were there several years before they had a convert. Her husband died in that place and she lost her only child there, too, and if she had not been perfected in the love of God she could not have stood it, but by His grace she had obtained the love that stood the test for seven years. She told how good the natives were to her and how she could trust them. There wasn't anything they would not do for her. Her health broke after she had the fever and she came home on a furlough. They were very much grieved when she had to come away. She had such love for the souls of those dark heathen that she was anxious to recover her strength and go back to the land where she had buried her husband and child, to labor until death. There she will rest until the resurrection. This is perfect love tested and this kind is the judgment test.

The Main Line

Just about the time I thought I was lost,
The train is coming in on the main line.
My dungeon shook and my chains fell off,
And I came right in on the main line.

CHORUS
The main line, the main line,
The train is coming in on the main line,
The main line, the main line,
The train is coming in on the main line.

I went down in the valley, I went for to pray,
The train is coming in on the main line.
My soul got happy and I stayed all day,
I came right in on the main line.

CHAPTER XXXIV
DEATH OF SISTER WITTEMAN

On the ninth day of May, 1925, Mrs. Ruey Witteman, superintendent of the Olive Branch Mission for nearly twenty years, passed away. Her death was a great shock to many. She had had two or three attacks of flu before this time, but she had rallied. Every one hoped that this sickness might prove to be temporary also. She was ill for weeks, and the workers at the Mission, with her many Christian friends, prayed much for her recovery, but it pleased our kind and heavenly Father to call her from her labors to her reward. She was a real mother, and she was loved by all who really knew her. She is greatly missed in her home, in the Mission, and in the church, and no one misses her more than the poor down-and-outs to whom she extended a hand of mercy and love in so many ways.

We worked under her ministry for twenty years and had learned to love and esteem her very highly for Jesus' and her work's sake. We all felt we had lost our dearest friend. We were in the Mission one night soon after her death when a man came in inquiring for the superintendent. When someone said she was gone, he went back up the steps, weeping. At the funeral one lady whom the Lord had blessed through Sister Witteman, fainted and had to be carried out. As the funeral procession moved away, some of the children who had come from a section of the city where she had built another church and Sunday-school, went down the street crying. There was scarcely a dry eye as the quartet sang the following chorus:

"Over and over, yes, deeper and deeper,
My heart is pierced through with life's sorrowing cry,
But the tears of the sower, and the songs of the reaper
Shall mingle together in joy by and by."

About eighteen years ago, when the Mission was having its greatest struggle to live, and workers were few, and the finances hard to get, there were many hindrances, as there always are, and much opposition. Sister Witteman called to see us one day and, as she talked over the work, her eyes filled with tears. When I first knew her I thought she had weak eyes, but later I found that it was caused by tears of sorrow for the lost. This day when we talked together, I thought the burden too heavy for her to carry, and said, "Why don't you give it up?" She said, "Let's pray," and praying, said, "O Lord, I can't give it up; I can't give it up." She prayed until it seemed that heaven and earth came together. She said, "See the souls that are not saved." I felt ashamed for having so small a faith. I could see a change for the better soon after this. The churches began to take hold of the work, and many hindrances were overcome. Some of those saved in the Mission are today ordained preachers, and others are evangelists.

We were glad for the one night through the week that we were permitted to work there. She often encouraged us by telling us that, as long as she was superintendent, she wanted us to have our Sunday night. The Lord gave her this wish. We never expected to outlive her, but the Lord knows what is best and is ever ready to comfort those who are cast down. The workers have taken courage, and once more the Olive Branch Mission is on the up-grade. May it live long to be a blessing to humanity and to glorify Jehovah.

CHAPTER XXXV
THE BE'S OF THE LORD
(God's Bee-hive)

Some of God's commands to be found in the Scriptures are very suggestive of a little insect called the honey-bee.

These commands, if received into our hearts, and obeyed in our lives, cause us to have an abundance of honey to give out to every poor soul we meet, whose life is embittered by the sin of this world.

One day while meditating upon the Word, a swarm of God's Be's rushed through my mind and into my heart, and oh, such sweet humming, singing, and honey-making. Hallelujah! There is the Saved Be--"Look unto me and be ye saved, all ye ends of the earth." And the Clean Be--"Be ye clean that bear the vessels of the Lord." The Holy Be--"Be ye holy, for I am holy." The Perfect Be--"Be ye perfect even as your Father which is in heaven is perfect." The Kind Be--"Be ye kind one to another, tender-hearted, forgiving one another." And others, such as, "Be courteous," "Be pitiful," "Be filled with the Spirit," and, "Be thou faithful unto death." We find it much easier to Do than to Be. But if we will Be what the Lord wants us to Be, we will Do what He would have us to Do, and we will not have to depend upon our feelings, or emotions, or loud shouts. Neither will we give place to the devil's "I can't be," or, "I hope to be," or, "I want to be," or, "I'm going to be some time," but we will just Be.

Notice what a little insect the bee is, as he constantly goes flying through the woods, fields, and meadows, gathering honey. So we, as servants of the Lord, can go on wings of eagles and bring in the lost from the fields of sin.

As the bee harbors no drones, and is loyal to his leader, knows and keeps his place, and carries both honey to eat and a poisonous stinger which is a sword with which to fight his enemies, so we should put on the whole armor of God, and ever use the "sword of the Spirit, which is the Word of God, quick and powerful, and sharper than any two-edged sword, piercing even to the dividing asunder of soul and spirit, and of the joints and marrow, and is a discerner of the thoughts and intents of the heart."

This experience can be obtained by being born from above and having our hearts made perfect in the love of God.

If you have not this experience, do go in for it and some day we shall be like Him, for we shall see Him as He is. Glory to His name.

Oh, to be like Thee--full of compassion,
Loving, forgiving, tender and kind;
Helping the helpless, cheering the fainting,
Seeking the wandering sinner to find.

Oh, to be like Thee. Oh, to be like Thee,
Blessed Redeemer, pure as Thou art;
Come in Thy sweetness, come in Thy fulness,
Stamp Thine own image deep on my heart.

--Mrs. L. P. Ray.

CHAPTER XXXVI
DOROTHY HERALD'S QUESTION

One time at a camp meeting a little girl by the name of Dorothy Herald, granddaughter of Rev. and Mrs. Haslam, asked why I was black. I do not believe she had ever seen a colored person before, and I seemed strange to her. Her grandmother made some reply, but it did not satisfy her, so she kept asking until her grandmother told her to ask me. She wanted to talk to me so her grandmother brought her over to me. She did not seem a bit afraid; she just seemed eager to talk. Possibly this would have offended some, but not me. The first Indian I ever saw, I was afraid. If someone had explained things to me, it would have satisfied my curiosity.

I took Dorothy by the hand and we went into a tent alone. She looked me right in the face as I told her the story of Jesus. Then I told her about the creation and how God made everything of its own kind, and that He loved variety. I told her of the different kinds of animals, birds, and flowers, and that He also made different colored people--some white, some black, some red, and some yellow, and that He loved them all, and that it was His choice to make me black and her white. She seemed perfectly satisfied with the explanation. I wish everyone was as simple and childlike. I was glad to explain to her what I believe is the reason for my color, and if He has another purpose I can gladly say, "Good is the will of the Lord." I am perfectly satisfied with my color, and I would be almost frightened to death if I should turn white. I can truly say that I have never seen anyone with whom I would change faces or places. I am satisfied with the way God made me. I want to be just myself in the Lord, because it pleases Him to have it so. The only thing I covet above everything, is to have a pure, white heart.

I learned a beautiful lesson one evening while sitting upon my front porch, which faces the west. As I watched the sun set I began to mediate and think of how God had made everything, and how the sun had done its work for the day and kept its course, and the thought came to me, "All nature obeys God." I watched until the sun went down behind the Olympic Mountains. It was a beautiful sight, and after it had gone clear out of sight and the evening shades were gathering, I looked up, and there to my surprise was the moon in its first quarter, and I said, "Oh, praise the Lord, there is the moon. She, too, is keeping her course and obeying the Lord." As I gazed, this Scripture came to me, "The heavens declare the glory of God, and the firmament showeth His handiwork. Day unto day uttereth speech, and night unto night showeth knowledge." I was surely learning something of the greatness of God. I discovered a little star not far from the moon, and it, too, was doing its duty. As I looked to the west, the evening star was twinkling, and again the words of the Lord came to me, "There is one glory of the sun, and another glory of the moon, and another glory of the stars." Then it came to me that they were all glorifying God.

It seemed as though the little stars and the big ones, as they twinkled, were saying, "Glory! glory! glory!" And of course my heart was responding as I gazed upon the night, "Glory! glory! glory!" The beautiful part of it all to me was, as they were glorifying God they kept their places. One was not jealous of the other. The little star, so close to the moon, did not seem to have anything to do but to twinkle and glorify God. Then I prayed, "It is but a little I can do in this world, but I want to keep my place. I want to keep my own personality and fill the little place that Thou hast given me and shine like the little star."

The Lord through the Holy Spirit has never permitted me to use any illustration that He has given to another, without first mentioning the name of the one that it was revealed to.

Neither do I want to preach another person's sermons. The Lord has a peculiar armor which just fits Emma Ray, and to be a success in Him I want to wear my own, for another person's armor is a misfit. I do not like misfits. A few times when holding revival meetings the preacher or some of the workers got nervous and some jealous, and undertook to steady the ark and thereby spoiled a whole meeting. Admonition and counsel, when given in the Spirit, bring good results, but given in the flesh, cause discord. Not that we know anything of ourselves. The Lord has let us see and keenly feel our own ignorance and weakness, but He has taught us that faith and humility of heart giveth power to the faint, and we take courage and go forth trusting in His strength alone. We remember how Samson slew the Philistines with the jawbone of an ass. David slew Goliath, his weapon being five small stones. The walls of Jericho fell by the blowing of a ram's horn. God has said He would cause mountains to become plains. He sent ravens to feed Elijah, His servant. He used Simon, the Cyrenian, to carry the cross of His holy Son to Calvary. Jesus Himself called common fishermen to be His disciples. Joseph, a rich Christian man, had the blessed privilege of laying the body of Jesus in his own tomb for three days. Our Savior was once dead, but now is a risen Christ and is interceding for us at the right of the Father.

What a glorious day that will be when Jesus comes with all the redeemed saints. Let us keep in our places, fight the good fight of faith, and lay hold upon eternal life.

CHAPTER XXXVII
CONCLUSION

We are still actively engaged in our chosen work and, as in former days, long for the salvation of souls, because "The love of Christ constraineth us." Amen.

We send out this book in the fear of God, praying that it may bring a blessing to all who read its pages.

We wish to express our thanks to Professor A. H. and Mrs. M. L. Stilwell, and also to Miss Agnes Green and to Mr. Kenneth Kohler, who have kindly assisted us in preparing this work for the press.

May the Lord bless them abundantly.

Yours in Christian love,

Mrs. Emma J. Ray.

Memoirs of a Southerner
1840 - 1923

BY

EDWARD J. THOMAS

SAVANNAH, GEORGIA
1923

Memoirs of a Southerner

1840—1923

BY

EDWARD J. THOMAS

SAVANNAH, GEORGIA
1923

PREFACE

My young manhood having spent in the South just before, during and after the War of Secession, I may say I lived in two distinct periods of our Southern history, for this war completely severed the grand old plantation life, with all its peculiar interests and demands, from the stirring and striving conditions that followed. The first was a life complete in all things to foster intelligence and honor; the second simply, for me, a constant struggle and a hard fight to keep the proverbial wolf from the door, but with pluck, frugality and endurance the fight was won, and now, in my old age, with kind relatives and good friends, I have found happiness and contentment.

Memoirs of a Southerner
[1840 - 1923]

MY FATHER was of Welsh stock descended from one John Thomas, captain of the first vessel that brought colonists to Georgia. My mother's maiden name was Huguenin, of the Huguenots, who, being Protestants, left France and settled in South Carolina after the revocation of the Edict of Nantes by Louis XIV in 1685.

I was born in Savannah, Georgia, March 25, 1840, but a few years after we moved to the old homestead in McIntosh County, some forty miles from this city. My first recollection was of this plantation. It was called "Peru" on account of its fertility - the legend of Pizarro's gold find being not yet forgotten - situated on South Newport River, a bold and wide salt water stream emptying into Black-Beard Sound. My grandfather lived at one end of this plantation of three thousand acres, and my father lived at the other. I remember my grandfather very distinctly; he wore no whiskers, and, not shaving daily, would catch me in his arms and rub his face against mine, scratching me with his beard, much to our mutual delight. This impressed me with the belief that old men had beards and young men had whiskers, for father wore whiskers except the moustache, which, to wear in those days, was considered "horsey." Grandfather, Jonathan Thomas, died a few years later, leaving his many plantations - Peru, Belvidere, Baker, and Stark, comprising some fifteen thousand acres and about one hundred and twenty-five slaves.

His remains are buried by a large oak in our private burying ground on the banks of South Newport River, and there he rests while the restless waters ebb and flow nearby. His portrait now hangs over my fireplace, and kindly smiles down on his great, great, great grandchildren.

Plantation life on the seaboard of Georgia was master and slave in its prettiest phase. It was the rarest thing to sell a negro, and but few were bought. The negroes on these places had been reared along with their young masters and mistresses, and the interest of each was the concern of all.

And just here permit me to say that of our one hundred and twenty-five slaves there was but one mulatto, and let me tell you how that one came. It became necessary, on account of mother's health, when I was about eight years old, for father to take her to one of the northern springs. Those were the days of *state* money, and no express, and I well remember the bags of gold father had to pack in his trunk, for Georgia money would not be good in Massachusetts, and vice-versa. Of course no Southern lady traveled without her colored maid. Mother carried "Fanny," and behold, sometime after "Fanny" got home, a chocolate boy was seen. "Fanny" told me that the red clay hills of the old North State did it. I was delighted. I claimed him as my special charge, to rear as my body servant. I named him "Ned," but he died a year or two after.

There was on the plantation a trusted and intelligent slave called the Driver, who was directly in charge of all field work, Sea-Island cotton, corn, peas, sweet potatoes, sugar cane, melons, and all garden stuff; another was in charge of the horses, cattle, etc., and a third was foreman of the plows.

The fields were all staked off in tasks, a quarter of an acre, and each slave was required to cultivate with hoe or plow a certain amount of these staked fields, and as near as possible the same area cultivated in the early spring would be constantly worked by the same person, that he or she might be rewarded for doing the work well in the beginning, as it would be less labor the second hoeing if it was well done at first. In this way the industrious and diligent negro seldom worked after the noon hour.

They were very well housed in two-room lumber cabins, a chimney to each house, and allowed a garden. Sundays no work was permitted, the slaves attending church. They could raise as many chickens as they pleased, could have boats and go anywhere fishing, so they came home by daylight to resume work.

They were given two suits of clothes a year, one of wool, the other cotton, two shirts, a pair of blankets, and a pair of heavy shoes. The clothing was given to them twice a year, in the early spring and winter; the shoes in the beginning of winter. During the summer they generally went barefooted. Each slave's foot was measured, and his name written on the stick showing the length of foot; these sticks were then bundled and sent to the merchant furnishing the shoes, and each shoe would come home with the stick inside of it. The master would then take up the shoe, pull out the stick, and call the name of the slave, who would receive it.

The ration on cotton plantations was corn meal and grits, potatoes, peas, and a little bacon or Louisiana molasses; on rice plantations, rice instead of meal. These rations were distributed weekly, the slaves coming with proper utensils to receive them. Having their own boats, they could always have fish and oysters, and in their gardens raised chickens and vegetables.

The marshes abounded in raccoons and the woods in 'possums, and nightly the baying of the dogs - their own - would tell you the boys of the plantation were on a hunt. Diamond-backed terrapin were abundant, and one never was brought to our dwelling that the bearer could not get in exchange a "thrip" (the old-fashioned six cents), or, if he preferred, a ration of bacon or syrup. Many old English coins were in use, the thrip - six cents - and the "seven-pence," twelve cents.

The women sold their chickens to mother, eight for a dollar. Baked 'possum and roasted potatoes, as these people would fix them, were always nice; at least I thought so as a boy, and many the time some old mammy would call "Mas' Ed" and give him a portion of what was in her little three-legged iron pot. Yes, "Mas' Ed" could have all he wanted, patting me on the shoulder, "Bless de chile, 'e spit image of 'e Granpa.

The older men were allowed to keep guns; to many they were supplied by the master. Many had horses and cows, permitted to run in a large free pasture. These pastures extended over thousands of acres of salt marsh, and in these pastures the horses were reared, hence the name they acquired, "marsh tackies." They were not quite so large as the horses reared on the Mexican plains, but for durability and deviltry they had no equal. On the eve of coming home from school, I would write the Driver to get many of these marsh tackies penned and fed, so they would be in good shape when I got there, and then, getting a half-dozen or more of our negro boys about my age, would bridle these devilish beasts, strap a saddle cloth on, and go bouncing and scampering over the plantation. Magnificent sport for boys.

The young negroes particularly looked forward to Mas' Ed's coming home, for they knew I would insist on a big barbecue of beef for our mutual enjoyment.

'Twas no strange sight to see many ponies and wagons on our route going to church, several miles away in some shady grove, driven by these families, for wherever the white folks attended church the slaves were welcome, and on Communion Sundays they all, master and slave, took wine from the same silver cup - the white folks, of course, first. They had their own meeting and prayer house on the plantation, built by the master, where "shouting" and singing and sleeping were enjoyed, and strange doctrines preached, but, by the master's order, never after twelve o'clock at night.

I can remember to this day the sweet chants of "our people," as we used to call them, when the young men and girls, on moonlight nights, would meet to grind their corn around the hand mills. The constant whirr of the mill stones and the plaintive ditties and merry shouts of these happy people frequently lulled me, when a boy, to sleep, the negro quarters being not so far away. Never more will such merry shouts be heard!

I remember the great big cotton house, three stories high and every window glassed, where the older women would sit and "pick and sort" the good cotton from the bad, where the youngsters would take the newly ginned cotton to the strong men with the iron pestles, who stood in a strong bag of stout bagging - no presses those days - until the contents were hard and fast, pestling in this bag some three hundred pounds of cotton; the horse gin, where Dick and Montezuma, the two horses, took turns with Lewis and Robin, the two mules, in pulling the lever that turned the machine that ginned the cotton; the two little black nigs who rode on the lever to keep the animals at even speed, and after a few hours, when the horses got accustomed to the noise, would fall off in the nearest corner fast asleep; the pleasant rivalry between the men and women to see who would pick the most cotton, and hence get the prize - a calico dress or hat or pair of Sunday shoes - that father would offer weekly to the one picking the most cotton. The picking season then was very long, no guano those days to hasten matters, so the cotton would not open until October, and the fields would be white until after Christmas.

Our family consisted of mother, father, and six children, and for the comfort and convenience of this family the following servants were employed in and about our house: Old "Mamma Chaney," who had held us all from babyhood, and rocked and soothed us to sleep by her lazy and loving pat and monotonous crooning. Her queer ways, high headgear, red shawl, and her black face and white bordered eyes, holding my little sister in her lap, I shall never forget. "Mamma Martha," the head servant, to whom the keys were entrusted, and who, during mother's absence, looked after our comfort; Fanny, mother's maid; Ann and Lizzie, seamstresses; Nancy, the washerwoman; Phyllis, the cook; old Lucy, looking after the chickens; little Lucy and Zelleau taking their first lessons to become maids to my sisters; Phil, the coachman; William, the hostler; Daniel, the butler; Bony, the fisherman; Henry, the gardner; and Joe, my body servant. These slaves were not housed or fed at our house, but were given the regular ration and served in all things at their own cabins.

THE YOUNG negro men, getting tired of cultivating the fields, would at times *run away;* that is, they would leave their cabins and seek shelter in the neighboring woods or some isolated "hammock," which so abundantly are found about plantations on the seaboard. When on these runaway frolics they would live by stealing cattle, or perhaps, robbing the nearest field or barn or potato cellar, and, of course, were always slyly abetted by those of their family at home. In this way they became outlaws, always a menace to the peace and good order of the plantation, and a source of extreme annoyance and vexation to the master, and, in fact, to the entire neighborhood.

Being accustomed to the use of boats and firearms, and knowing every little inlet through the marshes, which furnished all the fish and oysters they needed, these runaways could keep up their frolic of idleness and theft almost indefinitely. They would always be smart enough to provide themselves with good boats at the start; if they had none of their own suitable, they would steal the best they could lay hands on.

At night they would leave their hiding places and sneak to their respective cabins to get a change of clothing from mother or wife, or to replenish their rations from the nearest field or barn.

It can easily be imagined then what peculiar duties at times devolved upon the master. He had not only to be financier and executive, but at times detective. I remember early one morning going with my brother to the piazza of our home, and finding a sword broken in half and a heavy bar of lead. At breakfast table we asked father where they came from. He told this story. At twelve o'clock the night before he had an idea a runaway, by name Emmanuel, would be prowling about the negro quarters, and so he got out of bed and dressed, and before starting took his little bird-gun which was loaded with bird-shot, and not knowing what he might encounter, he rammed three buckshot (muzzle loaders those days) on top of one of the small shot charges. He walked a mile, perhaps, to where the cabins were and hid behind a tree. Soon he saw someone walking towards him, and when nearby he stepped from behind the tree, recognized Emmanuel, and ordered him to stop. Emmanuel stopped instantly, and put both hands behind his back. Father asked, "What have you in your hands?" He replied, "Nothing, sir." "Well," said father, "hand me what's in your right hand." He did so, and it was a sword; this father ran into the ground and putting his foot on it, snapped it. In the other hand he had a bar of lead. He surely came well supplied to carry off a beef. Emmanuel was then ordered to cross his hands, and father, placing his gun between his knees, took from his coat pocket a large silk handkerchief and was about to tie his hands when Emmanuel dashed for the woods. He was ordered to stop, but he kept on running. Father then fired the barrel with small shot, calling him to stop, and then the other barrel, but Emmanuel kept on his run to the woods. Father prided himself on his good shooting and could not imagine how it was he did not stop this man, who had been an outlaw for so many months - a perfect nuisance to the entire neighborhood.

The matter was almost forgotten, except that brother and I took our first lessons in swordsmanship with the broken sword, and had a set of new quoits from the bar of lead, when one morning while playing in the front yard we saw Daddy Emmanuel coming up the front avenue, a long straight way about a mile through the cotton fields from the woods to the residence. Father was absent. We ran to mother and told her. She came to the front door and asked the man why he had come home. "Missis," he said, "Massa hit me wid ebery shot in de gun, and me come home to dead." He was placed in a comfortable bed, the nearest physician called in, every attention given him, and he recovered very soon. This man belonged to us, was worth before the shooting some $2,000; afterwards, perhaps, only $500; that shot from father's gun cost him $1,500, but it was necessary, and today any outlaw would be treated by lawful officers in the same way. Daddy Emmanuel was always a good man after that; we children all liked him. He was put to light work, and, when his freedom came he preferred to remain on the old plantation, where a home was provided him to the day of his death.

It is strange that no negro ever thought of defending himself in these nightly encounters. Here was a man well armed, who made no resistance. Even if armed with a loaded gun, they would yield at the first command of the master. Father put the question to one of them, and the answer was, "My gun might snap, Massa; yourn neber do."

As a small chap I was given my milk and hominy or butter and hominy, fed me by my nurse, and put to bed before dark, and many the time I slipped from my bed and, looking downstairs at the lamps burning then with whale oil, and wondering, how funny it all looked. Then only whale oil, and wax and tallow candles made at home, were used for lighting purposes by the well-to-do; the negroes and poor whites - "poor Buckrers" we called them - used mostly lightwood in the chimneys, and even to this day many of these people use this same lightwood torch. Then came a fluid we called "burning fluid," somewhat like naphtha, and then, kerosene, gas and electricity.

My brother and I had a nice time catching birds in traps we made with sticks; the bulfinch, the red or cardinal bird, the speckle-breasted thrush - and, killing them, made a fire in the woods, broiled the poor little devils, and had a quick lunch; and as a boy I thought them fine until one day we caught a crow, but his meat was more than our appetites would permit. Sometimes we sat on the front porch in summer with bare feet and legs, to see which could kill the most mosquitoes.

When I was about ten years old, the biggest runaway squad in my remembrance almost worried my good father to death. He had arranged the planting of his crop for, say fifty or sixty slaves and the necessary mules, so much cotton and other crops to each hand. When the hot weather was the greatest, and the grass began to race with the crops for existence and the greatest diligence and energy were required of each hand to do his or her part, some eight or ten of his best men, with several from adjacent plantations, left their duties on a runaway. Of course this required that a certain proportion of the planted crops be abandoned, for there were none to hire to take their places. These were Solomon, Dick, Daniel, Jonas, Mark, etc., all fine boatmen and accustomed to firearms. They, as usual, lived by raiding the cattle ranches and corn bins, and gave intolerable trouble everywhere and to every one in the direct neighborhood. Besides it was like having twelve or fifteen thousand dollars taking wings to itself, destroying the proper ratio on the plantation as to the workers and consumers and thereby making the year's results perhaps unsatisfactory. After these men had been "cutting their capers" for a month or two, and after every individual effort on father's part to catch them had failed, the neighborhood decided to make a united effort to rid themselves of these outlaws. The idea was to provide a good boat, all equipped for ready action; then to scour the neighboring plantations with good dogs, and if they were not found on the mainland, then to take to the boats and search the "hammocks" and islands. A well known man from Savannah, with his trail hounds, was engaged.

I well remember the big eight-oared boat towed to the landing, the buffalo robes and blankets, and champagne baskets filled with hams and chickens and goodies of all kinds, the demijohns of good whiskey, in case of snake bite, the guns and ammunition, besides a sail to hoist if the weather permitted. I remember feeding the dogs and wondering how pretty "Musie," with her soft brown eyes, could prefer that ugly old man to anybody else. The dogs were docile and obedient, only intended to trail the outlaws, not to injure them. We were much interested in their welfare, for were they not our own? When everything was loaded in the boat and it was anchored in place, the neighborhood party mounted their horses and proceeded to do the first act in the drama, *viz.,* searching the mainland. Scarcely had the party gotten to the woods, about a mile distant, when a large party of these runaways came running up from another quarter, and in the happiest mood, bid mother, who happened at the back door, "Good morning, Misses," and walked towards the well furnished boat at the landing. They all shook hands with me, and with a hurrah pushed off the boat and were gone. A runner was sent after the scouting party, and returning, I remember father's remark: "Well, they have the best boat in the county, and nothing more can be done now." Some spy among the many house servants must have kept these runaways informed.

The man and his dogs returned to Savannah, and the hunt, for the present, was at an end. We heard no more of these runaways, except now and then that some cow had been killed by them, until about the first of December, when one cold night, happening at the back door, I heard some one outside in the dark say, "Huddy, Mas' Ed." I went down the back steps and said, "Hello! What you want?" And looking closely saw Solomon, one of the runaways. He said: "Mas' Ed, tell Massa we come in." I ran to the parlor where father was reading and I called out: "Father, Solomon and all the runaways have come in." Father said, "Tell Solomon and all his gang I wish them in hell. Will see them in the morning." Father then hired the gang to a railroad contractor for the balance of the winter, and the neighborhood was rid of them. When all this was happening on the plantation, we had no fear of them at home. Frequently we would be left alone for several days, mother and children, with the house servants, all our own slaves, and the doors of the residence not even locked at night. You may be sure, though, strong locks were on the barns, meat houses and chicken coops.

THUS OUR country life passed, mother teaching us our first lessons, and making us stand in the corners of the room, face to the wall, if we missed our lessons, and oh, what an awful time we thought we were having! If we got our lessons well, we were rewarded by going with her on her customary carriage drive, through the well kept roads draped with jessamins and overhanging trees, that ran through various parts of the plantation. Gero and Jerry, mother's chestnuts, with Daddy Phil, the coachman, and the pretty and sweet woods of the home plantation, will always have a warm place in my memory.

Christmas month we always spent with our grandmother, Mrs. Eliza Huguenin, in Savannah. There being no railroads in this section at the time, and in fact no railroads south of Savannah, the distance - a good day's journey by carriage - was made partly in our carriage, and partly by stage. At that time all communication south of Savannah was by stage. How well I remember one of these trips when about ten years old. We had driven some twelve miles to catch the stage, arriving at the little village of Riceboro. It grew very cold, so father provided each of us with a rough blanket to wrap our legs in. There was a lady in this stage dressed in a handsome black gown, on her way to the city, and the white hairs from our coarse blankets falling on her black dress, almost drove her wild, and all to our extreme delight. I fear we disturbed those coverings more than was necessary. A fine-looking, elderly gentleman was also a passenger, and was constantly teasing us, declaring that when we got to town the "big boys would grease our heads and swallow us whole." Little did I think then the relation I would bear to this jolly old gentleman in after years.

Father found it necessary about this time for us to have more regular instruction, so he engaged the services of a Miss Mary Boggs, a Virginia miss, for our governess. She came and she captured us all, with her great brown eyes, pretty brown hair, and large mouth filled with white teeth. I think she was my first sweetheart. She only taught English branches, so soon we grew beyond her acquirements. In truth she was so sweet and pretty that Judge McLaws, of Augusta, won her love and took her to his home, and this suited nicely, for he was our cousin and therefore she became our Cousin Mary.

At that time, 1853, there were good schools in Walthourville, Liberty County, some twenty miles away. So we went to live there. The premises we occupied were just across the road from the home of a Mr. George W. Walthour, and what was my surprise and pleasure to find him the jolly old gentleman of the stage four years back, and the lady in black who so disliked my blanket hairs, a relative.

In his family there was a daughter about ten years of age, and in my family there were two sisters nearly her age. It goes without saying that having no sisters companionable with herself, and living so near, my sisters and she became every-day playmates Her name was Alice She had dark brown hair combed back from her pretty face with the large circular combs used at that time. Her eyes were blue-gray and twinkled like stars, and as a thirteen year- old boy I thought this ten-year-old girl the prettiest thing I ever saw - chock full of mischief and fun, as straight as an Indian maiden, and supple as a reed. She took precedence in all our romps, and was never so happy as when catching a frisky calf by the tail, she made pandemonium with the chickens in the yard, and caused peals of laughter from all who saw her. Soon she was off to boarding school.

The first of May always brought us happiness in the way of a May party at the Academy's big shady grounds. Months before the jolly day everybody in the village was making preparations. The girls were getting ready their white dresses, ribbons and dancing slippers, the boys their natty coats and white pants, the mothers making cakes and goodies of all kinds, and the fathers cussing at the expense and yet more delighted than anybody else when the girls were rigged for the occasion. Of course the prettiest girl in school was chosen by the boys as our Queen of May, and I shall never forget our two queens of '55 and '56 - Miss Tilla and Miss Helen. Sweet and pretty girls they were sixty years ago, and today they are glorious matrons - the same sweet smile tempered with the cares of life. May the God of Love ever protect them!

I well remember the January of 1857, when not quite seventeen years old, I started for college. The railroad from Savannah southward and westward was only constructed thirty miles out, so I went by private conveyance, and then these thirty miles by rail to Savannah, where I took train to Augusta and thence to Athens, where I was to attend the University of Georgia. It took two days and two nights to make the trip in those days.

This was my first trip from home, and my first ride on a railroad train, and surely I expected some highwayman to attempt to rob me of my gold watch, or perhaps the small pieces of silver I had in my pocket, and as a college man I must defend my property, so I invested seventy-five cents in a sharp and shinning bowie knife (the kind they had in Kansas at that time), eight inches long, and a horn handle, and in a red morocco sheath, tipped with silver. I then cut a small hole in my waistband behind, and buttoned in my ugly armament. No sleeping cars, so when I got tired I twisted upon a seat, and wriggling in my sleep to get comfortable my coat pushed up and my big knife showed up in great shape. Some good old gentleman passing by unbuttoned my armament, waked me up, and quietly asked me if I had not better put it in my satchel. I never felt so cheap in my life. I quickly took it from him, thanked him, and threw it under the seat, and that is the last time I ever had such a thing.

COLLEGE LIFE was very pleasant but very uneventful. My first vacation, before going home, was spent with Col. Julius Huguenin, a kinsman in South Carolina. His mode of life was peculiar. Up early every morning, after a cup of coffee, he would take saddle-horse and ride over his home place; then getting into his carriage, to which were harnessed two elegant black stallions that tried so hard to chew each other up that an iron rod was fastened between their bits and their heads well checked - was driven to his second plantation, where saddle-horses would be in readiness, and with his overseer he would ride and direct the affairs of that place; then likewise to his third plantation, getting home about noon, when his breakfast would be served. About two o'clock - it was in December - all hands would prepare for a fox hunt, horns blowing the signal would be heard from the stable yards, the baying of hounds would testify to their readiness; saddle-horses, held by negro chaps in gay caps, would be waiting on the lawn, but not long waiting, for we would all soon be in the saddle and cantering to the forests. I never had anything to suit my taste as did these fox chases. We would take no guns, relying on the dogs and our swift horses, going pell-mell through fields, over fences and ditches, and once in a while bring home the tail of a fox stuck in some one's hat. Getting home about dark, a bounteous dinner would be served.

Cousin Julius took me into his cellar one afternoon, and all kinds of good things were there in evidence. He had a man who employed his time hunting, and hence venison, wild turkey and ducks, and birds were in abundance; the fisherman had also been industrious, and his catch was in evidence, clams and oysters were piled in the corners; portions of a fat ox and a small lamb showed that the dinner table would not be in want. This dinner was a long meal, and when it was over every evening, Cousin Julius, mellowed up with many glasses of good old brandy, would be lifted from his seat by two or three body servants, taken to his room, bathed and put to bed, like a veritable old Turk. Cousin Julius never drank wine, although his table was abundantly supplied with all kinds and enjoyed by the younger folks. When I went to college at seventeen I determined within myself not to touch a drop of any spirits until I was twenty-one, so I did not join the other youngsters in getting rid of the wine. I made one exception to this determination, for when I went home on vacation and mother exhibited her "orange cordials," "cherry bounce" and blackberry wines, I thought it would sound so unwelcome for me to say "Mother, I don't drink," so with her we drank her nice products, and I praised them to the sky, although to be honest, I did not care for them. This abstemious resolution made in early life has helped me wonderfully.

While Cousin Julius lived as I have mentioned, his wife had her three customary meals. Separate cook and kitchens were provided. Sundays the entire family took meals together, either at the husband's or wife's table. On this visit I met my cousin Tom Huguenin, who afterwards became the gallant defender of Fort Sumter.

Getting home after Christmas, father had arranged to give us a hunt on St. Catherine's and Black Beard's Islands. To make my story complete, I must tell about an old lady, Aunt Peggy Harris, as everybody called her, who owned a plantation and some twenty-five or thirty slaves, all being raised by her during a long life, from a few negro women inherited in her youth. She did not keep her plantation in very good discipline and hence father, her nearest neighbor, did not like to have his negroes companionable with hers. But she had a young man, very tall and strong, by name Landcaster, who wanted to marry one of father's women, by name Nelly. Father objected, as I said before, to having any of Aunt Peggy's people given the freedom of his plantation, and hence refused to sanction this wedding. However, his objection availed but little, for love found a way, and year by year Nelly's family grew larger. While father objected to Landcaster as a husband, because it would give him the freedom of his plantation, yet when he went on a hunt he would exchange hands with Aunt Peggy for the occasion - much to Landcaster's delight. He was a good oarsman (no naphtha launches then), sang songs merrily, knew every path through the woods, and where to get up a deer or find the best fish, a good cook, always jolly and willing - a complete rascal in all things; hence he was along on this trip.

The hunt and fish on the islands came off with the usual good luck, and we had enjoyed camping out under the large oaks, resting on the robes, and all the good things that boys do so enjoy. On our way home in this eight-oared boat, when perhaps half way home, my brother fell asleep, and when the boat made a sudden jerk he raised his foot suddenly, when out of the boat and in some ten feet of water, tumbled one of our best guns. Father immediately called out: "Landcaster, get that gun and I'll give you Nelly." Without even taking off his hat, Landcaster was overboard and into this ten feet of cold salt water, but in a shorter time than I can write it, up he came, gun in hand and a grin on his face. Immediately he was helped out of the water, three fingers of good old Bourbon floated under his shirt, his seat resumed and the oars feathering the water and driving the boat at fast speed ahead He knew he had Nelly.

A day or two after he got home, father fulfilled his promise to him and his dusky bride in, to them, royal style. The bride was diked out in one of mother's white dresses, ribbons *ad libitum* floated from head, waist and arms; the groom in the tallest white collar the community could furnish, and big yellow cravat. The large piazza was turned into a dance hall, and with fiddle and banjo they made merry, while a barbecue awaited them on the lawn.

To finish the story, Landcaster, so soon as the Federal gunboats in 1862 made their appearance off the coast and in sight of our place, took his wife and babes in a boat to find freedom After the war, he told me, he soon found freedom with a wife and six children very different from having a master to provide for them. Like the man he was, he did the best he could. When the war was over, he came back and lived on the old plantation until he died. I obtained a pension from the U. S. Government for his wife, Nelly. It seems he got his name on the payroll of the government by doing some trivial service and now his widow is receiving the usual pension. All bosh, I know, but while millions are being distributed to the undeserved, this poor woman might just as well get her mite. And strange to say that while I am writing, this same Nelly is now sitting in my kitchen waiting for a helping of whatever I may have, which she or any one of our old slaves shall have as long as the recollections of Peru Plantation, and those happy days, linger in my memory; and they all know it, for even to this day they bring all their big troubles to "Mas' Ed" to have him explain or correct.

I do not mean to imply that there was no cruelty between master and slave, but no more so than between husband and wife, or father and children, or employer and employed, but I do know that laws were enacted preventing a master's cruelty to his slave, as also that a husband should not bcat his wife. In all relations in life the tyrant will manifest himself.

FATHER DIED in the year 1859 in his forty-third year; was buried beside my grandfather in the old graveyard on South Newport River. He was not a church man; a man of good deeds rather than a man of faith, and goodness and sympathy beamed from him as naturally as light from the glowworm. A soul full of charity for every one, he has gone to his Maker to get that reward provided for the just.

The first of January, in my young days, was a day of rejoicing. Visiting the rule. About early noon we would gather in fours, get into carriages and visit everybody worth visiting; always the best of wines and cakes in evidence at every house, and perhaps we would have headaches the next morning, but 'twas all forgiven in the general good cheer. If you left your card New Year's Day, you were to have the civilities of that house for the year. For the disobedience of this custom, when quite a young chap, I got in much trouble. I was visiting my grandmother, who gave me a list of her friends to call on, she having driven to her plantation some five miles from Savannah. I had paid most of the visits; the last visit was to call on two old maids. They were close-fisted, sour old ladies, never had anything good to eat, but always a lecture on their tongues. Their house was near the Central R. R. depot on Liberty Street, and when we got near there, meeting friends, the idea struck us that we would switch off from that house - no cake, no nuts no nothing - and have a game of catcher on the cotton bales at the Central R. R. yard. In those days all the cotton that came to Savannah was unloaded at this yard, and then drayed to steamers, etc. The result was, in one of my leaps from bale to bale I slipped and broke my right leg, and had to be carried home in the arms of one of the big Irish laborers. When grandmother arrived home from her ride and found me lying down with my leg in splints, she wanted to whip me because I had disobeyed her in not going to see those old maids, and I thought I was pretty well punished. Father came from our old Peru Plantation home to see me, hunted up the laborer and treated him handsomely.

My dear old grandmother - how she used to indulge me, and how I used to fool her! Many little stories could be told of her confiding love and my infernal duplicity, but I suppose it is the experience of all boys.

About 1860 the papers rang out with discordant notes, the North against the South, the South against the North. How little we college boys knew what was before us! The beginning of this term, 1860, a chair of geology was established at the college for the first time, and Dr. Henry Hammond, fresh from the advanced schools in Paris, France, was consigned to it, and to us boys (we thought we were men) who had been sitting under teaching of good old Dr. Mell, Dr. Hammond's new ideas were surely confounding.

Dr. Mell taught that the world was made in six days, and Dr. Hammond that it took twenty-two thousand years to bring the earth to the present condition. Judge Joseph Henry Lumpkin, at that time Chief Justice of the Supreme Court of Georgia, once a week gave the Senior Class, of which I was a member, lectures on the Constitution of the United States. The Judge was a strong Secessionist, and delighted and enthused our young hearts with his word pictures of the glorious South, cut loose from the Union, with Cotton as King and free trade with the world.

Being so wise in our judgment, we boys thought surely he could and would decide whether Dr. Mell or Dr. Hammond was right - whether it took six days or twenty-two thousand years to make the world. After one of our lectures this question was put to him, and I shall never forget the result - at least to my mind.

The Judge was short and stout, wore very long hair much inclined to curl, and getting up he shook his head like an enraged lion, and almost swore at us boys for indulging in skepticism, declaring the Bible says "the world was made in six days, and you young gentlemen have no business to look further. You are losing that faith in Holy Writ which has brought not only individuals, but nations, to destruction. Beware! Beware!" Such was the answer given by Judge Lumpkin to the Senior Class of 1860, at that centre of learning, the University of the State of Georgia! How the world has progressed in thought, as in all things, in the last generation!

During my college course I paid much attention to religious matters; I became deeply interested in church work of all kinds. The various churches in Athens had protracted meetings, and eminent divines thundered orthodox doctrines in the ears of their congregations night after night. The gifted T. R. R. Cobb, an eminent lawyer, took active and enthusiastic part. The angry God and the loving Son was the burden of their song, and unless you were converted (?) you were sure of eternal punishment. I tried to get what these Orthodox called converted, that is, to feel that my sins had rolled off me like a mountain, and that I felt so happy I wanted to shout. I never got it. I even felt disturbed when some converted sinner would begin shouting his happiness; but I tried to keep not only my actions, but even my thoughts, "unspotted from the world." I tried to be too orthodox. I became too earnest. I wanted everybody to walk that narrow chalk mark, as it was chalked out to me by those who said they knew all about it. This would have suited very well, perhaps, if I had not begun to think too much, and ask too many questions of those who were teaching me. My teachers all had different views on all these matters, and I had sympathy for them all. I found my chalk mark grew wider as my sympathy and learning expanded, and soon I found the whole world chalked over, and the great and kind Creator, instead of the angry God, looking and lightening up the pathways for all mankind. Whereupon I opened my heart to that great Creator, discarded all the "isms" I had recently so fondly cherished, and simply put my trust in *Him*. Sympathy for all mankind and trust in God, I will live by and hope to die by.

I GRADUATED this summer in the class of 1860, and received my "sheepskin" as a Bachelor of Arts. On my route home, at most every station a liberty pole was erected from which flags of various designs were hung, always expressing something defiant of the Yankee. A rattlesnake coiled, with "Don't step on me" was frequently seen, and the secession badge pinned to every man's coat and lady's jacket; and the nearer I got home, the higher the poles and larger the flags. Father's death made it necessary for me to take charge of our plantation, and this, together with the unsettled condition of the country, made me forget my individual interest. The first of January, 1861 I assumed charge, and with the assistance of our old Driver, "Daddy John," prepared to plant the usual crops. Our family lived in Walthourville, Liberty County, twenty miles away, in order that the younger members of the family might have school privileges. I kept bachelor quarters on the plantation, with old "Mamma Peggy" as provider. About this time Federal gunboats could be seen out in the sound, and the neighboring planters became uneasy.

One of our neighbors, Mrs. Anderson, had a son about my age, a nervous and eccentric chap, and a very interesting daughter. I frequently rode or drove to their home, and was always welcome. They were distant relatives. One Saturday night about the first of March, riding over to this house, I saw quite a suspicious boat nearing the landing hard by, and suspected it to be one of those "Damn Yankee" trading schooners, selling, or rather trading with the negroes their products, such as skins and pelts of various animals, and frequently what stuff and cotton or corn they could steal from their masters, for mean whiskey and gim-cracks of all kinds. These vessels were not allowed about our landings without permission. Hence when I got over to Anderson's I told him about the vessel, and we agreed to visit this particular landing about midnight. Anderson had a young relative by name Jones visiting him. About eleven o'clock we started off. I took my long buggy whip, Anderson a gun loaded with buckshot, and Jones a gun loaded with small shot in which he rammed three large buckshot on top of each charge. I laughed at them, wanting to know whom they intended killing. We found nothing wrong at the landing, but returning, we heard what the negroes call shouting, in one of the cabins not far from the residence. It was a moonlight night, and this noise being contrary to rules, we walked over to see who the parties were and quietly stop the noise. Anderson and Jones were to go to the front door and rap, and I to the back door, and if any one attempted to get by me, I would intercept him. Anderson rapped, and the door by me was flung open and a negro boy, as well as I can remember about eighteen years old, ran by me before I could take hold of him. The idea immediately suggested itself to me that he belonged to some neighboring place, so I would at least have the frolic of catching him and finding out. Being quite swift of foot, I ran after him, and scarcely got beyond the corner of the cabin before Anderson fired his gun and the whole contents entered my right shoulder. He could not have been more than thirty feet from me, for it brought me down all in a heap. I suffered no pain, but I felt as though my body had been torn away and my head only rested on the earth. The nearest physician, eighteen miles off, was sent for, and the wound dressed. And thus I spent my twenty-first birthday, March 25, 1861, in bed.

Anderson never could give any reason why he fired the gun, and the name of the chap who ran by me was never known. The whole Anderson household did all in their power to alleviate my wretched condition. It seemed that when we stopped for a few moments at the landing, Anderson and Jones, by some means, exchanged guns. If that had not been done, I would have been killed, for Anderson started out with the gun loaded with buckshot. The doctor said that thirty-two duck-shot had entered my shoulder and back of my head, and three buckshot had passed entirely through my shoulder. Many of these shot have been taken out by the lances, but some twenty or more are still in my shoulder. I was in bed for about a month fretting that I was incapacitated to go and fight for my native land, for about this time companies of volunteers were being organized, through the entire South.

FROM THE writing of the Constitution there were always two distinct opinions as to the right of a state to secede from the Union. The New England states, Massachusetts, Connecticut, Rhode Island, were the first to declare for this right to secede, and openly threatened to do so July 4, 18 1814, on account of Jefferson's embargo, and then their right to do so was not particularly questioned. From the days of Hamilton and Jefferson - the first for a central control, the latter for state's rights - and then again in the time of Webster and Calhoun, later in the time of Lincoln and Davis, these two separate causes were championed. This ghost of secession was forever rising to disturb the Union, the Southern states always claiming the right; and hence we felt we were acting within our rights when, in 1860-61, we withdrew. Only such authority was delegated by the states to the General Government as would have this government function properly. All the other rights were reserved to the states.

The border states were loath to break from the Union. The great R. E. Lee and his state, Virginia, were for the Union until Lincoln called for Virginia's quota to make the desired number of troops to coerce the Southern states, and then Lee said, "The die is cast. I cannot fight for that." And Virginia, too, seceded. In fact, the Southern states have always felt that their first allegiance was to their state, and second to the Union. The Northern states have, so to speak, let down their state fences and are known more particularly by their large cities - as Portland, Boston, New Haven, New York, and so on, while we of the South have continued our state pride. For me, I am a Georgian first, and an American afterwards. This does not make us love our nation less, but our state more.

Before 1860 Georgia and Massachusetts were almost as distinct countries, under the Constitution of the United States, as are now Italy and Belgium under the League of Nations, for it was primarily for self-defense that these unions were effected. Yes, at times even the contrast is more favorable to the European countries, for a man can go from Belgium into Italy and not have his property stolen from him, but we of Georgia could not go to Massachusetts with our slaves - guaranteed to us under the Constitution as our slaves, and sold as such to us by these same Northern brethren, and also guaranteed by the Supreme Court of our land - without having them stolen from us, and then by underground railroad whisked off into undetermined places. It was not officially done, but connived at; and, perhaps, with the approval of the majority of the citizens of the state. Towards the end, it became a moral issue rather than a Constitutional measure.

The planters on the seaboard of Georgia found it necessary at this time to move further inland. Shot and shell from the Yankee gunboats would sometimes be thrown most too near. I took all the infirm and very old slaves, and many of the little negroes, to our home in Liberty

County, and found homes for the others among the farmers about Thomasville, Georgia. My object was to get them good homes during the war rather than to drive hard bargains as to wages. I had not a particle of trouble with them. They seemed to feel the emergency of the case, and assisted me in the work. Loyal they were to me, and they have never been forgotten for it. Although managing negroes from boyhood, I never whipped but two of them in my life. Jumping from my buggy one morning for a package I had forgotten, and rushing into my room buggy whip in hand, I found the house maid using my toothbrush. I struck her two or three cuts across the shoulder, threw the brush out of the window, and then resumed my trip in the buggy. I strapped my boy one day in camp for not having my horse ready when "boots and saddles" was sounded. While doing duty on the seaboard, a great many of us officers, non-coms and privates, had our body servants, and half a dozen forming a mess, our own negro cook; but when ordered to the front, all luxuries were abandoned, the servants sent home on the extra horses, and only the scantiest necessities kept. Nevertheless, how happy we were to go!

Knowing that I would be obliged to leave my mother, sisters and little brothers at home, without a male protector - for every white man was in the army - I called "Daddy Henry," one of our trusted slaves, to my room before departing, and told him that I left everything in his care. He must see that the many house servants were obedient to mother; he must take care of the old slaves and many young ones, keep mother well provisioned from plantation and garden; that, in fact, he must stand right square up, as he knew I wished. He was standing, hat in hand, and said, "Mas' Ed, 'fore God I won't betray you." I left with every confidence in the world. He proved faithful to the trust imposed, and when it became necessary for mother to take refuge in Savannah, on account of the raiding parties from Sherman's army, he did all in his power to aid her. When I met "Daddy Henry" at the old plantation after the war, he gave me a verbal accounting of his conduct, and seemed perfectly happy when I shook his hand and said "Daddy Henry, I knew you would be true." Before my visit at the plantation ended, I deeded to him his home and ten acres of land, as a home for him and his good wife, "Mamma Nancy," who had been our washerwoman as far back as I could remember. The South should never forget the loyal conduct of our slaves during the war of Secession; they not only took care of our families, but made bread for the soldiers at the front, and never a single instance occurred of improper conduct to any of these families. The day must come when a noble monument will be erected to their memory; and this loyal conduct refutes in burning language the assertion that the master was cruel to his slave, and I believe this same good conduct would still prevail, if the infernal fanatics had not insisted on their enjoying political preferences and social advantages, two privileges they were unfit for, and not prepared to receive.

During my vacation from college in 1859 I met Miss Alice Walthour, then sixteen years old, at a wedding, for the first time since we frolicked in childhood, six years before. She was one of the bridesmaids, and to say she was charming is only to be just. The pretty brown hair had grown in all its womanly luxuriance, and was becomingly arranged around the same sweet and saucy face. The pretty child had grown to be the beautiful woman. I only shook hands and said a few words, for Miss Alice was busy in her duties as first maid of honor, and I had taken a young lady to whom my duty as escort required my attention, but her image struck deep into my soul.

So, returning to college, the vision of that pretty miss, my former playmate, would not down at my bidding. I am not sure I bid it down. It kept dancing on the pages of all my text books, and I liked it. It smiled at me through the tangles of my calculus. I saw it in the deepest resources of my geology. I think it was in my eyes, and impressed itself everywhere.

After graduating from college I was so anxious to get into the army and help kill the d--n Yankees, fearing that the war would end before I got a chance. A cavalry company was organized in our county, which I joined, and we offered ourselves to the Governor of Georgia. He accepted us, and had us do duty watching the Yankee gunboats, always just off our coast, until the last of March, 1862, when we entered the service of the Confederate Army for the war. I stipulated for a thirty-day furlough in the beginning, and the second of April Miss Alice and I were married. The fond dream of my young manhood was realized.

The young men of the South were so afraid the war would end before they had a chance that a company was made up in my county and offered to the state, without compensation. I became one of them, although my right arm was yet in a sling. We were accepted by our Governor, and required to do picket duty along the coast, reporting the manoeuvres of the gunboats, always in sight along our ocean front. In 1862, April 1st, I enlisted for the war. Our victories had made us believe a few more months would see the end of it. How little we knew the feeling in the Northern states, and how determined Lincoln was to preserve the Union!

About this time our regiment was ordered to Florida to take part in the battle of Olustee, but General Colquitt, who was on the ground, made such quick work of the Federal attack that we reached there only in time to follow up the retreat of the enemy, and to see thousands of dead negro soldiers, dressed in blue. On this battlefield I found a dollar greenback, and didn't know what it was. I had frequently to pass through this stretch of woods, where the fiercest engagement occurred, and for a mile or more the dead horses were so thick and the stench so bad that, arriving at the place, I would hold my nose, put spur to my horse, and hasten through.

WHEN SHERMAN began his march on Atlanta, we were ordered to General Joseph E. Johnston's army to stop Sherman, and became a part of Joe Wheeler's cavalry, but we did not succeed. However, we all think if Johnston had not been retired at this time by President Davis, Sherman would never have made his hellish march to the sea. But who knows? Just before Sherman took Atlanta, the cavalry under General Joe Wheeler was ordered to the rear. *Why,* I, of course, don't know, but I expect because General Johnston wanted to cut off Sherman's railroad supplies, and because we had nothing for man or beast to eat. The order assembling us was strange. It commanded that we assemble without a change of clothing, without a blanket, but plenty of ammunition. Being acting Quartermaster of the Regiment, I was not included, but having a good horse, good pistols, and hungry for a fight, and from the nature of the order so poorly equipped for service, we all thought it a short raid, so I arranged to go.

Soon we found ourselves almost in Tennessee, living on what we could forage. At Dalton, Georgia, we captured - or stole, perhaps, is the better word - lots of goodies from the Yankees who had followed Sherman and opened shop. It was the first time I ever saw canned goods. We had been living on green apples and green corn since we left Atlanta, and to see the boys eat crackers and condensed milk was amazing.

The quartermaster had become forage master. With a squad of men to leave at crossroads, I was given the direction the march would take, and when about twenty miles distant, would provide the food, which would consist of a field of corn just maturing, making good food for both man and beast, but without salt or meat. We paid these obligations by giving a certificate of purchase, reading: "Two years after a treaty of peace between the Confederate States and the United States, the Confederate States promise to pay John Jones one hundred dollars for fifty acres of corn," I signing as quartermaster.

When the regiment or brigade reached this place, they would pull the ears of corn for their horses, and make large fires and roast the ears for themselves; then catch an hour or two of sleep on the bare ground, rain or shine, night or day, and, strange to say, the men and horses all kept well. The boys soon learned to put the green corn ears, just as pulled from the stalk, in the fire, and when the husk was burned off the ear was just properly cooked. The sharp line between officers and enlisted men was not severe in the Confederate Army. Although at first a sergeant in the army, the Colonel, a West Point graduate, would offer me his headquarters tent to entertain my sisters. The sharp command of an officer to attend to a duty was not necessary, each man seeming to realize that he was his own captain.

When leaving Dalton, I received orders the night before as to the route to provide the next night's forage for man and beast. Riding out of the city early in the morning, I heard a train stop just over the hill and out of sight. Soon the hill top was bristling with bayonets and blue coats, and the bullets spattered around me lively, but my good horse soon put the required distance between us. This occurrence cut me off from my command for four or five days, and when I put in an appearance I was warmly welcomed with the shout, "Why, here is Ed Thomas! He wasn't killed at Dalton after all!"

On this raid the horse I rode became lame on account of casting a shoe. At first I tried to put a shoe on; I found an old shoe at an abandoned blacksmith's shop, and having nails I fastened the shoe to the foot. Pretty bad job, and did not help much.

My Confederate "promise to pay" was all the cash the army had, and they were only accepted by these East Tennessee bushwhackers when handed out at the point of sharp sabres; but I had to have a horse. The question to decide was whether the bushwhackers should get me, or I get one of their horses. Being both judge and jury in deciding this matter, it did not take me long to come to a conclusion.

I started out early one morning determined to be sufficiently in advance of the corps to get a good selection. As forage master and quartermaster I had passes to go and come as I pleased. It wasn't long before I came to a farm yard. Just at the roadside I saw two horses in a pole stable. I opened the gate, went in with my lame horse, intending to force a swap for one more serviceable. The pretty sorrel mare I first examined, but her shoes were much worn, so I selected a gray horse, quite recently shod, and was about putting my bridle and saddle on trim when the owner came rushing from the house, some hundred yards away, swearing at the d--n scoundrel about to steal his horse. As he came he picked up an ugly, heavy stick, and when near me I ordered him to halt, with pistol in hand; but I believe he would have rushed on me requiring me to kill him, for horse I had to have, when he saw the head of our cavalry coming down the hill, and looking at my gray coat, he mounted the little sorrel and scampered for his life. Those poor border states! It was either the infernal Yankee, or the rascally Reb, who were constantly sapping their existence.

During the raid we lived by impressing what the country afforded, and whatever we did was done with despatch. To provide pork from an adjoining farm, and no hot water to get hair off, resulted in great waste; stripping the hide from a hog by amateur butchers, almost as much flesh was left at the pen with the hair as was taken away on the bones.

I remember going into a flour mill in Tennessee and asking for a certain amount of wheat flour, which the miller promptly furnished, and then, of course, wanted his pay. He would only receive my "promise to pay" after it was stuck on my sword and I quietly but determinedly let him feel how sharp it was when pressed against his abundant stomach. Then after getting the flour, how to prepare it for food? Found a lot of large flat stones, which I had the men heat very hot, and mixing the flour with water in a large barrel, spread it over the stones, and thus we had very large pones of eatable stuff. These, in large hunks, were handed the troopers as they rode by, and all shouting "Hurrah for Captain Thomas."

On these cavalry raids, which were within the confines of the seceding states, where our "promise to pay" was expected to be valid, we lived on what we could get in the immediate surroundings, but when Lee went into Pennsylvania, while he assessed the towns in accordance with military tactics, yet everything he consumed was paid for, and the strictest order maintained - no outrages or pilfering were permitted.

After feeding the boys, I began to scratch, for I was infested with what the boys now call "cooties" but we called "gray-backs." So the idea struck me I would beg a shirt of the good ladies living in this cozy town, stretched out for about half a mile on a pretty stream. I rode up to the first place and told the lady I had a sick friend who needed a shirt. "Certainly," she said, and presently she brought me what the boys call a "biled" shirt, all white and starched stiff. Of course I had to thank her for it, and stuffed it under my saddle blanket; and riding out of sight of this house repeated my lie to another lady, who brought me another "biled" shirt, which, as before, I thanked her for and again stuck under my saddle blanket. These shirts were about as much use to me as though she had given me a palmetto fan. So riding again further down the stream, in a quiet nook I took a bath, made a big fire, and holding my shirt and coat over the flames, singed those miserable things until I could hear them pop in the fire, and then, after throwing the biled shirts in the woods, dressed myself and caught up with the command.

After searching the country one night, I could only find a pen of sheep - no hogs or cattle and the boys did so dislike this horridly butchered mutton. But this or nothing, so I rode up to the pen where perhaps forty or fifty sheep were corralled in a good pen, and directed my men to get eight or ten of them. None of us knew anything about sheep, so the boys got down from their horses, found heavy sticks and went at the sheep. We knocked their horns off, crippled a few, but killed none. One of my men, coming up a little later, said, "That aint the way to kill them; just catch them and cut their throats." Soon we had all our horses could carry to camp. I have often wondered, when the owner came by daylight to see this destruction, what he thought had happened.

On this raid it was learned that the Yankees meant to destroy our salt works at Abington, Virginia, a small town in the southwest of this state. We were sent to defend the place, and quite a skirmish ensued. The Yankees retreated, and hearing of a mountainous short cut, our command was ordered to take it, hoping by this short cut to head off the enemy. 'Twas the darkest night I ever saw, and this mountain path as crooked and slippery as could be. In marching over it a large torchlight was carried at the head; each man dismounted, leading his horse and holding to the tail of the horse before him, for if the chain had been broken all might have gone over the precipice. At times the torchlight would be at our backs, so tortuous was the path, and frequently we would find ourselves slipping down a slide - but for God's sake don't let go the tail! By daylight we again reached the public road, just to see the rear guard of the enemy pass by. My comrade, Lawrence, was captured on this raid. The dead negro soldiers dressed in blue were lying so thick on the grass that it was with difficulty I rode without having my horse trample them.

While this raid temporarily destroyed the railroad over which Sherman received most of his supplies, I doubt if it accomplished any good to the Confederate cause. When we got back off the raid General Hood was on his unfortunate campaign northward, and Sherman on his march of devastation through Georgia to Savannah.

The Confederate cavalry furnished their own horses and equipment, and after we got to our line again, an order was issued giving a thirty-day furlough to any trooper without a horse. I had a good horse, but I gave him to a fellow trooper who had lost his horse in exchange for his thirty-day furlough. I made haste to get home, and there found my baby boy had grown out of my and his recollection. He looked upon me as an intruder, and if his legs had been strong enough would have kicked me out of the house. A few days, though, made him my staunch friend.

At this time Sherman was devastating the state, letting us know what he thought war was. Judging from what he was doing, I feared he would permit ill treatment of the women, so thought best to take my wife and son, two young lady sisters, and a niece who was stopping with us, out of the city. I stacked mother's store room with rice, about all that could be purchased in the city. No vehicles could be hired to leave the city, so I got from my grandmother's plantation near by, a horse and wagon to take the four ladies, my boy, and two negro girls - for the ladies must have their maids - and four or five big trunks, over the Savannah River to Hardeeville, S. C., the nearest railroad station; all other railroads were in Sherman's hands.

How I expected to accomplish the journey, I never knew; was like the darned fool who, knowing a thing could not be done, tried it, and did it. Good luck played in my hands, and at last we were in Hardieville.

WHEN I arrived there I saw a woman waving a handkerchief. Going to her, I found it was my wife, who told me that arriving at this station, the party was rushed on the train, saying that it was the last train to leave as the Yanks had cut off communication; that she began to cry, when General Beauregard, who happened on board, asked "why that lady was crying." Being told, he took from his pocket a small memorandum book and wrote: "Captain Thomas has permission to go to Charleston and return. G. T. Beauregard." But by and by another train did come, on to which we all tumbled, bag and baggage, and thus I had accomplished by luck what seemed at first impossible.

By some hocus-pocus I went as far as Columbia, S. C., where friends were met, and I turned my head southward, feeling for the first time since the war began that we could hold out but little longer. I never got back to Savannah to get my equipment. Sherman was there before me, and of course my horse and wagon were gone, and not knowing where my command was and not having any change of clothing or blanket to keep out the December cold, I felt disconsolate indeed. By some hook or crook, though, I got what I needed, joined my command, which, with the other troops, was endeavoring to make a junction with Lee in Virginia. Before this could be done, however, Grant had pressed the great Lee so severely, by overwhelming bodies of troops, that he had surrendered. Joseph E. Johnston was at this time again in command of what was left of the Western Army, after Hood's unfortunate battles, and with him I continued my duties until he, too, surrendered to Sherman.

As before mentioned, my wife and son and two sisters had refugeed to Limestone Springs, situated in the northern part of South Carolina. Hence my first journey was to see them. Riding a mule towards home, I took a mental inventory of my condition. The plantation we had bought in Baker County, we had given notes for; I had been informed by my brother that these notes had not been paid. When they became due they could not be found. It seems a firm of bankers in Savannah had purchased them, and knowing they were well secured by mortgage on the plantation, had taken the notes to England. Without the negroes to work the land, we could not make the cotton to procure the money to pay these notes. Hence that, too, was gone.

This is the way my inventory looked: a wife and babe to take care of; a mother, four sisters and little brother to help to support. How? It is true I had a good education. I had taken special work in engineering; but no money to make improvements, and hence nothing for the engineer. I could not look to that for support. The negroes were all free, and in fact I had no money to hire them if I desired to plant. Well, I will say one thing; to be sure I had the desire and the pluck, and these two carried me through.

Arriving at Limestone Springs about May first, I was truly rejoiced to be with my folks again, although I was almost as destitute as though I was an immigrant from another country. All the earnings and savings of my forefathers had been destroyed by the effects of the war. Yet I felt hopeful and confident that I could pull through.

Limestone Springs had been noted for its fine female college, founded and operated by one Dr. Curtis, who married my wife's oldest sister. His idea was to open the seminary again, and he offered me the position of teacher of mathematics if he succeeded. As a beginning I immediately opened a free school for the neighboring community and the doctor canvassed the state to see how matters looked. He returned in less than two weeks, disheartened; everybody too poor to send their daughters from home. I remained with Dr. Curtis for a while, but after seeing no prospect of his college opening again, I was convinced that I had got to get other work. The railroads were, of course, all destroyed; so saddling my mule, I rode to Savannah with only my two silver dollars, and how I did it seems strange to me now, yet I remember giving a small piece of even those two dollars to a poor family I met on the road just before entering Savannah. There I met my good mother and sisters and little brother, and what a lot of things they had to relate!

Sherman's entering the city had proven a blessing in disguise. He maintained good order; the soldiers had plenty of money to buy whatever the citizens had, and paid well for it. My mother had reserved a sack or two of peanuts, which my little sisters roasted, and sitting on the front steps sold to the soldiers passing by. The ladies made cakes and pies of all kinds, and sold to the soldiers. The officers roomed or boarded at the various dwellings, and materially assisted the inhabitants, and in this way everybody was doing very nicely.

I remained in Savannah only long enough to extend such assistance as the emergency of the case required, and then mounted my mule and rode to my place in Baker County, two hundred miles west, to see if anything was left there to assist me in my efforts for a living. Walthourville was directly on my route so, of course, I passed that way to see my wife's folks. I found these ladies, who had owned abundant slaves to do their bidding, doing their own work, and they were very cheerful. Luckily I found Mr. Bernard in Walthourville, with wagons and teams preparing to make the same trip I had set out on. Of course I joined him. In due time we reached Baker County, where I found I was still possessed of four mules, a horse, wagons, and several bales of cotton. I made preparation at once to arrange for vehicles to go after my folks at Limestome Springs in South Carolina. Proper harness could not be purchased, so I bought leather and thread, and, with the exception of the mules' collars, which were made of corn shucks by one of our slaves, I made harness for a four-mule and a two-mule team. These I loaded with cotton, six bales, and returned to Savannah where I easily sold it at a good price.

After assisting my mother in many ways, I started for Limestone Springs. Arriving there I rested for a day and again turned my head homeward, with wife and boy, sisters, the two maids and my brother Hugh, who had made the trip with me, camping on the way at night. We finally reached Savannah in very good shape. But the high prices of all things prevailing then, and the necessities of the occasion, soon depleted my pocketbook to such an extent that I found it necessary to renew it before beginning my return journey to the Baker County plantation. Freights from Savannah to Augusta were $4 a hundred. So, taking three thousand pounds of cotton bagging and my six-mule team, and hiring a colored man, Frank, to accompany me, I made the trip there and back in seven days, getting my $120. The day I left Augusta on my return, the man Frank complained of feeling sick. He soon became so ill that I had to take his driver's seat and allow him to lie in the wagon. This made the three days' trip down very laborious, as I had to drive all day and watch most of the night, the country being full of stragglers always ready to steal a horse or mule. On approaching Savannah, I went to the rear of the wagon where Frank lay sleeping and removed a cover from his face to find that he had an awful case of smallpox. He feared on my finding this out that I would abandon him on the road, and cried out lustily for my clemency. I relieved his fears, drove him to his home in the city, helped him out of the wagon, paid him for services rendered, and gave him over to his kinsfolk. Frank recovered, and today is one of my most loyal friends. I had spent three days in company with this man, riding the same feverish saddle he left, and yet did not take the smallpox.

In a few days I started off to Baker County to finally settle up matters there. The plantation was too firmly held by that unfortunate mortgage to bring that away, so by the first of January I found myself in Savannah with two wagons, six mules, and several bales of cotton - my entire available resources. In this short space of time, either on mule back or in wagons, I had made three trips across the state of South Carolina and four across the state of Georgia. I arranged for my wife and boy to remain in Savannah with my mother, and I went on my grandmother's plantation, seven miles out of the city, to plant cotton, rice, corn, and so on, and only visiting my folks once a week. There, with my soldier's blankets, which I found as I had left them on my going from the city on the eve of Sherman's coming, and a bale of straw for my bed, I lived for about three months; but I found it luxury, for an ex-soldier. I was up early and late, encouraging my hands in the performance of their various duties, untiring and indefatigable at all hours. The second year I fixed up the old residence, doing most of the work myself, and had my wife and son with me. While these years were laborious to me, I yet was happy with my little family.

I HAD NOT as yet, since the slaves were free, visited our old plantation home, Peru, in McIntosh County, but I had heard that a goodly number of our old slaves had returned, and, without leave or license, simply considered it their privilege to come home, after they were scattered by Sherman's raid.

They had taken up their abode in what cabins were left standing and had begun to cultivate the land. I was pleased to hear this and made up my mind to pay them a visit. So, just before Christmas, with a pair of mules to a buggy, I drove to the old plantation. If I had been a king returning to his subjects, I could not have been more regally received. The men gathered around my buggy, and bodily carried me to the front piazza of the old home, and some of the women pulled out an old arm chair in which I was deposited in state. I had soon, however, to get up from the chair and stand as erect as possible, to keep old Mammy Peggy from putting her arms around my neck and kissing me. My mules were soon stabled and well provided for, and then the preparations began for entertaining "Mars' Ed." One provided a mattress, another the sheets, and so on until a most comfortable bed was secured. At supper I found that each of my old friends insisted that something should be on the table from his or her larder, and I never expect, during my life, to sit down to such a supper again: fried chicken, pork, smoked raccoon, eggs, fried fish, oysters, crabs, shrimps, honey, rice, corn, corn bread, peas, collards, potatoes, and coffee! And Mammy Peggy insisted on my eating some of her stewed 'possum, which she brought me in a nice little bowl with a silver spoon. When leaving home I had intended spending my nights at my cousin's, Mrs. Anderson, who lived on the adjoining plantation, but they would not listen to it! "Marse Ed wan't gwine to leab 'em to go nowhar else."

That was not long after the war when they had many of the comforts provided them by their masters. Should I go there today, I know I would find no such bed and supper, and as the old folks are almost all dead, no such welcome. The feelings of the old slaves for their master, and of the masters for their slaves, will never be understood by coming generations.

While living on this farm near Savannah I was elected magistrate of the district. I accepted the place that I might use my influence for good, for the Freedmen's Bureau was stationed in Savannah, as also in other cities, and gave us much trouble in the proper discipline of our laborers, who thought that freedom was to be idle, to be untrammeled by law, and I used my office to counteract these unfortunate ideas.

About this time a negro man, by name Dick, killed another in cold blood. Governor Bullock of Georgia, a carpet-bagger elected by the negroes - most whites disfranchised - offered a reward of $500 for his capture. I found out where Dick was in hiding across the river in South Carolina, and made up my mind to catch him and get the $500 reward. I had a great big negro man as my constable, who was forever begging me for a horse I drove, so I told him if he would do as I directed and bring Dick to me, I would give him the horse. His reply, naturally, was that it would be necessary to have a requisition from the Governor of Georgia to the Governor of South Carolina before he, a Georgia constable, could arrest over the river in South Carolina. I told him I had the requisition. I got my sister to make me a rosette of red, white and blue ribbon, which I pinned to his inner coat and told him to keep it hid until he saw Dick, when he must approach him with great dignity, throw open his coat, display the rosette, and say "Requisition from Governor of South Carolina. You are my prisoner" - and just take him and bring him along. I gave him the needed money, and two days after he brought me the man, whom I turned over to the proper authorities, and in due time got my $500 and the constable got the horse. This was my first piece of detective work, and my last.

It was about this time that my sister Mattie died, and was buried in Bonaventure Cemetery. This sister was particularly gifted, remarkably pretty, large black eyes and light hair; was very smart; wrote well, and had a decided talent for drawing and music. Her young life was spent during the hard times of Civil War, and her opportunities for schooling were very small. Father died when she was quite a little thing, and it was always to my lap she ran to be petted and loved. Poor girl, she passed to her eternal home before the devastations of that cursed war were mended, having spent her entire young life in the midst of strife and confusion. A noble, gentle and modest girl. How I have wished she could have lived to spend some happy days. As a young man, when she nestled on my knee, and even then showed such undeveloped talent, I resolved to give her the best opportunities to develop her talents for music and drawing. But even as I was building these castles in the air the murmurs of war were heard over the land, which soon dispelled all my well laid plans.

THE CONFEDERATE ARMY in and about Savannah consisted of only such scattering stragglers and men on furlough, as could be rounded up for the occasion. It was more of a mob than an army, and when this mob was safe over the Savannah River, the mayor of the city, with an escort, visited Sherman and surrendered the place to him. His entrance into the city was made with so little noise and beating of drums, that the citizens were surprised upon awaking in the morning to find blue coats everywhere. Many encamped in the pretty parks in and about the city. The magnanimous terms that both Grant and Sherman gave to Lee and Johnston took out much of the sting of defeat, and I am sure every Southern soldier, when Lee said "Stop," obeyed, knowing we had done our duty to our state, as demanded of us. Yet - "My country! Right or wrong, my country!"

I was in Greensboro, N. C., at this time, in charge of a large quantity of stores and some two hundred men, and was given a certain amount of silver dollars (I think $300) to pay to the command I was attached to. It counted $6 to five men, and as we had no change, each man was given a dollar and the sixth was drawn for. By luck I got the extra dollar. This was all the money we got for some three years' service to our states; but no murmuring was heard. We asked nothing in return for doing our duty but health and powder. And if Lincoln had not fallen a victim to fanaticism, the horrors of reconstruction would have been averted. He always declared: "Let the Southern states come back into the Union, we don't want to punish them further;" "stop your fuss and come home" - and I am sure, after our three years and a half fighting we were anxious for peace.

My state, Georgia, by election, sent to the Senate the two most noted Union men of the state, Alex R. Stephens and Hershell V. Johnston, for neither of these men advocated secession, always declaring we should contend for our rights within the Union, and we so hoped that, now slavery was abolished, the trouble was settled; but at this time the Northern Radicals were in the saddle, the great heart of Lincoln was still in death, and our poor bleeding South passed through a period, called reconstruction, that cannot now be approved even by the most radical of our land. To quote from a Northern writer (H. T. Peck, LL.D., Columbia College):

"The bitterness of the war would soon have passed away, but the horror of reconstruction sank deeper into the soul of the South than even the memory of devastated lands and of cities laid in ashes. It is painful now to dwell upon the folly and fanaticism which made that period the darkest in all American history. The wise and conciliatory plans of Lincoln were forgotten by the Northern Radicals. Legislative halls which had been honored by the presence of learned jurists and distinguished law-givers, were filled with a rabble of plantation hands, who yelled and jabbered like so many apes. . . ."

Is it to be wondered at, then, that the South, of almost pure Caucasian blood, would not submit to this indignity? Surely the real man of the North must have sympathized with us when, as by magic, thousands of white-robed, resolute men sprung from the womb of our dear old Southern mother and scattered the wretched scalawags to their own respective slums! The poor black man was not to blame. He reaped none of the reward - was only used as a tool; he was accustomed to follow his white master, and when this master was supplanted by the scoundrel, he knew no better.

Well, my story is finished. I am an old man now, in my eighty-third year, but young in every feeling. I am white and wrinkled, but my soul shall be young. Providence has been good to me; my health is good, and I have the respect and confidence of all who know me; my children are all grown and are my greatest comfort. Many grandchildren have come to me, all fine chaps, and at my knees frequently my two little great grandsons sit and hear me tell of that war which I passed through fifty-seven years ago.

As time passes how vividly is reflected from Memory's mirror the stirring events of those historic years. How loyal we of the South have always been to the teachings of the Constitution of the United States, and the highest decisions of our Courts, and how safe we felt under these protections, when lo! to our amazement, we heard these things classed by our Northern fanatics as "being in league with the devil." All this is now in the past; but we shall always stand in the presence of our God, proving by our pious homage to the dear old Confederacy, our loyal devotion to the living Union.

EDWARD J. THOMAS,
Savannah, Georgia

THE END

Made in United States
North Haven, CT
07 September 2023